D1521392

DIVINE REVELATION AND HUMAN LEARNING

How do we learn about God? In an age of competing world-views, what is the basis of the Christian claim to offer the truth about God, the world and ourselves?

David Heywood charts a path through the study of human knowledge, showing how the insights of theology, philosophy and psychology complement and amplify one another, and bringing the experience of revelation within the scope of the study of human learning. He shows the relationship between human psychology and the work of the Holy Spirit and demonstrates the credibility of the Christian claim to a transforming knowledge of God in Jesus Christ. Offering a new model for the relationship of theology to the natural and social sciences, David Heywood shows how the claim of Christian theology to deal in issues of universal truth can be upheld. For Christian education, this book provides a theological rationale for the use of methods of teaching and learning of educationally proven effectiveness.

Explorations in Practical, Pastoral and Empirical Theology

Series Editors: Professor Leslie J. Francis, University of Wales, Bangor, UK
and Professor Jeff Astley, University of Durham and Director of the
North of England Institute for Christian Education, UK

Theological reflection on the church's practice is now recognized as a significant element in theological studies in the academy and seminary. Ashgate's new series in practical, pastoral and empirical theology seeks to foster this resurgence of interest and encourage new developments in practical and applied aspects of theology worldwide. This timely series draws together a wide range of disciplinary approaches and empirical studies to embrace contemporary developments including: the expansion of research in empirical theology, psychological theology, ministry studies, public theology, Christian education and faith development; key issues of contemporary society such as health, ethics and the environment; and more traditional areas of concern such as pastoral care and counselling.

Other titles published in this series:

Ordinary Theology
Looking, Listening and Learning in Theology
Jeff Astley
0 7546 0583 3 (Hbk)
0 7546 0584 1 (Pbk)

The 'Empty' Church Revisited
Robin Gill
0 7546 3462 0 (Hbk)
0 7546 3463 9 (Pbk)

God, Human Nature and Education for Peace
New Approaches to Moral and Religious Maturity
Karl Ernst Nipkow
0 7546 0863 8 (Hbk)
0 7546 0872 7 (Pbk)

Divine Revelation and Human Learning

A Christian theory of knowledge

DAVID HEYWOOD

ASHGATE

Published by
Ashgate Publishing Limited
Gower House
Croft Road
Aldershot
Hants GU11 3HR
England

Ashgate Publishing Company
Suite 420
101 Cherry Street
Burlington, VT 05401-4405 USA

Ashgate website: http://www.ashgate.com

British Library Cataloguing in Publication Data
Heywood, David
    Divine revelation and human learning : a Christian theory of knowledge. – (Explorations in practical, pastoral and empirical theology)
    1. Knowledge, Theory of (Religion) 2. Christian education – Philosophy 3. Learning, Psychology of – Religious aspects – Christianity 4. Revelation 5. Psychology, Religious
    I. Title
    231'.042

Library of Congress Control Number: 2003052238

ISBN 0 7546 0850 6

Typeset in Times by LaserScript Ltd, Mitcham, Surrey
Printed and bound in Great Britain by MPG Books Ltd, Bodmin, Cornwall

Contents

Preface

It has taken me almost twenty years to write this book. It began life as a doctoral thesis in the University of Durham in the 1980s at a time when cognitive science was still in its relatively early stages. It has been tested in over sixteen years of parish ministry as an Anglican curate and vicar including stints as a part-time trainer of candidates for lay and ordained ministry.

The subject of the book grows out of a fascination with broad, abstract questions such as the form of our knowledge and how it arises but equally with practical questions such as how the Church and its ministers can teach most effectively the Christian faith. If I can make a contribution to the effective teaching and training of Christian people, especially those offering themselves for lay or ordained ministry in God's Church, I will be very glad.

Over a period of twenty years, things move on. Nevertheless I was fascinated, on returning to concentrated study in order to write the book, to find out just how many of my original questions and conclusions were still relevant. In some areas, as I shall argue at greater length in the book, there are fields of enquiry which have failed to move forward because they have not recognized the important questions relevant to the research being carried out.

Among the many people who have supported me in the writing of the book I would like to thank especially Revd Dr Jeff Astley of the North of England Institute for Christian Education for his unstinting advice and generous allocation of time as my supervisor and editor. Revd Jeremy Whales had the dubious honour of being the vicar with whom I served as curate, during which time he allowed me a great deal of time to complete my thesis. Some years later my team rector Revd (now The Ven) Chris Skilton allowed me time off to make a start on what eventually became this book. To all of these I offer my profound gratitude.

Stylistic Note

I have sometimes written about human beings in the feminine gender and sometimes in the masculine. In nearly all such cases, 'she' implies 'she or he' and 'he' implies 'he or she'. I believe that this shorthand is acceptable provided that it is adopted in both forms.

Acknowledgements

The author and publisher are grateful to Jeff Astley and David Day for permission to rework most of the material previously published as the author's, 'Theology or Social Science? The Theoretical Basis for Christian Education', in *The Contours of Christian Education*.

Introduction

Christian Discipleship

A disciple is not above his teacher, but everyone who is fully taught will be like the teacher.

(Luke 6:40)

Christian discipleship is a particular kind of learning. A student is initiated by the teacher into a branch of knowledge. An apprentice learns from the master the skills of the job. A disciple learns *with a view to becoming like* the teacher. In some ways the learning involved in Christian discipleship is like that of a student. Christians learn the basic doctrines of Christian faith and the story of God's people in the Old and New Testaments and in Church history. In other ways it is like apprenticeship. Christians learn to find their way around the Bible and interpret it. They may enrol in a course of training leading to a role in the community of faith – leading intercessions in worship, leading a young people's group or becoming a minister. They may also learn through secular agencies skills such as musicianship, accounting or the care of the bereaved, which may be offered to the work of God's kingdom.

But these elements of Christian education and training take place against the background of the call to a deeper kind of learning. To be a disciple of Jesus means learning with a view to becoming like him – in personal qualities such as compassion, humility, patience and steely determination; in the way he related to others – rich and poor, young and old, outcast and complacent; above all in his relationship with his Father. Jesus knew himself as the Son of God, a knowledge which at least one of the gospel writers sees already evident as a young boy (Luke 2:49), which was confirmed at his baptism (Mark 1:11) and put to the test in the wilderness (Matthew 4:3, 6). The privilege of Christians is to enter by adoption the relationship with the Father which belongs to Jesus by nature, to know ourselves as children of God (Matthew 6:1, 4, 6, 9; Romans 8:15–16; 1 John 3:1–2). Thus the kind of knowledge appropriate to discipleship is the transforming knowledge of a person.

In view of this it is not surprising to find that the Hebrew word 'to know', *ya'da*, is a relationship word. In the words of one writer its real meaning is

1

'to have a formative relationship' (Downing, 1964, p. 42). Criticizing King Jehoiakim for his wasteful building projects and the oppression of his people, the prophet Jeremiah compared him with his father Josiah who 'defended the cause of the poor and needy' and went on, '"Is that not what it means to know me?" declares the Lord' (Jeremiah 22:16). For Josiah to know the Lord meant both sharing his compassion and justice and practical obedience. Towards the end of his life the apostle Paul declared his deep desire for a knowledge of Jesus which would radically change him. 'All I want', he wrote, 'is to know Christ and the power of his resurrection and the fellowship of sharing in his sufferings, becoming like him in his death, and so, somehow, to attain to the resurrection from the dead' (Philippians 3:10–11). For the author of the fourth gospel the one who holds to Jesus's teaching is really his disciple. He will 'know the truth', which will set him free (John 8:31–2). To know the truth is to know Jesus himself since he is the truth (John 14:6) and to know Jesus is to know the Father (John 14:7) and to have eternal life (John 17:3).

But the knowledge of God comes by revelation. According to the gospels it is available only to those who love both Jesus and the Father (John 14:21–4). Those 'on the outside' see and see but never perceive, hear and hear but never understand (Mark 4:12). The deep things of God are deliberately hidden from the wise and learned yet revealed to babes (Matthew 11:25). The world in its wisdom does not know God; instead he offers a wisdom of his own to those who believe in him and are saved (1 Corinthians 1:21). The saving knowledge of Jesus is not revealed by 'flesh and blood' but only by the Father in heaven (Matthew 16:17).

Thus revelation is a transforming knowledge which both guides and enables a process of psychological change – the process by which disciples become like their teacher. It is therefore *a process of learning* – learning in its fullest sense, the learning that consists not only of intellectual growth but of personal change.

Theory and Practice

Nothing is so practical, Jeff Astley reminds us (1994, p. 2), as a good theory. Having set out in the mid-1980s to research the practice of adult Christian education (by which I refer to the efforts of Christian churches to teach and nurture their members in the faith), I came to the conclusion that what was most needed was a theory of revelation. One reason for this was that Christian education had then, and still has, no unifying paradigm. One recently published collection of essays was entitled, *Who Are We?* (Westerhoff, 1978b). Seymour and Miller's book *Contemporary Approaches to Christian Education* (1982) listed five separate approaches, each with contrasting understandings of scope, aims and method. If, as D. Campbell Wyckhoff claims, 'Christian education as a discipline is an enquiry into teaching and learning as modes and means of response to revelation' (1967, p. 173), a theory of revelation is what is needed to provide unity and direction to an otherwise fragmented field.

However this is precisely where problems arise. There is no single shared understanding of what revelation is and how it is given. Instead there is, in the words of one writer, 'a buzzing multiplicity of individual Christian opinion' (Sponheim, 1984, p. 197). The same lack of unity is a feature of Christian education. Traditional transmissive approaches draw their justification from traditional propositional views of revelation in which 'revelation' is identified with the Bible or the Church's tradition. On the other hand more subject-centred, experiential methods of learning rely on a contrasting experiential model of revelation (Astley, 1987, pp. 32–3). Even the definition of revelation is in question. For the one approach 'revelation' consists of a certain definitive content, the other an experience of a particular kind. Such uncertainty over the manner in which the knowledge of God is available can only lead to a profound malaise not only for Christian education but for theology as a whole. It has always been the case that theology offered several different 'paradigms', each with a different framework for the interpretation of the relation between God and human beings, each paradigm continually modified by the work of successive generations of scholars. But 'a multiplicity of individual opinion' on a subject as central as the knowledge of God itself seems to indicate the breakdown even of such unity as the various paradigms and the well-charted relations between them may once have offered.

The lack of an agreed paradigm in Christian education is partly due to a further lack of agreement over the correct theoretical basis for Christian practice. Christian education is a religious undertaking and as such needs to be informed by theology. Christian education is a form of education, which has its own body of theory in which the social sciences play a major role. In Christian education the practices of education and theology meet. Yet what is to be the relationship between them? Is Christian education simply a particular variety of education, or is it a branch of practical or pastoral theology? Which is to be the dominant or foundational 'macro-theory' for Christian education, theology or the social sciences?

For those who take the 'theological approach', the teaching and learning of the faith is an aspect of the Church's mission and it is thus theology, the discipline of reflecting critically on that mission, which provides the 'clue' to Christian education. In a book of that title, Randolph Crump Miller writes, 'The centre of the curriculum is a two-fold relationship between God and the learner. The curriculum is both God-centred and experience-centred. Theology must be prior to the curriculum! Theology is "truth-about-God-in-relation-to-man"' (1950, p. 5).

Thirty years later, concluding a chapter on educational philosophy, Miller wrote that since 'Christian education deals with the data of common experience, the problem is to work out some coherent unity for our belief system. Thus Christian education comes back to theology for its primary content and its organising principle' (1980, p. 180). In Miller's view, theology provides the definitive understanding of the learner as a person in a particular relationship with God. It provides a definitive understanding of the context of Christian education as part of the Church's pastoral ministry. Finally, theology judges the methods of Christian education. In the words of John Westerhoff, 'Our theological presuppositions provide the screen for understanding both theory and practice' (1978a, p. 285).

For other writers, Christian education is a variety of education. These writers look to educational theory for the basic models guiding the Church's educational practice. Among the most outspoken is James Michael Lee, whose trilogy outlining his 'macrotheory' of 'Religious Instruction' has the subtitle, *A Social Science Approach.* In Lee's words, 'Religion is learned according to the way the learner learns and not after the manner of its own existence' (1973, p. 58). Lee is expressing an educational commonplace. Whatever may be the formal structure of Christian theology, as indeed of any discipline, effective teaching does not consist of asking the learner to digest the textbook. It requires engaging with the learner at the point of her interest and concern, helping her to make sense of new information in terms of her existing experience and understanding and giving her the opportunity to explore each new concept for its potential significance in her own life and make connections with other areas of interest. The ground rules of effective teaching find their empirical and theoretical basis in educational rather than theological theory.

Lack of a unifying paradigm and disagreement over the theoretical basis for Christian education form the background. A third and for me even more persuasive reason for concentrating on a theory of revelation is the lack of unity among both theorists and practitioners about the role of God himself in the Christian learning process. Non-interventionist positions see God working only through the natural dynamics of the teaching situation and the social and psychological mechanisms of learning. Interventionist positions give varying degrees of weight to God's immanent presence in the natural ways through which people learn but see greatest significance in particular interventions over and beyond these. The danger is that without a theory to relate the natural and supernatural, learning outcomes become 'in the last analysis a personal decision that rests in the mystery of God' (Miller, 1980, p. 162). All the human educator can do is to prepare the ground and pray for divine intervention. 'What is needed – but rarely forthcoming – in this discussion is any attempt to work out a link or hinge between the human educator's preparatory ("horizontal") work and God's decisive ("vertical") activity' (Astley, 2000, pp. 15–16).

Some two decades after my original decision, these issues seem no nearer resolution. In fact Astley, Francis and Crowder (1996, pp. xi–xvi), introducing a collection of seminal articles on all aspects of Christian education, cite the question of the relation of theology to Christian education, the manner of God's intervention, if any, in the natural processes of human learning and the lack of an agreed theory of revelation as central issues still to be resolved. Moreover in the wider field of 'practical theology' the relation between theology and the social sciences remains an issue, not only for Christian education but for other areas of the Church's mission such as pastoral care and counselling, church management and leadership and the local church's role in and for its community.

One very significant development in the last twenty years has been the development of what is now called 'practical theology'. In the 1980s teaching and learning in the Church, pastoral care and counselling and community work were seen as practical skills of ministry, outside the scope of theology proper. Twenty years later these activities are seen as necessary and integral parts of the Church's activity in the world, which is the proper focus of a fully contextualized theology. From the point of view of the practical theologian, all theology is practical theology, since all theology serves the mission of the Church. With the development of practical theology has come a sea-change in the perceived relationship of theory and practice. No longer is it sufficient to see theology as reflection only on God's self-disclosure in revelation. Theology must reflect also on what actually happens in the world and in the Church, the experience of Christian people in their daily lives and mission. In place of a straightforward 'theory to practice' model, in which academic theology, the interpreter of revelation, dictates to the Church her proper shape and focus, practical theology substitutes a 'practice–theory–practice' model or, as Don Browning puts it, 'From present theory-laden practices to a retrieval of normative theory-laden practice to the creation of a more critically-held theory-laden practice' (1991, p. 7). Our theology is inadequate until we discover by engagement and reflection the key features of the particular situation we face, whether on a global or local scale. Only then, by reflection on Christian tradition, can we arrive at the wisdom needed to interpret the situation aright and apply the Christian gospel effectively.

Nevertheless the move to a methodology thoroughly rooted in practice should not be allowed to obscure the need for good theory. For me at least, experience of trying to lead local churches in mission has reinforced the vital importance of knowing *what* we are hoping to achieve and *why* we hope to achieve it. Without good theory, the Church quickly loses its focus and direction. Still more important, the Church must always hold before itself the question of whether its aims and practices are a genuine expression of the gospel. Overt evangelism may be *less* Christian, because of the methods involved, than a church's involvement alongside local residents in service to its community. As Browning points out, all practice is theory-laden and good theory is essential for good practice.

Viewed in one way, Christian education is a division of practical theology, alongside such fields as pastoral care and counselling, worship and liturgy, evangelism and mission. In another way, reflection on the methodology of each suggests a paradigmatic link between Christian education and the whole of practical theology. Central to both is a fourfold cycle, in practical theology the 'pastoral cycle', in Christian education the 'learning cycle'. The pastoral cycle proceeds from *experience*, in which some event begins a process of change; through *exploration*, in which those involved think about what is going on and gather evidence to help them understand it; through *reflection*, in which the information gathered about the situation is allowed to challenge the underlying beliefs and values which have guided previous activities and responses; to *action*, in which a considered response is made to the original events, the result of which is a new starting point for future experience (Ballard and Pritchard, 1996, pp. 77–8). In a similar way the learning cycle proceeds through *experiences* such as an event, conversation or formal learning experience; through *reflection*, closer in sense to the 'exploration' of the pastoral cycle, in which a person or group analyses the original experience in order to make sense of it, perhaps linking it with other relevant experiences and memories; through *conceptualization*, in which a new understanding or new values are formed; to *action*, in which this new understanding is put into practice in some way (Baumohl, 1984, pp. 23–32).

A number of explanations suggest themselves for this obvious link between Christian education and practical theology as a whole. On the one hand, Christian education can be seen as practical theology in miniature. The act of learning is a dialogue between the learner and the tradition resulting in personal change and growth (Astley, 2002, p. 34) just as engagement with the pastoral cycle might be for an individual Christian, group or community. Or to take the relationship from the other end, 'Religion itself is a kind of learning' (Astley, 2002, p. 4, quoting Paul Holmer). Practical theology, as critical reflection on religious practice, can be seen as a variety of Christian education. Taking a broader perspective, both the pastoral and the learning cycle express what we might call the hermeneutical mood of postmodern society. The defining characteristic of postmodernism is resistance to overarching theories of explanation. Its mood is to eschew a theory to practice understanding of life as a whole in favour of a practice–theory–practice way of living. Given this mood it is not surprising that practical theology should have made such progress in recent years, nor that learner-centred approaches should have gained ground at the expense of authoritative transmission in Christian education.

The long sway of theory to practice approaches to both life and thought was based on 'foundationalism', the belief that the theory in question could be traced back to a solid foundation of objectively verifiable, philosophically derived or supernaturally revealed truth. Based on universally valid principles, all that remained was to apply the particular theory to experience. In traditional Christian terms, this means living out the revealed principles of Christian faith. The characteristic of the postmodern world is to deny general theories this degree of authority. There are no more 'metanarratives' capable of making sense of the whole of life. Against this background, the attempt to construct a theory of revelation is problematic. By its very nature, revelation ought to be authoritative. Included in the concept should be the possibility of definitive truth about God, the world and humankind. Thus grounded in the truths of revelation, all that remains is for Christian theology to be applied in the life and ministry of the Church and individual believers. 'Revelation' as traditionally understood and practice–theory–practice methodology appear to clash at the level of their most basic presuppositions. What I am going to attempt however is to uphold *both* the authoritative character of revelation as definitive truth *and* a practice–theory–practice understanding of how revelation is assimilated and applied in experience.

For the liberal theologian and Christian educator, 'There is no fixed and final form of Christian faith, and this is why there can be no fixed and final form of nurture into it' (Astley, 1992, p. 42). In the words of a British Council of Churches Report,

> When Christians seek to nurture their young into Christian faith, they literally do not fully know what they are nurturing them into. They only know what they are

nurturing them out of, i.e. out of the Christian past. They know the resources but not the use which will be made of them. What we pass on to our children is not the painting but the paintbox.

(1976, p. 23)

In other words, Christianity itself is no overarching theory of life or 'metanarrative' but a way of life that needs to be reinvented in each new generation using the resources of its own tradition. On the other hand, while admitting the need for each new generation to grasp or be grasped by its faith afresh and reapply it to its contemporary situation, can we nevertheless maintain that those aspects of the faith whose significance may be newly grasped belong to a truth which existed all along 'out there' to be discovered? Christian theology claims to investigate a truth that is eternal, definitive and authoritative, capable of transforming both individual human lives and whole communities in the direction of true humanity. The scientist who adopts a critical realist perspective on his work assumes that he is in touch with a reality existing over against him, even though his theories may come short of a full and adequate description of it. In the same way the theologian is entitled to believe in the reality of God and the possibility of ultimate truth however adequately or inadequately his theories may describe it (Peacocke, 1993, pp. 11–16).

Practical theology moreover requires a theory of revelation because it requires a theory of knowledge. In their introduction to the subject, Ballard and Pritchard (1996, pp. 58–70) mention four models for practical theology. The Enlightenment model of 'applied theory'; 'critical correlation' based on the hermeneutical theories of thinkers like Hans-Georg Gadamer; the 'praxis' methodology which emerged in Latin America as part of the movement of liberation theology; and the 'habitus' model offered by Edward Farley in which *habitus* is understood as a wisdom for living rooted in character. Each of these presupposes and is more or less explicitly based upon a theory of knowledge. All depend on assumptions about how people learn as well as how theory arises and is related to practice. In Christian education in particular, the learning cycle is based on outward observation of the way people actually learn most effectively. It requires an 'inward' explanation for why it is that people learn that way. Christian theology exists in a learning context, and its shape is influenced by the way people learn (Astley, 2002, p. 4). Like the truth of God himself, the theorist is entitled to believe that there is a consistency about human learning that is open to discovery.

The 'Christian theory of knowledge' I am presenting here is intended as a contribution both to practical theology and to Christian education in particular. The key question is *how we learn about God*. On the one hand, the transforming knowledge of God without which Christian discipleship could not take place is available only through revelation. On the other, discipleship is a process of learning in its fullest sense involving intellectual growth and personal change. What is the relation between the action of God in revelation and the psychological and social processes characteristic of human learning? Can we develop a theory of *revelation as a process of learning in which the learner is open to God*?

The Scope of the Argument

How is a theory of revelation to be discovered? The root of the problem is the place of the doctrine of revelation in theology as a whole. Revelation is not just one theological topic among many to be placed alongside the doctrine of God, Christology, the Church, ministry and so on. Revelation is the source of theology. The way the knowledge of God is deemed to be available through revelation governs the parameters of theology. The doctrine of revelation dictates what kind of knowledge of God is available, what are its limits and, most important of all, how this knowledge is available to human beings. Thus while there must be some congruence between revelation and other doctrines – of God, of the 'revelation' of himself in Jesus Christ, of the Church, ministry and so on – any move from the content of theology to a doctrine of revelation is a purely circular argument. Revelation tells us how knowledge of these other aspects of theology comes about. Until this is established no conclusions in these areas are warranted.

There is thus no approach to revelation from the discipline of theology and no theology without a prior understanding of revelation. The understanding of God and his ways in the world requires some other starting point, and this implies a need to cross disciplinary boundaries. According to William Abraham, theologians are nervous about engaging with other disciplines, especially philosophy, fearful of questions that may distract from their primary focus on the Church's life and witness. However arduous a task it may be, however, the necessity of grappling with the source and manner of our knowledge of God remains. Explicitly or implicitly, theologians need to refer to the nature and actions of God – and to justify their statements with an account of the sources of our knowledge of these things. *How we know* remains a central question (Abraham, 1997, pp. 202–3). Practical theologians need not be daunted since practical theology is an interdisciplinary pursuit. They are accustomed to employing the social sciences in the service of theology, drawing on their insights as part of their critical reflection on the Church's ministry. 'What is needed is the courage to make connections and to see things as a whole. Interdisciplinary dialogue has become a necessity' (Ballard and Pritchard, 1996, pp. 106–7).

However, the difficulties in the way of an interdisciplinary investigation are many. First is the tendency to specialism encouraged by the exponential growth in knowledge of all kinds. Relatively easy livings are to be made, especially in the North American Academy, by knowing 'more and more about less and less'. A contemporary textbook, such as Bly and Rumelhart's *Cognitive Science* (1999), includes sections on 'physical movement', 'attention', 'categorisation', 'brain architecture', 'emotion' and so on, each written by a different specialist. Examination of the reading lists at the end of each section reveals virtually no cross-fertilization between the different areas. Even within a single subdiscipline, researchers pursue the work in their chosen field in virtual ignorance of the possible impact on their own work of key questions raised in closely related fields. Secondly these researchers are not used to examining or criticizing the philosophical presuppositions of their own research methods and as a result they fail to spot the significance and implications of their own discoveries. In the chapters to come I will be giving examples of significant developments in research fields like memory selective attention whose importance has gone unrecognized because the research led to an explanation based on human agency, which clashes with the mechanistic presuppositions of the discipline as a whole. A third danger applies more to the theologian or philosopher than to the social scientist – the danger of using the results of empirical research either anecdotally or uncritically. There are no short cuts in interdisciplinary working. Intellectual integrity requires a thorough awareness both of the presuppositions on which empirical evidence is based and of those on the basis of which that evidence is to be reapplied. Science, social science, philosophy and theology must all be incorporated in a completely critical practice–theory–practice methodology.

It is my hope that the theory I am about to present will avoid these dangers. Its starting point is empirical: the results of several experiments which took place over a period of almost a century. The argument proceeds by means of a dialogue between theory and practice, in which I attempt to fit the results of empirical research in an ever-widening number of fields into a consistent theoretical framework. The end result is intended to be a 'Christian' theory of knowledge incorporating a theory of learning that draws on empirical research recognized as significant by the experts in the relevant fields and a theology of revelation capable of winning the acceptance of theological specialists.

Rather than beginning with a concept generated within a particular theological paradigm of the way divine revelation is *given*, what is attempted here is to begin with an investigation of the way revelation might be *received*. The approach is a deliberate 'turn to the subject', an investigation from the side of the knower rather than the known. It involves the further assumption that the 'how?' of learning and the 'what?' of knowledge are interrelated. Knowledge does not exist in a vacuum, nor is it structured according to a universally available system of logic unaffected by the processes of learning. The way in which information is learned affects the way it is known. In relation to the knowledge of God this implies that any conclusions about *how God can be known* will suggest *what it is possible to know about him*. To take this argument boldly one stage further, it involves the assumption that God chooses to make himself known in a way that respects the human capacity for learning. The way revelation is received conditions the way it is given rather than vice versa.

Since it cannot start with theology, a Christian theory of knowledge ranges widely across disciplinary boundaries. It involves not only theology but the formal disciplines of both epistemology – the philosophy of knowledge – and the psychology of learning. Equally important, this turn to the subject involves a full account of anthropology – the study of human beings. Anthropology is both a doctrinal area in theology and a division of philosophy but its scope is still wider. The study of human beings is also the province of the social sciences. This approach to revelation thus brings together philosophy, theology and social science. It also requires an account of how these disciplines are related and how it is possible to use each one in pursuit of the single goal of understanding the Christian disciple in receipt of revelation.

I have begun with an investigation of the psychology of learning and delved into the past to examine the significance of some much-remarked but relatively neglected experimental work on perception and memory. I have used the work of cognitive psychologists to explore the interaction between the external environment as a continual source of incoming information and the structures of memory developed over time and deployed as the means by which external information is recognized, understood and itself stored in memory.

This approach to the study of learning and knowledge throws up some important and wide-ranging philosophical issues. It challenges the received wisdom of empiricism, on which until relatively recently most philosophy of knowledge and social science practice has been based. In the light of this challenge it is necessary to re-evaluate several firmly held conclusions about the relationship between philosophical and psychological approaches to knowledge. One result of this re-evaluation is to offer the possibility of a liberation of theology from the stultifying effects of empiricism. It also opens up the subject of anthropology, challenging the prevailing determinism of the human sciences in favour of a teleological approach to humanity – a view of human beings as agents with purposes.

The break with the rigidly logical framework of empiricism also opens the way to a further departure. It becomes possible to admit the importance in human knowing of the affective elements of personality: attitudes and feelings. Rather than extraneous biasing factors in our knowledge, I have argued that these are integral to the process of knowing. Knowledge of facts and opinions is based on and affected by those more fundamental elements of personality: values, goals and purposes.

The reason for this is the vital importance of identity as the area of knowledge around which all other awareness of the world revolves. Identity or self-understanding and the 'world-models' through which we understand the external environment are two sides of the same coin. Together they affect the way we understand the world, relate to others and make important life choices. Because identity develops in social relationships, all knowing is a 'knowing with'. Accordingly, I have rejected the idea of objectivity as the 'foundation' of valid knowledge integral to empiricism in favour of inter-subjectivity, the shared frameworks that make up culture and undergird the life of society. Crucially, the search for identity is the primary motivating factor in learning. This search for identity as well as knowledge of the world is the work of the 'knowing subject', the person with goals and purposes.

Having sketched out a theory of learning, I make the transition to theology to explain how this understanding of human knowledge and personal development contributes to a theory of revelation. Drawing on the theory of knowledge already presented, I develop a 'meta-theory' to explain the relationship between the natural sciences, social sciences, philosophy and theology. The point at which these discrete disciplines intersect, I argue, is the study of humanity and human nature. All are attempts to explore and hopefully answer the age-old questions of human existence and identity. Yet despite hundreds of years of human endeavour these questions, which lie at the heart of human understanding, still have no definitive answer.

The content of revelation, if such a revelation were to be given, would have to be an 'image of humanity'. It would need to supply a foundation beyond the flux of inter-subjectivity for human knowledge and self-understanding. As well as conveying truths about God, revelation must also convey the truth about human beings and human nature. In Christian theology two important themes answer to this requirement. In the opening chapters of the Bible human beings are said to be created 'in the image of God', suggesting that knowledge of God supplies the key to the understanding of human nature. Secondly, in the New Testament the same phrase, 'the image of God', is applied to Jesus Christ, who is said to reveal the nature of God through his incarnation as a man. It is concluded that Jesus is not only the revelation of God but the exemplar of human being, the 'proper man' in relation to God. He is the source of a new identity for the Christian believer made available by the gift of the Holy Spirit. The Spirit is a gift of new dynamism, who joins with human personality at the level of the knowing and acting subject to provide the power to live a radically changed life with the life of Jesus himself as its exemplar.

This conclusion has implications for the traditional formulation of the doctrine of revelation. It suggests that 'general revelation', the idea of a knowledge of God available to all humanity, is not only a reality but a necessary condition for the receipt of saving revelation in Jesus Christ. It is expressed imperfectly in a variety of philosophical positions as well as in the world's religions. Attention is drawn to the importance of history as the medium through which Jesus himself is understood in his concrete reality, through the guidance of the indwelling Holy Spirit. Finally the place of the Bible, traditionally the locus of definitive revelation, is explored.

Revelation stands at the meeting point of nature and grace, natural and supernatural. It is an aspect of divine grace, God's action for the salvation of the world. The involvement of God in the learning process is shown to revolve around the role of the Holy Spirit in revelation, energizing and redirecting the natural processes of learning and human development. Far from an alien intervention into a universe governed only by its own inherent lawfulness, the action of God in revelation fulfils the purpose for which the world was created. That purpose was the creation of human beings capable of growing in relationship with God, expressed in the calling of men and women to live as disciples of Jesus Christ and to be transformed 'into his image'.

In the conclusion I will return to the three issues identified as crucial to a coherent discipline of Christian education: the choice between theology and social science as theoretical basis; the tension between authority and experience in the adoption of teaching and learning strategies; and the manner of God's involvement in the learning process. Finally, I make my own plea for attention to be given to that most underrated and neglected quality, without which Christian education cannot hope to thrive – the skills of good teaching.

Chapter 1

Knowing the World

Seeing and Looking

Most of us assume that seeing is believing; our senses tell us the truth; what we see is what is in front of us. Experiments in perception however tell a very different story.

Card Trick

Some fifty years ago Jerome Bruner and Leo Postman recruited 28 students from Harvard and Radcliffe Universities for an experiment in perception. They showed their volunteers a series of ordinary playing cards for small fractions of a second, testing to find out how long it took them to recognize them (Bruner and Postman, 1949). The experiment made use of a piece of equipment known as a tachistoscope, which presents an image for fractions of a second. The length of the exposure is gradually increased until the subject recognizes the image correctly and the number and duration of exposures required is recorded. A tachistoscope parallels situations like moving around an unfamiliar room in the dark, when we may be uncertain of what we are actually looking at, and experiments with it can be used to show how we go about making sense of what we see.

Among the playing cards the students were asked to recognize Bruner and Postman had included some 'trick' cards: a black three of hearts, a black four of hearts, a red two of spades, a red six of spades, a black ace of diamonds and a red six of clubs. Following the usual procedure, they were presented with the cards one by one in exposures of increasing duration until they correctly recognized each one. Not surprisingly it took much longer, that is more exposures of longer duration, to recognize the trick cards.

The most interesting outcome of the experiment however was what happened when the volunteers failed to recognize the trick cards. One common type of failure was the 'dominance reaction' in which either colour or, more often, shape was dominant. Faced with a black four of hearts, the participants would report seeing a four of spades or, more often, a (red) four of hearts. Another type of failure was the compromise. Subjects would report a red six of spades, for example, as purple, brown, black on a reddish card, rusty colour or 'black but with redness somewhere'.

From time to time most of us have the experience of coming across a mis-spelled word and struggling to remember the correct spelling. This type of recognition failure, disruption, also occurred in the experiment, usually after the students had exhausted their previous 'hypotheses' about what the card might be. A first attempt to recognize a black ace of diamonds might be to name it as the (red) ace of diamonds. On being told that this was wrong the volunteer might switch to colour dominance and label it as the ace of spades. When this failed he might try compromising and suggest a brown or purple ace of diamonds. By the time the third hypothesis proved wrong his expectations of normality were thrown into disarray. One exclaimed, 'I can't make the suit out, whatever it is. It didn't even look like a card that time. I don't know what colour it is now or even whether it's a spade or a heart. I'm not even sure what a spade looks like!'

Sometimes a particular type of recognition failure such as the dominance reaction would fixate. The students would go on insisting that a black four of hearts was a four of spades until the time was up. Recognition, when it did come, was often preceded by a sense of wrongness. The subjects would say, 'There's something wrong about that card but I can't quite work out what it is.' When they finally recognized the trick cards the light usually dawned quite suddenly. All at once they realized that they were seeing 'odd' cards and began to allow for them. Bruner and Postman called it the 'My God!' reaction in which the students would say things like, 'Good Lord, what have I been saying? That's a red six of spades!' The delay in recognition came about not only because they had to allow for new possibilities but also because they had to discard their previous expectations about what playing cards are supposed to look like. Once these expectations were overturned and replaced by a new 'set' in which the anomalous cards were allowed for, they began to recognize them much more quickly.

Schemata

Bruner and Postman's results are the kind of thing we might intuitively expect but what is the explanation for them? First it is obvious that their previous experience was preventing the students from recognizing what they were actually seeing. Some, looking at a black six of hearts, perceived it as a six of spades. Others, struggling to account for the unfamiliar, actually made up brown or purple cards. In these cases the effect of previous experience was to distort perception of a new and unfamiliar pattern. In others, however, the unaccountable new experience had the effect of thoroughly disrupting and throwing their previous expectations into question.

In every case the observers were using their prior knowledge of what playing cards look like to cope with the task of recognizing the cards shown to them. We might say that each of them had a 'schema' (plural: 'schemata') for playing cards based on their previous experience. The schema told them what playing cards were supposed to look like and generated a strong expectation of what they were to see in the experiment. The schema made it possible for the participants to recognize the ordinary playing cards very rapidly after seeing them for only a small fraction of a second. But it also made the task of recognizing the unexpected cards considerably harder. Sometimes and in some people the schema was powerful enough to distort their perception, leading them to report seeing cards which did not exist. Sometimes their awareness of the actual visual image was more powerful, powerful enough in some cases to throw the schema itself into crisis. But even more significantly, in every case the result of the experiment was to modify the participant's schema. Having recognized the presence of trick cards in the batch, their expectations changed intelligently to take them into account.

The Bruner and Postman experiment is one of many which suggest the vital role played by past experience in perception, recognition and learning. Most of the time it is easy to assume that what we hear, see or touch is what is there. In fact what is going on is a much more subtle process. When we see, touch or hear successfully it is because we *already know* what we are perceiving. The relevant schema, based on past experience, organizes the raw data available to our senses quickly and efficiently. Every so often, however, we meet situations when our expectations, based on past experience, lead us astray. We see someone in the street we think we recognize. We touch something in the dark which gives us a fright until we discover what it is. We think we hear someone nearby mentioning our name. We misread a word or phrase in a book or on a poster. Very rarely, however, do the schemata based on our previous knowledge fool us for long. We seem to be sufficiently open to the physical environment to allow our five senses to put us straight very quickly. The expectations generated by our schemata may be strong but there exists in most people an even more powerful desire to understand the world correctly.

Remembering

The word 'schema' was introduced into modern psychology by Sir Frederic Bartlett in his ground-breaking book of 1932, *Remembering*. Like Bruner and Postman, Bartlett noticed in his experiments what he called an 'effort after meaning'. A particular pattern of lines so readily evoked an aeroplane that practically all the participants overlooked the 'error' in the accompanying words: 'An Airoplaxe', and recalled them as 'An Aeroplane'. The only person who did not make this error was a man who failed to recognize the drawing as representational in any way. A picture of a notice-board by a gate suggested to 80 per cent of observers the words 'Trespassers Will Be Prosecuted', although in practice the lettering was too small to be distinguishable. It seemed to Bartlett that perception was not so much a process of passively receiving stimuli from the external environment by means of the senses as an action in which those stimuli are given a meaningful context. 'A great amount of what is said to be perceived,' he concluded, 'is in fact inferred' (1932, p. 33).

Another experiment Bartlett called the method of repeated reproduction. He asked his volunteers to read a piece of writing through twice and after 15 minutes to try to write it down from memory. He then asked the volunteers to come back after various periods of time, sometimes a few hours, a day or two, a few weeks or in some cases even years and write the piece again. Bartlett tried this method with eight different short stories as well as descriptive and argumentative pieces and found a surprising uniformity about the way his volunteers both remembered and failed to remember the details of what they had read. His findings offer further interesting insights into the way schemata work.

The story Bartlett reports in *Remembering* is a North American folk-tale called 'The War of the Ghosts'. He chose this piece, about three hundred words in length, because it came from a culture obviously different to that of the 14 young men and 6 young women who read and tried to remember it. It included a number of dramatic incidents but the links between them were far from obvious for people of our culture. Finally it had a rather strange and supernatural ending in which a young man dies after fighting with ghosts and Bartlett was interested to see what his volunteers would make of the supernatural.

First he found that 'odd' details in the story could be made acceptable by labelling the story or the characters in it as 'non-English'. Just as the volunteers in the playing-card experiment had been able to adjust their expectations when they realized that they were being shown a number of trick cards, Bartlett's Cambridge students of the 1920s were able to adjust their expectations of the stories by accepting a 'strange' or 'different' character. Even so almost every participant inserted familiar details in the stories in place of unfamiliar ones: 'canoes' became 'boats' and 'hunting seals' 'fishing'.

Another change was the links in the stories. Hardly any of the volunteers accepted the lack of obvious connection between incidents in the story. Words like 'nevertheless' and 'and so' began to creep into their retellings right from the start and the more incomprehensible features of the story were simply left out. Some of the volunteers supplied a whole context for the story. A student of anthropology decided that the 'ghosts' were in fact a rival clan and retold the story accordingly, omitting all reference to the supernatural. A young woman produced a version based on the idea of dream symbolism. All the participants strove to make the story 'make sense' by supplying links based on their own culture and experience for those based on the story's own inner logic. Over time their memories of the stories were gradually assimilated to the pattern of their everyday experience.

Bartlett also noticed that when they came to retell the stories his volunteers would often begin by remembering one important detail. Their memory of the whole story would then gradually crystallize around the particular event or item they had first called to mind. Interestingly, however, it was not its part in the story which made the first remembered detail important but the interests or temperament of the storyteller. It might be a familiar word, a comic association or a link with a participant's own particular interest. It was the schemata of the teller's own previous experience which made those particular details memorable rather than anything intrinsic to the story itself.

Finally, Bartlett's volunteers usually supplied an overall tone to the stories they told. Not only did they remember the stories as happy or sad, frightening or mysterious, but their reconstructions tended to fit in with the emotional label they gave to the story as a whole. Events were subtly changed, links made and motives attributed to the characters in such a way as to make sense of the tone of the story. Bartlett called this sense of tone an 'attitude', which he described as a complex psychological state hard to analyse and mainly a matter of emotion.

Although Bartlett's experiments were conducted in the 1920s, interest in them resurfaced with the emergence of cognitive psychology in the 1960s and 1970s. More recent experiments have confirmed and developed his findings. One particularly interesting example of the influence of schemata on memory is the transmission of a North Carolina ballad called 'The Wreck of the Old "97" ' (Wallace and Rubin, 1988). The song describes a train crash that took place in 1907 and was transmitted in a variety of versions. By the 1930s it had been recorded four times in two different versions and the discrepancy eventually gave rise to a celebrated copyright trial in 1934, at which five ballad singers performed five different versions of the song, in which the number of verses ranged from 5 to 14 and crucial differences included the name of the driver, the name of the train and the cause of the crash itself. In the 1980s the researchers visited North Carolina and searched out ballad singers who were still performing the song. They discovered five, each of whom was asked to give a second rendering six months later. Not one gave exactly the same performance both times. Words were added or deleted, phrases sung in a different order and even whole verses added or omitted.

Yet despite the fluidity of its performance a number of constraints appeared to be operating which ensured the survival of the song in recognizable form over several generations. Interestingly these constraints reflect the ballad tradition within which the song is set as much or more than the story of the train crash itself. As well as the narrative structure of the story, they include the number of beats in a line, the number of lines in a verse, the meaning or gist of the verses and the order of the verses. Wallace and Rubin comment, 'It is as if the rules or constraints, rather than the particular telling, are being transmitted' (1988, p. 286). Furthermore beyond all these is the influence of existing models in the ballad tradition – the story of the ship that never returned or the tragedy of parted lovers. These models and the musical and poetical constraints form the schemata that guarantee the continuity of the song even while specific details of the story change over time.

Not only is a great amount of what is said to be perceived in fact inferred but a great amount of what is said to be remembered is reconstructed. In the story experiment the process of remembering worked almost like rationalization, as Bartlett's volunteers subtly shaped their memories to fit their overall impression of the tone of the story and substituted familiar and comprehensible details for the strange and unfamiliar, or like crystallization, as one detail, selected on the basis of its importance to the teller, provided a clue to the reconstruction of the rest. In 'The Wreck of the Old "97" ' the structures and patterns of the local ballad tradition have shaped the transmission of the song and the story within it. Bartlett's work has given rise to a tradition of research which demonstrates that memories are not just passively recorded but actively shaped by means of the schemata derived from past experience.

Schemata as Mental Processes

But what is a schema? Bartlett defined it as 'an active organisation of past reactions' (1932, p. 201). Schemata are the way past experience is organized and made available to interpret the present. They are a tool for both recognition and remembering. Moreover, schemata must be both psychological and physiological – psychological because they handle processes such as memory and interpretation, physiological because they handle the raw physical data of perception, the light and sound waves available to the senses and the neural messages which carry them. A schema is therefore a feedback mechanism whereby physical experience is assimilated, stored and made available in psychological form for future use.

Bartlett lived in the days before computers. But his ideas have immediate relevance in the field of computer modelling of human thinking. A computer has a physical basis consisting of electrical connections and its function is to store and use information. Computers have memories and can be programmed to use stored information to recognize patterns of both light and sound. Since the 1960s cognitive psychology using computer-based models has grown to become a major force in psychology (Bruning et al., 1995, p. 1) and schemata accepted as a standard account of the data-structures of which our memories consist (Baddeley, 1999, pp. 152–4; Smith, 1998, pp. 402–10).

The Structure of Memory

The earliest influential attempt to describe the kind of data-structure a schema might be was a paper entitled 'A framework for representing knowledge' published in 1975 by Marvin Minsky of the Massachusetts Institute of Technology. Taking as his starting point the use of computers to simulate visual processes, Minsky proposed a theoretical framework by which to understand the way in which the knowledge required by the computer for the simulation of vision might be represented. Minsky called his hypothetical data-structures 'frames' but explicitly stated that his work was to be seen as an attempt in the tradition of Bartlett and also Thomas Kühn to investigate the representation of knowledge in memory. In view of this the terminology of frames and schemata can be taken as interchangeable.

The frame or schema is a data-structure representing a stereotyped situation such as the layout of a room, the routes between home and work, correct etiquette at a formal dinner or the way to service a car. The 'top level' of a schema is the information which is always true of the situation to which it relates. In the schema for a room, for example, walls, floor and a ceiling are mandatory. If we open a door and they fail to appear, the expectation of finding a room on the other side must be revised: a coal-cellar perhaps, or else a roof-garden. If we walk into a building expecting a restaurant but find ourselves in a place with no chairs or tables, expectation switches to something related, perhaps a bar or disco.

Items at 'lower levels' of the schema however are not specified. A room may be decorated and furnished in a variety of different ways according to its function. The schema for a room leaves these items to be filled in and they may serve as clues to the function of the room in question. Conversely what we know about the function of a room leads to certain expectations about the appropriate furniture and decor. Just as in Bartlett's experiments the participants supplied information like the wording on a noticeboard according to their sense of what was appropriate, schemata create expectations about what to expect in certain situations. Having discovered the bathroom on the upstairs floor of a house, for example, we normally assume the other rooms to be bedrooms but we may be more or less surprised to find a study or a model railway layout, depending on what we know of the occupant.

A schema provides the setting or context for comprehending incoming information. As the playing-card experiment nicely demonstrates, it is predisposed towards certain expectations based on the regularity of previous experience in a given area. The 'settings' or 'situations' which form the content of a given schema are extremely varied. They might represent a situation or task such as one's route to work or what to expect on a visit to the dentist. The ability to read or to speak a given language can also be understood as schemata. Schemata also vary from person to person in respect of their detail. An interior designer will notice far more features of a room than someone without her interest and training, a professional musician may 'hear' more of a concert than an amateur enthusiast, a chess master 'sees' more of a game than a beginner.

The Deployment of Memory

It is rare for only one schema to be operating in any given situation. On the way to work, for example, we may need the skill of driving a car and the ability to read the road signs as well as the knowledge of how to get there. In all three our prior knowledge is organized in such a way as to be instantly available to help us to understand and respond to the present. In addition, if we decide to listen to the car radio we will be deploying schemata for the understanding of music, drama or news events. The bodily skills involved in driving the car usually work at a subconscious level as hands and feet respond semi-automatically to the condition of the traffic. The possible routes between work and home will be represented by a mental map. A mental map is not the same as the printed road map. We may in fact be aware only of the roads we need and one or two favourite short cuts. During the drive the schema is continually updating our position on the mental map so that we know which turning to take next as well as absorbing any relevant information like planned road works. To listen to the car radio we need the schema learned in childhood for understanding the language as well as that which tells us which stations are available and how to locate them. If our choice is the early morning news the schema for current affairs together with its component sub-schemata for political events, sporting events and so on will be needed to understand all that we hear and it too will be continually updated as new information is taken in and yesterday's situation discarded. In virtually any situation the schemata of our understanding are capable of searching for information through which to become more effective. All experience is potentially a lesson for the future. It becomes so by incorporation into the active settings by which the past is organized and the present comprehended.

The sum total of all a person's schemata forms a 'model' of the world, which he carries 'in his head', a framework which enables him to comprehend the day-to-day 'real' world. A schema works by filling in the gaps in the information available through the senses, generating expectations, closing off less likely alternatives and in general supplying a meaningful context within which our experience of the world makes sense. Take for example the following three sentences:

1 Mary heard the ice-cream van coming.
2 She remembered her pocket-money.
3 She rushed into the house.

Without a context these three sentences have no connection. They only describe a comprehensible sequence of events when we know the facts which are required as essential background – that people like ice-cream, that ice-cream is bought with money and that money is often kept in houses. These facts are supplied from our existing knowledge by the schemata for money and ice-cream. In addition we expect a story. We expect that the three sentences will have something to do with each other and on this basis we construct a context which includes motives and feelings. If in place of 'ice-cream van' and 'money' we were to read 'teacher' and 'homework' the motives and feelings we supplied might be very different.

Another aspect of schemata, which we will examine in more detail at a later stage, is the way they express *shared* understandings (Bruning et al.,

1995, p. 8). A story-teller could use the sentences about Mary and the ice-cream van confident in the expectation that knowledge of ice-cream and money, teachers and homework and the connections between them is widely shared. One of the reasons a person driving to work can expect to arrive safely at her destination is the fact that the schema for driving includes both written and unwritten codes of driving behaviour which, as long as everyone sticks to them, help to ensure safe travel. The reporting of any given piece of political and sporting news on the car radio will in fact omit most of the information relevant to the situation because the news editor is entitled to assume that the vast majority of listeners already share it.

Another example of the corporate nature of schemata is the way they also act as 'scripts', which guide our actions (Schank and Abelson, 1977). For example, a visit to the dentist consists of a typical sequence of events. After a few visits the script becomes familiar. It tells us we need to make an appointment, to check in a few minutes before the appointment is due, to wait in the waiting room, to bring something to read if we don't want to be bored and so on. The script supplies rules for actions and decisions, such as 'If it goes on hurting, contact the dentist'. It also tells us the way the dentist is supposed to carry out his role – firmly but with sympathy, without being too apologetic, making light conversation but nothing too personal. By scripting our actions and expectations in this way schemata enable us to cope with life by reducing its unpredictability and giving us a modicum of confidence and control of our own destiny, even in the dentist's chair! (Schank, 1981).

Tacit Knowledge as Bodily Knowing

Another name for the model of the world each of us carries in our heads made up of schemata which guide our actions and enable us to comprehend the world is 'tacit knowledge', the term coined by Michael Polanyi and used extensively throughout his writings, including his major work, *Personal Knowledge* (Polanyi, 1958). Polanyi shared with Bartlett two crucially important insights: that tacit knowledge is based on physical or bodily mechanisms and that it is holistically or globally organized. We have already noted that perception has a physical basis. The external world, the physical and human environment in which we live, is always supplying new information through the five senses while the internal world, our previous experience actively organized in the form of schemata, is continually sifting and interpreting this new information in a search for meaning. While we have also seen that schemata can be physically modelled on computers as data-structures, the insights of both Bartlett and Polanyi on the relationship between memory and bodily mechanisms highlight the importance of understanding memory in terms of *skill* rather than *structures*, intentional activity rather than inert data.

Bartlett discovered the vital clue to his description of schemata in the work of physiologist Sir Henry Head (Bartlett, 1932, pp. 198–201). Head was interested in a certain type of brain damage in which his patients lost what he called their 'ongoing postural model'. Normally we all know what position our bodies are in. We can shut our eyes and touch the end of our noses without too much trouble. When we start to overbalance we automatically correct ourselves. We know when lying down whether our legs are bent or straight. Head's patients, however, had lost this sense and found it difficult to orient themselves. They could not get out of bed for example without checking to see whether their legs were in the right position. Head called this 'ongoing postural model' a schema. Thus in Head's definition a schema is a holistic or globally organized representation of a physical reality, continuously modified by a process of feedback.

Thought of in this way the schema is a kind of continuously updated and highly flexible bodily memory. In a game of tennis, no two movements are exactly the same. Each backhand, forehand or overhead shot is a variation on a theme. Any particular game involves a large number of shots, no two exactly alike. The essence of a bodily skill, such as tennis, Bartlett believed, was the use of the body's ongoing postural model continually to update the awareness of the position of the body coupled with the outwardly-directed intention to play the ball in a certain way. During a practice session it is possible to 'work on' a shot by consciously paying attention to the co-ordination of the movements involved but during a game the focus of attention shifts to responding to the opponent's shots and putting the ball in the desired place and the movements required to achieve these are almost always unconscious.

Thus in the performance of a skill there is a considerable tacit element. It involves 'knowledge' held by the body in the form of schemata, the content of which cannot be reduced to explicit description. Polanyi gives several examples of similar skills. The ability to stay on a bicycle can be explicitly defined by a complicated mathematical formula but it is quite unnecessary for the would-be bicycle rider to learn that formula. What is learned is the art of keeping one's balance. The knowledge represented explicitly by the formula is comprehended tacitly in quite a different way. By the same token, Polanyi argued, the knowledge of the expert chef is more than can be set down in a cookery book and learning to drive involves much more than simply reading the manual (1958, pp. 49–50; 1966b, pp. 6–7).

Polanyi proposed that perception be understood not as the passive contemplation of objects but as a bodily skill. Significantly he used the sense of touch rather than sight as his paradigm. With touch the active, exploratory role of the perceiver is much more obvious than with sight or hearing. One example he frequently repeated was the use of a stick in the dark or by a blind person to feel his way (1967, pp. 12–13). What the blind person feels are the movements of the stick but what he is actually thinking about and paying attention to is the picture of the surrounding environment which the movements of the stick convey. Each individual perception goes to modify or enrich a global psychological representation of the person's immediate surroundings. Equally important is that this global representation is being used for a purpose: to find one's way.

Like a blind person's stick our schemata are an extension of our bodily senses. We use them to interpret the data we receive from touch, sight, hearing, taste and smell in order to tell us what is there. Our tacit knowledge is thus an extension of the body's ability to orient itself to its surroundings. It consists of a mental picture of what to expect in a given situation. And like the tennis player's bodily skill the schemata of tacit knowledge constitute a continually updated, flexible feedback system, enabling a person to respond flexibly and 'intelligently' in any given situation. Based on the sense of touch and an understanding of perception as the activity of orienting oneself in the world, Polanyi draws attention to the necessity of focusing on the skill of 'remembering' rather than the hypothetical structures of 'memory'.

Interaction and Learning

Active and Passive Processing

The experiments of Bartlett and Bruner and the theories of Polanyi suggest that far from consisting only of the passive reception of sensations from the environment, perception involves an active process of selection and interpretation. Nor is it difficult to see why this should be so. The sheer amount of information available to the senses at any one time is so great that if we tried to pay attention to it all we would soon be overwhelmed. The capacity of long-term memory, the ability to store past experience, has no known limit. The bottleneck occurs in short-term or working memory, the amount of information we can deal with at one time (Baddeley, 1999, pp. 22–6).

It has been recognized for some time that the capacity of working memory is limited to about seven items (Miller, 1956; Bruning et al., 1995, pp. 49–53). But a unit of memory may be of any size so long as it contains within itself the key to recovering all the information included in it. For example, an isolated letter or digit makes up a single unit but so also does a word, a phrase, a sentence or even a whole story. The capacity of short-term memory is increased by 'chunking' or 'unitizing', packing as much information as possible into one unit, a skill our minds seem to perform automatically. In Bartlett's experiment on the way stories are remembered his volunteers often found a whole story stored as a unit in long-term memory, so that remembering one vital detail was the key to recalling all the rest. In his experiment with the 'Airoplaxe' he found his volunteers consistently imposing a single overall meaning on an objectively 'meaningless' combination of lines and letters. The sentences about Mary and the ice-cream van illustrate the tendency to impose a single context of meaning on otherwise disconnected statements. Experiments have also been done in which participants are presented with words and letters for a short time and asked to remember as much as they can. When the image consists of about 25 random letters, only four or five are usually recalled. If the 25 letters are arranged into four or five words what is recalled is usually two or three words, or about 10–15 letters in total. But if the 25 letters are presented in the form of a meaningful phrase, then it is likely that the whole phrase will be successfully recalled. The skill of reading a page effectively consists of the ability to extract the importance cues, the key words and sentences, and use these to reconstruct the sense of the rest (Smith, 1982, pp. 28–31).

One of the functions of schemata is to bring together separate items of information in a single meaningful context. Stored in long-term memory, they provide the units for working memory enabling us to process the largest amount of information possible at any one time. But the same feature by which schemata help to overcome the problem of limited capacity often proves a drawback. Schemata work by providing a stereotype of a given situation, be it a physical location, such as a room, or a psychological one, such as a political issue discussed on the radio. By so doing they impose expectations about the nature of the incoming information, reducing our openness to novelty and surprise. It was the very efficiency of their schemata for playing cards which made it difficult for the participants in Bruner and Postman's experiment to recognize the trick cards. And Bartlett's volunteers consistently substituted familiar details for unfamiliar ones and links based on their own culture for those of the original stories.

Interaction

All this means that in perception and in the way the mind processes the information we receive there must be a balance between passive receiving and active shaping of information. As cognitive psychologist Ulric Neisser puts it, 'There is a dialectical contradiction between these two requirements: we cannot perceive *unless* we anticipate, but we must not see *only* what we anticipate' (1976, p. 43). In cognitive psychology the passive and active processes are known as data-driven and concept-driven processing. Data-driven processing is what is involved in receiving the incoming information. This is essentially an automatic physical and to that extent passive process. In the case of human perception light strikes the eye and causes a neural reaction. The information acts as a stimulus to which the organs of perception and the brain respond. Concept-driven processing involves the deployment of existing knowledge in such a way as to generate a 'set' or expectation. In other words it is essentially active involving the 'effort after meaning'. Incoming information acts not just as a stimulus but as a cue to which the brain responds by offering an interpretation. Perception has to be understood as a process of *interaction* in which the data-driven and concept-driven processes successfully combine.

Both Neisser in *Cognition and Reality* and Jerome Bruner in his paper 'Personality dynamics and the process of perceiving' (1951) offer accounts of perception and learning as interaction, embracing both the active and passive sides of the process. Each of them suggested that at any given time the perceiver has to be understood as *doing* something, whether this is reading, travelling, working, playing or even taking part in an experiment! The demands of the task prepare us to utilize a certain set of schemata. At the most basic level these include our knowledge of the world about us and of the language, spoken and written. They include our knowledge of our physical surroundings and, finally, the schemata specific to the particular task in hand – playing football, operating a lathe, doing the weekly shopping or engaging in a political argument. Each of the schemata in operation can be understood as a *hypothesis* or, in Bruner's words, 'a determining tendency or cognitive predisposition', the readiness to receive certain types of information and to respond in a certain set of ways. These hypotheses vary in strength according to a number of factors, especially our familiarity with the task in hand and the relative probability of different alternatives: it takes far less mental readjustment to register a bus coming round the corner of the street than, for example, an elephant!

Our schemata can thus be understood as continually and intelligently *sampling* the environment (Benjafield, 1997, pp. 33–4). Although schemata stereotype the situation in a certain way and impose certain expectations, they also have gaps ready to be filled in – the decor of the room we have entered, the number on the bus coming up the street, and so on. In other words, there is an inbuilt readiness for the data-driven element in the perceptual process. If the first stage in perception is the presentation of a 'hypothesis' in the form of a schema, the second is the input of the information the schema is waiting for and ready to respond to. The third is the checking of that information against the range of expectations generated by the schema. As soon as information is picked up the various possibilities offered by the schema can be rapidly readjusted. If we did see an elephant in the street unexpectedly, the idea of a circus in town or an escape from the zoo would leap from distant possibility to distinct probability! Incoming information may also correct a schema, such as when our mental maps have to be readjusted to take account of a new roundabout or one-way system.

Learning

What is true of perception is true on a broader scale of the whole of learning. Learning too is a process of interaction in which we make sense of our surroundings. The difficulties experienced by the students in the playing-card experiment nicely illustrate one of the main characteristics of human learning, our tendency to *assimilate* new information to the pattern of our existing understanding. When learning a new skill we often misunderstand the instructions through lack of experience. We do not have enough information in our existing schemata to help us make sense of the task demands. When studying a complicated passage in a book we may distort the new information we intend to learn simply because we do not understand it well enough. When reading the newspaper we may interpret the political news of the day in a way which confirms our existing views and prejudices. Assimilation of information to the existing structure of our tacit knowledge is much easier and takes much less effort than that required to alter the shape of our schemata – to learn new skills or change our minds about the things we believe.

In both perception and learning, one of three things may happen to the information with which the world supplies us:

1 We may *ignore* it. We may decide the new information is irrelevant or uninteresting. We skip over articles in the newspaper we don't wish to read and forget TV adverts as soon as they are finished. Alternatively we

may not be capable of understanding the new information. We possess no schema by which to make sense of it. In this case the information may not be noticed at all or, if noticed, passed over as beyond comprehension. A conversation in a foreign language, a friend's explanation of some aspect of his own particular hobby, an item on the news about business affairs, may be impossible to understand and so never remembered. Finally the new information may be too threatening; the emotional or social consequences of attending to the new information may be seen as too great. So for example members of some right-wing groups deny the Holocaust and many left-wingers formerly denied the existence of Stalinist labour camps.

2   We may *assimilate* it to the structure of our existing schemata. In this case the new information may be distorted or even falsified. We have gone some way to understanding it but our existing schemata were not capable of comprehending it completely. Most teachers are satisfied with a degree of assimilation. When our daughter Susie looked at the lighted gas ring and called it a candle we were pleased with the evidence of her learning rather than disappointed with the error. The student has to make sense of what she is learning in her own terms. The seriousness of any distortion can only be measured by a generally accepted norm of what a person should have learned in a given situation. Small children are generally allowed more leeway than adults, but even as adults we usually allow each other to look at things differently and individuals like artists frequently suggest new ways of looking at familiar things.

3   The third possible response is *accommodation* to the perceived structure of the new information. In accommodation a new schema is created or an existing one modified in order to make way in the understanding for what is clearly seen as something new and not previously understood. Sometimes this takes place in a moment of inspiration, often in a gradual way. Accommodation is, or is intended to be, the characteristic of formal learning, but all experienced educators appreciate that in practice accommodation is usually preceded by at least some degree of assimilation, which must be allowed for and if possible made use of.

While accommodation may be the goal of formal learning situations, in practice all three strategies are likely to be found in differing proportions as we interact with the world around us. All learning is a balance between assimilation and accommodation.[1] In order to learn something new the learner must *do something* to the new knowledge. To be learned, knowledge must be changed by assimilation to the schemata of the learner. Not only is the new knowledge changed, however, but the schema is also changed in order to *accommodate* the new knowledge. Learning changes the learner.

This poses an important question for the study of revelation. The concept of revelation involves new information about God in some form or other being received and understood. Most Christians are familiar with Jesus's parable of the sower in which some of the seed fell on stony ground and was trampled underfoot and we can probably accept that there are many people who ignore the revelation offered to them. We will probably be comfortable with the idea that this new information changes the person who receives it. Who could discover the truth about God and not be changed by it? But can the knowledge conveyed about God in revelation be subject to assimilation? Can revelation submit to change in the course of interpretation and still be revelation? In the course of the following chapters this is precisely what I hope to show. As David Brown argues (1999, pp. 127–33), revelation is a personal dialogue between God and individuals, God and communities in which God *accommodates* to the conditions of the time in order to preserve human freedom. This conclusion has potentially an enormous impact on theology. It leaves behind the neo-orthodox framework, in which nothing is said to prepare humanity for the receipt of revelation but the action of God in revelation itself. It gives back an important role to the human understanding in the construing of God's self-disclosure. Rather than consisting solely of reflection on revelation, theology reflects the interaction between revelation and human experience (Browning, 1991, pp. 5–6).

However, before exploring the implications for theology we need to explore the process of learning in more detail. Earlier we noted the tendency to assimilate our reading of the daily paper, for example, to our existing beliefs; or a person's conscious or subconscious decision to ignore new information because she finds it unwelcome or threatening. The study of learning is not complete without an investigation of the role of attitudes,

---

[1] The use of the terms 'assimilation' and 'accommodation' to describe the action of the mind in cognition was originated by the philosopher and child psychologist, Jean Piaget. However, Piaget's structuralist theory, underlying the use of these terms, cannot be accepted without considerable modification. See, for example, Donaldson (1978) and Siegel and Brainerd (1978).

values and emotions. Before embarking on the investigation of these important elements in learning, however, there are a number of philosophical issues which arise naturally from the account of perception and learning set out in this chapter. It is to these issues that we now turn.

Chapter 2

The Big Picture

Psychology and Philosophy

Empiricism

If our ability to perceive and understand the world depends on the deployment of schemata based on past experience, if each of us constructs a 'model' of the world 'in our heads' to help us understand the 'real' world of experience, if new and unfamiliar information is assimilated to the structure of our existing understanding, it follows that there can be no such thing as a purely objective point of view. All new experience is interpreted and every new discovery takes place within a context provided by our past experiences. While our schemata enable us to perceive and recognize the familiar quickly and accurately, they actually prevent us from recognizing and cause us to distort the unfamiliar, whether the unfamiliar consists of a trick playing card, a story from a different culture, a chapter of a book or an item on a news programme. Yet despite the fact that schemata generate powerful expectations which influence our perceptions of the world, they are also capable of change. The expectations they generate may be strong but not strong enough in most people to counteract the desire to understand the world more fully. Existing expectations in the form of our schemata and new observations in the form of our perceptions interact with one another. Anomalous playing cards are eventually recognized for what they are and the schema for playing cards modified accordingly.

This understanding of perception, recognition, remembering and learning, easily demonstrable from a few simple experiments, actually contradicts not only the everyday 'common sense' idea that facts are facts and seeing is believing but the much more fully developed philosophical position that has dominated the English-speaking world for several hundred years – empiricism. The empiricists include among their number such names as John Locke in the seventeenth century, David Hume in the eighteenth, John Stuart Mill in the nineteenth and A. J. Ayer and Bertrand Russell in the twentieth. According to empiricism all valid knowledge is derived from the outside world via the data of our senses. We may have to be taught the use of an ace of hearts but simply recognizing an ace of hearts presents no problem. The red vehicle moving towards us up the street reveals itself as a bus without the help of schemata. Learned experience tells us only what we need to do if we want to use the bus to travel. The concepts through which we learn to associate experiences and form an intelligent picture of the world are arrived at by repeated observation and logical deduction. Thus having seen windows broken by stones or footballs once or twice we learn to associate flying stones and footballs with broken glass. More important still, true knowledge is held together with the glue of correct logical deduction. Animals are mortal, a cat is an animal, so my pet cat will die one day. Buses belong to a class of public transport vehicles whose function is to carry people along certain designated routes. The number 57, which passes my home, is an example of such a bus, therefore it is possible to use it to travel to my destination.

Thus the empiricist claims to be capable of constructing what Stephen Toulmin calls the 'City of Truth' on the foundation of clear and certain observation using the architectural principles of correct logical deduction (1976, pp. 82–90). Moreover these two elements of our knowledge, clear observation and correct deduction, are independent of one another. True observations are those on which all independent observers can agree and depend only on the reliability of our senses, not on any concepts the observers might hold in common. Correct concepts built on logic hold true for all experience and are unbiased by any particular observations. This approach gives rise to what W. V. O. Quine called the 'two dogmas' of empiricism. 'Modern empiricism', he writes,

> has been conditioned in large part by two dogmas. One is a belief in some fundamental cleavage between truths which are *analytic*, or grounded in meanings independently of matters of fact, and truths which are *synthetic*, or grounded in fact. The other dogma is *reductionism*: the belief that each meaningful statement is equivalent to some logical construct upon terms which refer to immediate experience.
>
> (1961, p. 20)

Quine concludes that these dogmas are in fact unsupportable. Analytic truths – those based on logical analysis – and synthetic truths – those arrived at by observation – cannot be conveniently isolated from one another. There are no observations of fact 'uncontaminated' by theoretical assumptions because empirical observation takes place in the context of assumptions based on previous experience and learning. New knowledge is inevitably assimilated, at least in part, to the structure of existing knowledge and belief. However, empiricism rules out the contribution of the subject in perception, comprehension and learning.

Empiricism and Metaphysics

Following on from their presuppositions, empiricist philosophers from Locke to Ayer and beyond tended to concentrate on analysing the conditions of perception and devising systems of logic and, since mathematics seems to provide the perfect system of logic, it plays a key role in the work of many of these philosophers. In fact as long ago as the 1650s Thomas Hobbes compared thinking to calculation (1651, p. 82). The titles of empiricist philosophy include John Locke's *An Essay Concerning Human Under-standing*, George Berkeley's *A Treatise Concerning the Principles of Human Knowledge*, David Hume's *An Enquiry Concerning the Human Under-standing*, A. J. Ayer's *The Foundations of Empirical Knowledge* and Bertrand Russell's *The Principles of Mathematics*. Moreover, because empiricists hold that clear observation and logical deduction alone hold the key to true knowledge, they tend to dismiss anything outside these pursuits as unworthy of the name of philosophy. 'If we take in hand any volume', wrote David Hume on the last page of the *Enquiry*,

> of divinity or school metaphysics, for instance; let us ask, *Does it contain any abstract reasoning concerning quantity or number?* No. *Does it contain any experimental reasoning concerning matter of fact or existence?* No. Commit it then to the flames: for it can contain nothing but sophistry and illusion.
>
> (1748, p. 165)

The best modern example of this position was the verification principle introduced by the school of logical positivism in the early twentieth century. The classical expression of this position in English is A. J. Ayer's *Language, Truth and Logic*. According to the logical positivists the meaning of a statement is equivalent to the method of its verification. A sentence can only be said to mean anything at all if it can be shown to be true or false by a process of observation and reasoning. Nothing that is not based on demonstrable fact and clear deduction qualifies as a 'statement' in the strict sense of the term. This implies, as the verificationists were not slow to point out, that any statement about morality, aesthetics, religion or metaphysics is meaningless since it cannot be shown to be either true or false. Good or bad, beauty or ugliness, the existence of God and the purpose of the universe are not philosophical questions, only fruitless speculation.

The empiricism of the philosophers has its echo in the everyday 'common sense' of western culture. Here it is widely assumed that there is a certain class of facts which are matters of public and verifiable truth, chiefly the domain of science. Everything else, including politics, morality and religion, is a question of personal opinion in which one person's belief is as good as anyone else's. A politician or public servant's 'private life' is supposed not to influence the performance of his public duties. If science has not yet quite disproved the Bible, at least the Bible and religious 'truth' generally is less reliable than other kinds of truth. Nor has theology itself managed to remain immune to this assault; in fact quite the reverse. In 'An empiricist's view of the nature of religious belief', R. B. Braithwaite (1971) laid it down that statements of morality or metaphysics could only be taken as meaningful if understood as expressions of attitude or emotion rather than statements of fact. This position influenced the tone of theology, at least in the English-speaking world, for more than a generation and even as late as the 1980s it was common to find theology texts paying homage to Ayer, Braithwaite and verificationism in general (for example, Sponheim, 1984, pp. 199–210).

In education the effect of empiricism was to enforce a rigid distinction between the philosophy of knowledge and the psychology of learning. While psychological study may concentrate for example on those factors which contribute to the effectiveness of learning, the conceptual analysis of the acquisition of knowledge falls within the field of epistemology – the philosophy of knowledge (Hamlyn, 1974). Knowledge, argues Paul Hirst (1965), may be divided into a number of publicly specifiable 'forms of understanding', achieved over the course of generations, each form of understanding having developed its own distinctive logic. Learning, he argues, consists of initiation into the different types of logical relationships appropriate to the various forms of understanding, but the logical structure of the different forms of understanding are to be strictly distinguished from the psychological processes by which they may be learned.

Concepts and Observation

In practice, however, it is not difficult to see that a philosophy which depends on the interpretation of such things as the data available to our senses involves implicit psychological assumptions. The same is true for a large number of philosophers. Descartes's *Meditations*, which was in many ways the foundation stone of modern philosophy, is a particularly good example. His theory of knowledge is dependent on the analysis of data received by the senses, on considerations as to the reliability of the sense organs and notoriously on his conceptualization of 'mental substance' as separate from and interacting with 'physical substance'. Locke, Hume, Berkeley, Price and Ayer, to name but a few, all make use of psychological generalizations. Expressions such as *ideas, impressions, imagination, sensible manifold, sense data* and so on are all psychological terms. Yet even twentieth-century philosophers, writing in the period when the discipline of psychology was expanding and finding its feet, failed to recognize the need for adequate experimental grounding of these basic expressions of empirical reference.

Take for example A. J. Ayer's *The Foundations of Empirical Knowledge*. Ayer makes use of a number of empirical examples to illustrate what he calls his 'argument from illusion', the idea that what we perceive may be unreliable or illusory. The inference Ayer draws is that we do not perceive 'material objects' but only 'sense data'. 'Sense data', he maintains, are the basic level of perception, the 'foundation of empirical knowledge', and as such they are 'incorrigible', in contrast to material objects, whose existence is simply an inference from the experience of sense data. Ayer's examples include mirages and hallucinations, the perception of a coin which, although circular, appears elliptical for some observers, and that of a straight stick which appears to bend when put into water due to refraction. His assumption is that the use of these examples is unproblematical, that they can all be taken at 'face value'. He fails to see the need for a process of interpretation involving careful empirical investigation before they can be used to provide evidence for his theory. 'When I look at a straight stick, which is refracted in water and so appears crooked,' he writes, 'my experience is qualitatively the same as if I were looking at a stick that really was crooked.' This example, like all the others Ayer uses, is anecdotal. He has performed no tests to establish the regularity of or the conditions for the experiences he describes. Nor does he bother to define, in terms which could be experimentally verified, what is meant by the phrase 'qualitatively the same'. Moreover there are several factors which Ayer has failed to take into consideration. The fact that along with the 'bent stick' we also see the surface of the water makes a significant difference. Most people are familiar with the effect from past experience, and this, with or without a theoretical understanding of refraction, in fact prevents virtually every intelligent observer from interpreting their perception as a 'bent stick' (Ayer, 1940, pp. 3–9).

Another example of the philosopher's tendency to ignore psychology is Gilbert Ryle's *The Concept of Mind*, in which he put forward a theory he called 'logical behaviourism'. This was an attempt to derive the principles of behaviourism purely by deduction with virtually no reference to empirical observation. In fact Ryle virtually ignored the actual practice of the psychological school of behaviourism, which at the time of his writing was in the process of becoming the dominant approach to human psychology and the study of human thought. Interestingly enough Ryle's book was in turn virtually ignored by behaviourist psychologists, most of whom were unaware or dismissive of the philosophical foundations of their own work. Nor is this surprising since, following the same empiricist principles as Ryle and Ayer, they, like most psychologists, believed that empirical observations and the conclusions they drew from them owed little to theoretical presuppositions.

The effect of empiricism has been to maintain strict lines of demarcation between philosophers and psychologists. Many philosophers, rather than admit the interdependence of empirical and conceptual questions, insist on a one-way logical dependence of the study of 'learning' upon that of 'knowledge'. The result is a tendency to ignore the implications of the results of psychological research and a resistance to any 'psychological idiom' in philosophy.[1] Equally, the work of psychologists has suffered until relatively recently from a failure to recognize the philosophical foundations of their own work. Psychology has been and remains to a large extent divided, with little cross-fertilization between separate areas of research or awareness of the possible implications of even the basic theoretical assumptions of one branch for those of another (Mischel, 1973). I have already noted the isolation of each separate sub-field of cognitive science revealed by Bly and Rumelhart's textbook (1999). In a similar way, Baddeley's standard textbook on memory (1999) discusses the half-century-old theories of Benjamin Whorf on the role of language in the development of concepts but ignores the far more relevant and recent work on language acquisition by Jerome Bruner and others (Baddeley, 1999, pp. 156–60).

Small wonder therefore that many psychological researchers show little awareness of the relevance of the philosophical questions which underlie and inform their discipline. As long ago as 1976 Ulric Neisser criticized the lack of 'ecological validity', or contact with everyday reality, of the

---

[1] See the contribution of G. E. M. Anscombe in Brown (1974) and Strawson (1966, p. 19) (objecting to Kant). Among philosophers who have given their attention to the activities of psychologists and their implications for philosophy is D. W. Hamlyn. But Hamlyn operates within the traditional empiricist framework and maintains a rigid distinction between the work of the psychologist and that of the philosopher (see, for example, 1967). See also Hamlyn's exchange with Stephen Toulmin on this subject in 'Epistemology and conceptual development' (1971). The relevant article of Toulmin's is 'The concept of "stages" in psychological development'.

theoretical approaches in cognitive psychology prevailing up to the mid-1970s. Even more important, he noted the lack of awareness of the need for a new philosophical anthropology to undergird the picture of human beings as information-processors (1976, pp. 1–9). Yet even though Neisser's *Cognition and Reality* was in many ways a ground-breaking text, in subsequent work he himself has failed to appreciate the theoretical and methodological consequences of the interactionist perspective and the even greater potential impact of the role of purpose and goals in perception and memory (Neisser, 1997). Psychological texts generally contain few references to philosophers and philosophical questions, indicating that few practitioners appreciate the background of philosophical questions against which they work. Perhaps the most outstanding example of this lack of awareness occurred in the early days of artificial intelligence research. Confident predictions of finding solutions to all the major problems in a decade ignored the fact that the basic philosophical question behind AI is the old mind–brain problem – the relationship between the physical mechanisms of the brain and our experience of consciousness – a question which has not yielded a solution in hundreds of years! Conceptual progress in many areas is still hindered by the continuing influence of empiricism. For example, in social psychology rational, 'objective' and measurable processes rather than individuals' interpretation of their situations constitute the preferred explanation even for the development and maintenance of attitudes or relationships (Fishbein and Ajzen, 1975; Schlenker, 1980; Clark and Woll, 1981; Weldon and Malpass, 1981).

Nevertheless cognitive psychology has given rise to some significant theoretical developments. The old purely empiricist model has finally and with some difficulty begun to lose its dominance, to be replaced by the 'cognitive orientation'. During the period of behaviourist hegemony in the 1950s and 1960s 'mental events' were outlawed as subjects for investigation since they could not be observed. The first crack in the structure came with the possibility of modelling mental events on computers. Further developments followed from the growing realization of the complexity of the 'information' required by a computer to simulate even the simplest types of human thought. The actual experience of attempting to model human thought processes on machines led to progressive change in the underlying theoretical assumptions governing the field. Marc de Mey summarizes the 'cognitive orientation' as follows:

> The central point of the cognitive view is that *any* such *information processing*, whether perceptual (such as perceiving an object) or symbolic (such as

understanding a sentence) is *mediated* by a *system of categories* or *concepts* which for the information processor constitutes a *representation* or *model* of his world.

(1982, p. 4)

Most significantly of all, de Mey traces four stages in the development of the cognitive view. The first is the *monadic*, in which information is assumed to consist of small, self-defining pieces. In the second, *structural* stage, scientists attempted to define the way individual 'bits' of information might combine in more complex structures. In the third, the *contextual* stage, they began to recognize that meaning depended on the provision of a suitable context. In the final *cognitive* stage it was recognized that modelling the visual recognition of even the simplest objects required a total world-view. The information-processor's 'context', whether human or machine, was recognized to be the whole of that information-processor's existing knowledge or world model.[2]

In fact the conclusions of Bruner and Postman's playing-card experiment and these observations on the relationship between philosophy and psychology clarify and confirm one another. In order to recognize anomalous playing cards correctly, the participants in the experiment needed both to use and modify their pre-existing theory while observing the cards. In the same way, the psychology of learning requires a framework of philosophical theory, while the philosophical theory of knowledge throws up generalizations about perception and learning that require psychological investigation. Philosophical framework and psychological investigation interpret and correct one another. However, the fact that this is imperfectly recognized by both philosophers and psychologists means that a considerable amount of care and re-evaluation is required as we use the work of each to investigate the relationship between learning and revelation. In particular, the significance and implications of experimental results may vary according to the philosophical framework within which these are interpreted.

---

[2] De Mey also traces his four stages in the history of philosophy of science. The monadic stage is represented by classical positivism, the structural by logical positivism, the contextual arrives with the interpretation of scientific progress in terms of sociological factors and ideology and the cognitive stage with the development of paradigm theory associated with Thomas Kühn. Kühn's theory is sometimes mistakenly understood, especially by his opponents, as an example of a contextual stage theory.

Intention and Interpretation

The basic assumption of empiricism is that explanations of human behaviour are to be found in the relationships of cause and effect appropriate to the study of the natural world. However, the way people understand the world is both *intentional* and *hermeneutical*; the schemata of our understanding are formed as a result of an 'effort after meaning' and by a process of interpretation. This raises the basic philosophical question which affects every branch of human science: can the intentional and hermeneutical nature of human understanding of the world be fully understood in terms of the causal relationships appropriate to the study of nature and natural phenomena? How far is the reductionist tendency of scientific method to explain everything in terms of natural cause and effect appropriate in the study of human behaviour? Or does the explanation of human action and motivation require another kind of explanation altogether?

Selective Attention

An interesting case study with which to begin our attempt to answer these questions is the study of *selective attention*.

The earliest investigations of selective attention concentrated on what was known as the 'cocktail party phenomenon'. A guest at such a gathering has the task of 'paying attention' to one particular conversation in a room full of sound. This is achieved by attending strictly to the words of the speaker with whom he or she is engaged and 'filtering out' the rest. But if someone in another part of the room mentions the guest's name or if a neighbouring conversation turns to a topic of interest, concentration on the original conversation becomes more difficult and the effort of selective attention becomes conscious. Experiments were begun in 1953 by E. C. Cherry, who played recordings of different messages simultaneously to participants over headphones, varying the subject matter, voice and position of the messages between the right and left ear (Neisser, 1976, pp. 79–80; Barber and Legge, 1976, pp. 77–90). The subject was instructed to 'shadow' one of the messages, that is to repeat it, in order to divert attention from the other message, and the aim was to find out what characteristics, if any, of the 'rejected' messages are retained. The results indicate that in fact surprisingly few details of the rejected message even register. 'Crude physical characteristics' such as whether the voice is male or female were usually recalled, very few participants could give an account of what was in the rejected message. However, this did not mean that the rejected channel was not heard at all. 'Highly probable stimuli' such as clichés, the sudden appearance of something new, such as a new voice, and 'emotionally important stimuli', such as the subject's name, frequently caught the attention.

The earliest attempts to explain these results postulated various types of 'filters' between the ears and the brain by means of which information was filtered out at various stages of processing. The problem with these explanations was the difficulty of explaining the great variety of information which may get through on the rejected channel if the conditions were right. In particular it was variation in the task demands of the experiment, the information the subject was asked to listen for, which most affected the range of information that was perceived. In 1973, however, Neville Moray put forward a different kind explanation based on the theory of sampling (Moray and Fitter, 1973). This was a model developed from the experience of aeroplane pilots, who are required to pay attention selectively to a wide range of instruments. In this model the pilot is not a passive receiver of information filtered for him by a hypothetical mechanism; instead he is actually *doing something*, actively looking for the information he needs to fly the aeroplane safely. What the pilot has to do is to construct an *internal model*, a schema, of the source of information he needs. This schema will include the likely *importance* of information coming from various directions. The schema has to be continually updated as the information is sampled, bearing in mind the relative importance of the information conveyed by the different instruments. For example the lower the aeroplane comes to the ground the more important becomes the information from the altimeter. Information about the level of fuel, taken for granted in ordinary circumstances, becomes crucially important if a decision is required to divert to a different destination.

Moray concluded that selective attention is an intentional phenomenon. An observer or listener constructs a schema for the likely relevance of information coming from different sources and uses it to distribute his attention. However, despite the close fit between Moray's theory and the cognitive orientation, it has still received little attention. Bly and Rumelhart's textbook (1999) gives eleven possible explanations for selective attention, mentioning the idea of 'effort' only in passing. This apparent lack of recognition that Moray's theory is of a different *kind* to the various hypothetical filtering mechanisms postulated by other researchers seems to reflect a lack of awareness of the potential role of philosophy in clarifying the questions with which psychology is dealing but also a general resistance to explanations based on purpose and intention in favour of causal mechanisms.

Causal and Teleological Explanation

The scientific community is used to causal explanation. Natural events, from spots on the sun to the fall of the leaves in autumn, have *causes*. The physical universe is governed by a chain of cause and effect. Moreover the scientist assumes that this chain is closed. Sunspots and falling leaves are indirectly linked and might conceivably even affect one another because they occur in a closed universe in which there are no extra causes acting from 'outside' undetectable by the scientist. Everything that happens in the physical universe falls within the scope of scientific explanation.

However, people are different. We inhabit the physical universe and are subject to the same laws of cause and effect as other objects. Our bodies consist of the same chemical elements that are found in the rest of creation. We have weight because of the law of gravity and require nutrition to survive like all plants and animals. We also act as causes in the physical universe, instigating motion and change, creating new chemical elements and regulating the domesticated part of the world of biological nature. But we also have purposes and make decisions. The study of intention and purpose introduces a new type or level of explanation, *teleological* explanation. Dispute rages as to the relationship between these two types of explanation, with many philosophers insisting that explanation by purpose has to be seen as completely separate from natural or causal explanation. As Aurel Kolnai puts it:

> Action is not a 'resultant' of psychic urges, pressures, yearnings, cravings, attractions and repulsions, forces or bents, nor an emergent product of motives relevant to its context; rather it is the execution of a decree issued by something like a unitary 'self' or 'ego' or 'sovereign rule' who consults these motives and is influenced ('inclined', 'pressured', 'instigated' or 'coaxed') by them, but who in its turn is in control of motility and directs its workings.
>
> (Kolnai, 1968, p. 24)

The idea that agency, purpose and the 'self' might be in some way independent of the workings of causal laws is highly unpopular in the social sciences. In the study of human behaviour, scientists have to set up carefully controlled experiments, isolating the factors whose influence they wish to investigate, hoping to achieve results which can be both quantified and repeated. The idea that the people recruited to take part in their experiments might have their own reasons for behaving in certain ways and that these reasons may profoundly affect the way they respond to the various influencing factors introduces a disconcerting level of uncertainty. Moreover the success of the experiments, the fact that human behaviour does display regularities which can be explained by means of causal factors, appears to justify the scientists' faith in its regularity and predictability. The agent and his decisions can be left outside the picture. For example, Bartlett, in framing his conclusions, successfully avoided the use of the term 'self' by defining it as the interplay of appetites, instincts, interests and ideals, and 'temperament' and 'character' as due to 'the order of predominance or perceptual tendencies' (1932, p. 213). Paul Barber and David Legge avoid the term 'purpose' by substituting the 'motivational need-state of the organism' (1976, pp. 82–3).

Reductionism, the belief that the explanation of human behaviour can be *reduced* to the laws of cause and effect, has a long history. In the seventeenth century, Thomas Hobbes maintained consistently that all 'voluntary motion' arose from 'appetite' or 'aversion'. In the nineteenth, John Stuart Mill confidently proclaimed the 'unity of science'. A complete description of the causes of human behaviour was, he believed, only a matter of time. The obstacle was not one of principle but only the extreme complexity of the laws. The twentieth century has seen several attempts to construct complete explanations of behaviour. According to B. F. Skinner and the behaviourist school all the factors controlling human action were to be explained in terms of 'operant conditioning' through which certain patterns of reaction are either punished or reinforced. The commitment of behaviourists to seeing human beings as another part of animal nature can be judged by the fact that all their experimental work was carried out on rats and pigeons. In more recent years the mantle of the attempt at a complete causal explanation has fallen on the proponents of 'strong' artificial intelligence, many of whom are avowedly reductionistic in tone. Here is Douglas Hofstadter, a computer scientist at Indiana University, for whom reductionism is the 'ultimate religion':

> Perhaps my lifelong training in physics and science in general has given me a deep awe at seeing how the most substantial and familiar of objects or experiences fades away, as one approaches the infinitesimal scale, into an eerily insubstantial ether, a myriad of ephemeral swirling vortices or nearly incomprehensible mathematical activity. This in me evokes a kind of cosmic awe. To me, reductionism does not 'explain away', rather it adds mystery.
>
> ('Commentary' on Searle, 1980)

However, despite Hofstadter's confidence, it is precisely the failure of artificial intelligence that offers the most important indications that natural cause and effect are insufficient to explain the workings of the human mind.

Artificial Intelligence?

The Physical Basis of Intelligence

The enormous growth of cognitive psychology in recent years is based on a perceived analogy between the functioning of computers and the human mind. Computers supply terminology such as 'data-driven' and 'concept-driven' processing. As in Minsky's 'frame' paper, schema theory draws heavily on computer-based models. In a computer-based age, information processing provides a powerful model of human functioning which has begun to influence a number of related branches of psychology. Unheard of a matter of thirty years ago, cognitive models now prevail in areas such as the study of attitudes, emotions and social judgements. But the computer potentially provides more than a basic analogy or style of thinking. In human beings, just as in computers, cognitive processes depend on underlying physical mechanisms. In computers those mechanisms are the electrical connections supplied by the computer's 'hardware'. For the human mind 'thinking' is dependent on the neural connections between the brain and the sense organs and within the brain itself. In fact the study of which parts of the brain are involved in which kinds of information processing is gradually but surely advancing.

Just how close is the analogy between a computer and the human brain? Proponents of what is known as 'weak' artificial intelligence are content to regard information processing as a fruitful analogy of the functioning of the brain and to concentrate on developing the powers of the computer to carry out tasks formerly possible only for human beings. Whether or not the computer is performing the task in the same way as a person is not important. The fact that the chess computer 'Deep Blue' could beat the world's best player does not prove anything about the relationship between human and computer intelligence, since the machine functions in an entirely different way from Gary Kasparov. The computer uses its speed and capacity to search through the consequences of hundreds of possible options before every move. The chess master uses his experience of patterns in the game to tell him which moves are worth considering. For the proponents of 'strong AI', however, the victory of the computer is a major step on the road to simulating human intelligence and convincing the doubters. The aim of strong AI is to produce a total computer-based model of human intelligence. The success of this venture. would be the equivalent of a total scientific explanation of human life (Boden, 1979, p. 113). The 'unity of science' postulated by John Stuart Mill would be achieved and, like Mill, the proponents of strong AI see the difficulties involved as those of complexity rather than principle.

However, AI has been slow to justify the claims of its proponents. In the early days the possibilities appeared immense and Marvin Minsky (1967) could claim that 'Within a generation the problem of creating "artificial intelligence" will be substantially solved'. However the formal rules underlying human intelligence remained stubbornly elusive and problems constantly dogged the attempt to model even the simplest of intellectual tasks on the computer. Fifteen years after his optimistic pronouncement, Minsky wrote, 'The AI problem is one of the hardest science has ever undertaken' (Kolata, 1982, p. 1237). In the 1980s computer scientists in Japan and the USA raced to be the first to design an 'expert system' capable of diagnosing medical conditions such as blood disorders. After ten years none was any closer to success. The team at Rockefeller and Cornell Universities commented, 'Well trained and experienced physicians develop the uniquely human capability of recognising common patterns ... they are unable to spell out in detail how they do it' (quoted in Dreyfus, 1992, p. xlvii).

The basic problem with which the researchers had to contend was to work out how much information the computer needed in order to recognize a symptom and respond with an appropriate question. The results of their efforts pushed them continually in the direction of more and more information until it appeared that, even to perform the simplest of tasks, the computer required a total world-view. Thus the progress of this particular piece of research parallels the growth of the cognitive orientation from viewing information as small and separable pieces to recognizing the role of the information-processor's total prior experience in each action of recognition and judgement. Yet the problem of providing the computer with a sophisticated enough context for its operations proved harder even than this. More and more it appeared that what the computer required in order to simulate human 'common sense' was not 'knowledge' *per se* but 'know-how' or skill in using the knowledge at its disposal. As Hubert Dreyfus, one of the leading opponents of the idea of artificial intelligence, commented:

> The problem precisely was that this know-how, along with all the interests, feelings, motivations and bodily capacities that go to make a human being, would have to be conveyed to the computer as knowledge – as a huge and conceptual belief system – and making our inarticulate, pre-conceptual background understanding of what it is like to be a human being explicit in a symbolic representation seemed to me a hopeless task.
>
> (1992, pp. xi–xii)

Dreyfus states precisely the question at issue: is it possible to reduce the experience of being human to something that could be modelled by a machine? Or do we, in the words of Michael Polanyi, 'know more than we can tell' (1967, p. 4)? And if tacit knowledge is irreducible to explicit explanation, is there something in the experience of being human and having purposes that lead to action, that cannot be reduced to causal explanation? Is the problem of artificial intelligence one of principle rather than one of complexity?

The answer to these questions calls for closer examination of the relationship between mind and body, thinking and the activity of the brain. First of all, schemata have a physical basis. Bartlett's idea of a neural feedback mechanism was drawn from the work of Sir Henry Head with brain-damaged patients. Not only does damage to the brain impair the function of the intelligence but the way the schemata of intelligence work is analogous to the way the body's 'postural model' works during a game of tennis. Or, to draw a similar analogy from Michael Polanyi, the functioning of tacit knowledge is based on the ability of the brain to draw together the separate particulars of perception into a single representation. Moreover we are familiar with physical systems that exhibit 'intentional' behaviour. The 'purpose' of a thermostat is to maintain the temperature of a room above a certain level. In order to achieve this purpose it carries a simple 'internal model' of its immediate environment. The thermostat 'knows' how hot it is in the room. Its 'behaviour' is to switch the heating system on when the temperature drops below a certain level and off again when it reaches that level.

What is 'Knowing'?

I have used the word 'know' for the thermostat's 'awareness' of the temperature in the room, but does the thermostat really 'know' the temperature in the way that a human being does? The 'weak AI' sense of the word 'know' in the sentence in question is that the function of the thermostat and the way it is programmed to perform that function offers an analogy (in this case a distant one) of human intelligence. 'Strong AI', however, is strongly reductionistic. The strong AI sense of the word 'know' in connection with thermostats is that the instrument does in fact 'know' what the temperature of the room is in the same sense as a human being can be said to 'know' it. Human 'knowledge' is simply the output of a physical system. If a computer like Deep Blue can play the game of chess, then it can be said to understand the game of chess, since being able to play the game is in itself the definition of understanding it.

For the opponents of strong AI all the computer is doing is making a series of calculations on the basis of information fed into it. In a celebrated article John Searle (1980) used a thought experiment to explore the differences between the two sides. He asked his readers to imagine themselves locked into a small room, able to communicate with the outside world only by means of written instructions. The first written communication to arrive is a large batch of Chinese writing and since we don't understand Chinese we can make no sense of it. Shortly afterwards another batch of Chinese writing arrives together with some instructions in English for correlating the first batch with the second. Next a third batch of Chinese symbols arrives, this time with further instructions in English on how to give back certain Chinese symbols in response to those which arrived in the third batch. Outside the room the people feeding in the Chinese writing call the third batch of symbols 'questions' and the symbols we feed out to them they call 'answers'. But inside the room all we know is that we have been asked to make particular responses to the appearance of certain combinations of Chinese symbols. To provide a bit of light relief a story in English may arrive together with some questions in English to which answers are requested. Since we actually understand both the story and the questions this is far pleasanter and less tedious work. But if the instructions on how to answer the Chinese questions are good enough and if we do our work well enough the answers we provide to the Chinese questions should conceivably satisfy a Chinese speaker every bit as much as our answers to the English questions satisfy an English speaker. The crucial difference is that whereas we produced the answers to the English questions by 'understanding' them, we managed the answers to the Chinese questions only through following a series of rules about how to respond to certain symbols with other symbols of the same kind.

The point Searle wished to make with his experiment was that of course the manipulation of formal symbols, which is all the computer can do, is different to what we are accustomed to call 'understanding'. The weakness of his article is that he is appealing only to our everyday common-sense experience of understanding. He does not actually explain what this 'understanding' consists of. The strong AI position is precisely that this everyday common-sense experience is misleading. Our conscious awareness of having understanding is not an extra something which distinguishes human understanding from that of the computer. Real understanding is simply the ability to manipulate formal symbols in the way both brains and computers do. Consciousness of being able to do so is simply an 'epiphenomenon' of the activity of the brain and has no significance in itself. Despite the immense appeal of Searle's 'Chinese-room' experiment to a 'common-sense' approach and similar anti-reductionist arguments, such as Roger Penrose's (1989) immensely complex attempt to demonstrate that thought processes are irreducible to computation, hard-line proponents of strong AI remain unconvinced. What is required is an explanation of what our everyday common-sense experience of understanding actually consists of.

Hardware and Software

Like the computer, the mind is a processor of information. And like the computer, the information to be processed exists in two forms, or can be described at two levels. At one level 'information' describes the physical state of the mechanism – the pattern of neurons in the brain or the state of the electrical connections in the computer. At another level the information exists in the form of symbols which represent elements of the outside world. In the computer simulation of vision the image of a tree has to be converted into a particular pattern of electrical signals, the one which 'means' a tree. In order to 'see' a tree and know it is a tree, a human being requires the brain to register the neural signals arriving along the optic nerve which 'describe' a tree and convert these into a pattern of connections which 'mean' that there is a tree in front of him. The same neural connection in the brain may be brought into play when a human being reads a description of a tree in a book. Likewise the computer may be fed a written description of a tree in order to ascertain whether it can correlate this with the actual image of a tree previously encoded.

In computing the two levels of description are the 'hardware' and the 'software'; in psychology the brain and the mind. In computing everything represented by the computer's 'software', that is the program and the words and images which appear on the screen, must also be represented by the hardware as a pattern of electrical connections. Without this the program will not work. At the software level the representation is expressed in symbols of the same kind as an ordinary language. At the hardware level the electrical state of the machine also constitutes a 'model' of the state of affairs described in the program expressed in physical terms. Without the ability of the hardware to reproduce all the relations of the software the machine could not run. The same is true for the human mind. In order to see, hear or think, our images and thoughts must be represented at a physical level by a pattern of neural connections.

This relation between hardware and software, mind and brain, is also analogous to that between grammar and meaning, syntax and semantics.

The distinction between syntax and semantics is also used by computer scientists. The hardware is the grammar or syntax of the computer, the software its meaning or semantics. The question, 'Is the phenomenon of the mind to be understood in terms of the physical functioning of the brain?' can also be expressed, 'Is there a level of meaning expressed in the software or semantic level of a computer which cannot be reduced to the terms of the physical syntax of the machine?'

Grammar and Meaning

The solution to this problem requires an excursion into the field of linguistic philosophy, the natural home of terms like 'syntax' and 'semantics'. Early this century the programme of logical positivism was to reduce meaning to grammar by proposing the idea of an ideal language in which the logical relation between states of affairs in the real world would be exactly reflected in the grammar of the sentence used to describe them. The success of this programme would have reduced the experience of meaning to grammatical syntax in much the same way as the proponents of strong AI hope to reduce it to the physical relations of the computer. Unfortunately for strong AI the conclusion already reached in philosophy is that this programme has failed. Ironically it was one of the chief inspirations of logical positivism, Wittgenstein's *Tractatus Logico-Philosophicus*, which also demonstrated its impossibility.

In the *Tractatus* Wittgenstein put forward his 'picture theory' of meaning, in which he maintained that language is to be understood as picturing reality. Language is made up either of 'logical atoms' which have a one-to-one correspondence with the reality they describe or else, as in the normal state of affairs, of complex statements, which need to be analysed into logical atoms. The logical atoms were intended to refer to immediate sensory experience and the relationships between them to picture the logical structure of reality. Despite the enthusiasm with which the *Tractatus* was received, however, Wittgenstein soon began to have his doubts about it. In fact he was unable to produce a single example of a logical atom, which is hardly surprising since, as we have seen, sensory experience is always mediated by a system of concepts based on past experience.

But perhaps more important than this practical failure to implement the programme, the *Tractatus* contained within it the seeds of its own destruction. On the last page of the book Wittgenstein writes: 'Anyone who understands my propositions recognizes them as nonsensical, when he has used them – as steps – to climb up beyond them. (He must, so to speak, throw away the ladder after he has climbed up it.) He must transcend these propositions and then he will see the world aright' (1921, 6.54, p. 74).

What Wittgenstein means by these enigmatic statements is that, although it is possible to assume that language pictures reality, it is impossible for language to picture this assumption. The relation between language and reality cannot be pictured by language alone. He calls his statements 'nonsensical' because they all fall within the area which it is impossible to express in the ideal language. To *understand* something is *to recognize the existence of a relationship between syntax and semantics*. Since this relationship can never be reduced to syntax alone, understanding is more than the ability to manipulate formal symbols. The difference between giving answers in English and manipulating Chinese symbols is a real and not an imaginary one, not just because we have no knowledge of the realities to which the Chinese symbols apply but also because in the English questions and answers, we are capable of picturing to ourselves the *relation* between the realities described and the symbols which describe them.

The computer model of mental functioning is valid therefore up to a point. It is valid to the extent that both computers and human beings exhibit two levels of information processing, the syntactic, dependent on physical causation, and the semantic or representational. But in neither case can the two levels be simply equated or the one reduced to the other. You can teach a computer to make all the correct moves in a chess match but you cannot give it an understanding of what chess actually is.

Bodily Knowing

One highly significant question remains to be explored: 'What is it about human beings that enables us to picture this relationship between syntax and semantics?' Or to put it another way, 'What is the characteristic of human beings that gives us an awareness that what we experience as a pattern of neural connections has a meaning outside itself?' The answer is that human beings have bodies. As Bartlett and Polanyi make clear in their different ways, perception is a bodily skill. It is an integral part of the work of schemata, the physical feedback mechanisms through which the body orientates itself in the world. Our understanding of the world, our ability to recognize objects, construct imaginary situations and build concepts, is an extension of the work of schemata. The body, says Polanyi, is the one thing of which we are never normally aware as an object. Our bodies mediate between the outside world of 'reality' and the inner world of experience and interpretation we build for ourselves.

All the parameters which govern our ability to interpret the world of experience are mediated by our bodies. It is through our bodies that we are aware of the outer world of reality and through our bodies that this outer world continually corrects the ideas we form about it. It is through our bodies that we are part of the natural world of cause and effect and by means of our bodies that we act in the world. It is through our bodies that we communicate with others, not only in language but by means of gestures, facial expressions and tone of voice.

There is something peculiarly significant for human life about incarnation. It is the basis of the process of interaction through which we experience the world and ourselves in it. If divine revelation were to enter this process of interaction it would be appropriate for it to do so by means of incarnation.

The Postmodern Climate

In the stages traced by Marc de Mey the cognitive orientation was preceded by three others, the monadic, the structural and the contextual stage. The underlying assumption of the third of these stages, the contextual, is that the meaning a person gives to any new knowledge depends on the context in which it is placed. Only at the fourth stage does the required context expand to include the whole of a person's previous experience and world-view. Moreover the argument of the preceding section suggests that there is a stage beyond the cognitive at which the required context for understanding is in fact our tacit awareness of what it means to be a human being. Nevertheless it is at the third stage that understanding is first recognized to be hermeneutical in character, depending on interpretation in a given context. The weakening of the culture of empiricism, represented by de Mey's first and second stages, has allowed the flowering of a variety of hermeneutically based styles of philosophy and social science, of which one of the earliest was the sociology of knowledge.

In his massive study of political and economic power and conflict, Karl Marx pointed out that knowledge is a cultural product. The assumptions shared by a particular society, the knowledge the members of that society share in common, is controlled by the dominant group in that society. According to Marx the function of the common stock of knowledge is to legitimize the power relations of that particular society. Feudal and other hierarchical societies, for example, are sustained by the shared assumption that to be high-born is to be in some undefined way 'better' and with a greater entitlement to wealth and status than the mass of people. Patriarchal societies are sustained by ideas about the natural roles of men and women. Moreover the whole universe is brought in to sustain the established order and God himself made to play the role of patriarch or feudal lord.

'Only with the appearance of a new generation', wrote Berger and Luckmann, 'can one properly speak of a social world' (1966, p. 79). The world created by the older generation is experienced by the young born into it and growing up in it as given, the way things always have been. Only by exercising the 'hermeneutics of suspicion' is it possible to delve into the power relations which make the world of our experience appear to be the natural and only way. When we do so we recognize the power relations which are legitimized by the shared assumptions of society and realize the possibility of alternative ways of ordering society and understanding ourselves. The tremendous growth in South America of liberation theology is based not on Marxism pure and simple but on the exercise of the hermeneutics of suspicion, through which priests and teachers, with the benefit of education, enable the poor and oppressed to escape the system which defines them and see themselves in a different light as objects of God's love and care.

In the sociology of knowledge it is not objective experience and logical deduction which form the foundation of knowledge but the person in society. 'Legitimations', the overarching structures of knowledge which hold societies together, are human products. They develop over time to meet the needs of human beings to live together in society. The ultimate 'reality' and source of human identity is simply cultural agreement. For example, Berger and Luckmann pointed out that on the island of Haiti people understand themselves and their lives in relation to voodoo practices. In New York people with problems visit a psychiatrist. Both psychoanalysis and voodoo have a foundation of theory which legitimizes them as ways of meeting the social needs of society. But whatever we might want to say about the 'objective' rights and wrongs of voodoo or psychoanalysis, these structures of legitimation *must be understood* as strictly human products. 'Neither the Voudun gods nor libidinal energy', they write, 'may exist outside the world defined in the respective social contexts. But in these contexts they do exist by virtue of social definition and are internalised as realities in the course of socialisation. Rural Haitians *are* possessed and New York intellectuals *are* neurotic' (1966, pp. 197–8).

There is an exact analogy here with the arguments over demon possession and the New Testament. Conservative Christians in general wish to accept the real existence of demons because they are part of the New Testament world. Other critics prefer to interpret the unclean spirits as evidence of mental disturbance in line with the assumptions of the modern world. Berger and Luckmann would say that in the New Testament people *were* demon-possessed, whereas today they are simply mad or disturbed. What matters is not whether demons do or do not exist but the beliefs of the society within which the behaviour in question is experienced. The arbiter of reality is cultural agreement.

In many ways the sociology of knowledge looks forward to the full flowering of postmodernity in society and postmodernism in philosophy and culture which we are experiencing at the beginning of the twenty-first century. The characteristics of modernism, based on the Enlightenment, include belief in a stable world of identifiable facts. In the study of literature they include the belief that a text has a given meaning related to the intention of its author. In postmodernism the commitment to a solid basis of rationally guaranteed knowledge is thrown into question. As the sociology of knowledge illustrates, the goalposts for what counts as 'reality' have been moved. Science is just as much a human and cultural product as anything else. In the study of texts the intention of the author no longer has a privileged place. The author has created an 'artefact' which it is open to each new generation to interpret. Meaning resides not in the text but in the interaction between text and audience. As the idea of objective meaning and firmly established facts recedes, so does the idea that the world itself has a meaning. We now know that in different times and places societies have understood the world very differently. The 'big stories' which in different cultures and periods of history have given meaning and coherence to our experience of the world, such as belief in scientific objectivity or the dignity of human persons or the great religions of the world, can now be seen to be simply the products of those particular cultures. The postmodern, writes Jean-François Lyotard, can be defined as 'incredulity towards meta-narratives' (1984, p. xxiv). By this he means that there are no over-arching beliefs capable of unifying society and culture. Each person must discover or make their own identity using the variety of cultural resources available in a world of fast travel, instant communication and information overload.

The jury is still out on the question of whether postmodernism represents the overthrow of modernism or is simply a stage within it. Like the fish in water, however, and like the peasant in feudal society, it is sometimes difficult to recognize the medium in which we actually swim or the structures of thought which give meaning to our lives. My suspicion is that, rather than signalling the end of metanarratives or 'big stories', postmodernism may in fact be an expression of the big story which prevails in a great part of science and culture, namely reductionism. By subjecting human life to the natural laws of cause and effect, reductionism abolishes any source of meaning for human existence outside nature and imprisons human beings in a universe with no discernible purpose. The result is precisely that loss of overall meaning and purpose in human existence on which the philosophy of postmodernism is based. With the development of the contextual stage in philosophical thought, the field is free for a hermeneutical approach which floats free of the restraints of Enlightenment criteria of rationality, and in which meaning is relative to the shared interests of society or the particular interests of each individual.

If this analysis of postmodernity and postmodern thought is correct, the way out lies not in a return to the supposed objectivity of empiricism but in a way of thinking based on the total context of all human experience. This can only arise as part of a shared understanding of what it means to be human, which in turn requires the explication of what Dreyfus calls our 'inarticulate, pre-conceptual background', the uniquely human characteristics of tacit knowing. In the chapters that follow I shall argue that revelation holds the key to the solution of this problem.

Chapter 3

Thinking and Feeling

Tacit and Explicit Knowledge

All we know about the world, based on the sum of experience, is organized to form a 'world model' which we carry 'in our heads', generating expectations and guiding actions. Our world models are formed by a process of interaction in which new information is interpreted in the light of existing experience. In the process of interpretation new information may be assimilated to the pattern of existing knowledge; or the pattern of our existing knowledge may change to accommodate the new information. In practice both are likely to take place. We may begin by understanding an unfamiliar situation in terms of our existing schemata but in the process of learning, the new situation soon acquires a schema of its own and our world model is reshaped. If revelation is to conform to the pattern of the ordinary processes of understanding, the knowledge of God must first become part of our world models and then begin to shape them. But before we can understand how this takes place we need to know more about the way the model of the world in our heads is organized. We need to delve more deeply into the structure of 'tacit knowledge' and the schemata which compose it. What we shall discover in the course of this chapter is that this exploration will lead us into the realm of *feeling*.

Already we have seen that tacit knowledge is not simply a copy of the world. It is formed when we actively engage and interpret the information coming from our surroundings. Tacit knowledge is more closely comparable to a physical skill than a library of information. This means that it is structured very differently from 'explicit knowledge', the way we express our understanding in speech and writing and co-ordinate it with one another. Using a schema to understand the world is more like performing a skill than writing an essay. The knowledge stored in our schemata is more than can be expressed in words. It consists of the 'know-how, interests, feelings and motivations' that go to make up 'what it is like to be a human being'. In the words of Michael Polanyi's dictum, 'We know more than we can tell' (1967, p. 4).

Exemplars

A further important issue surrounding the representation of knowledge in memory concerns the role of concrete exemplars. Should the form of our knowledge stored as schemata be understood as consisting of generalizations or abstractions or should we understand them as based on concrete instances (Anderson, 1995, pp. 164–5; Smith, 1998, pp. 410–19)? A major contribution to the understanding of the way knowledge is represented in the mind is found in the work of the American scientist and philosopher Thomas Kühn. Kühn became famous for his book *The Structure of Scientific Revolutions*, first published in 1962, in which he put forward his theory that science progresses by a series of revolutions in which the governing 'paradigm' in a particular field is overthrown and replaced by another. The examples he gave included the Copernican revolution in astronomy and the way Newton's gravitational theory was succeeded by Einstein's theory of relativity.

Kühn's observations on the role of paradigms led him to wonder about the way the shared knowledge in a given paradigm is represented and passed on. His ideas were first set out in the 'Postscript' to the second edition of *The Structure of Scientific Revolutions* and then more fully in the paper 'Second thoughts on paradigms' (1977). According to paradigm theory a group of scientists form a community which is defined by the knowledge it holds in common. In fact the 'scientific community' has various levels from all scientists, down through all biologists or all physicists, to all nuclear physicists, to all working in a given specialist field, to a particular laboratory team. Each community or sub-community is united by the knowledge its members hold in common in the form of a shared paradigm or paradigms. Explicitly this knowledge consists of a set of formal rules or generalizations. An example might be Newton's Second Law of Motion $f=ma$ or 'the force of an object is equivalent to the mass of the object multiplied by its acceleration'. Another might be Einstein's theory of general relativity, $e=mc^2$. As part of their apprenticeship in the scientific community, students have to learn not only how these generalizations are derived but also how to apply them to concrete scientific problems. At this point Kühn found again and again that his students' understanding broke down. Despite reading and understanding the textbook's explanation of a new topic, they were unable to do the example problems at the end of each chapter. The theoretical relations were perfectly clear and coherent; it was the way the rules could be made to apply to reality that eluded them. Kühn's conclusion was that the ability to apply formal scientific rules to experience did not come automatically with the understanding of the rules. It was in fact a separate and distinct type of knowledge.

Kühn found that what removed the mental block and enabled the students to solve the problems they found so difficult was noticing a resemblance between the new problem and an old, familiar one. The problems given in textbooks, he pointed out, are frequently variations on a few standard examples or 'exemplars'. Students extend their knowledge not simply by learning general rules but by increasing their stock of exemplars. This is done by making connections between them, by observing points of similarity, and so by extending the old, familiar exemplar by small steps to cover new situations:

> The student discovers, with or without the assistance of his instructor, a way to see his problem as *like* a problem he has already encountered. Having seen the resemblance, grasped the analogy between two or more distinct problems, he can interrelate symbols and attach them to nature in the ways that have proved effective before. The law-sketch, say *f=ma*, has functioned as a tool, informing the student what similarities to look for, signalling the gestalt in which the situation is to be seen. The resultant ability to see a variety of situations as like each other, as subjects for *f=ma* or some other symbolic generalization, is, I think, the main thing a student acquires by doing exemplary problems, whether with a pencil and paper or in a well-designed laboratory.
>
> (1969, p. 189)

An 'exemplar' is a pattern for the way a general rule applies to a concrete real-life situation. Kühn's theory is that an exemplar is a form of knowledge in its own right. In fact, he concluded, the working knowledge of a given scientific community consists of a set of exemplars – standard working examples. What distinguishes scientific communities from each other is not the different scientific generalizations with which they work but the different exemplars they use.

Kühn went on to describe instances of scientific progress that came about through the application of a generalization originally worked out in one area to a new area of investigation. In the seventeenth century Galileo worked out the rules governing the behaviour of a ball rolling down an inclined plane. Huyghens was able to apply the rules Galileo had worked out for an inclined plane to the motion of a pendulum. Finally Bernoulli was able to apply Huyghens's solution for the pendulum to problems in hydraulics. The key to progress in each area was discovering a resemblance or analogy between the new problem and another similar situation for which a solution already existed. The extension of the generalization came about by means of the extension of standard examples. As early as 1961 N. R. Hanson suggested that the 'logic of scientific discovery' might be analogical in character (Hanson, 1961). By pointing to the importance of similarity relationships in both scientific progress and student learning, Kühn's work strongly suggests that he was right.

Natural Categories

Having established the relevance of exemplars to scientific knowledge, Kühn went on to explore their place in everyday life. The example he gave was a young child on a walk in the park with her mother or father. During this walk the child encounters a variety of different kinds of birds – ducks, geese, sparrows and so on. Her parents point out the different type of birds and teach her how to group them into categories. She learns how to distinguish water-birds from other types of bird and the difference between ducks, geese and swans. She also learns, without explicitly being told, that each category of bird forms a 'natural family' separated from neighbouring families by a 'perceptual space'. In other words, as well as learning to group objects into families, the child also learns not to expect to find objects half-way between families, no birds half-way between sparrows and ducks and no water-birds half-way between ducks and swans.

The existence of natural categories as a basic form of cognitive organization has been confirmed by the work of Eleanor Rosch (Rosch, 1975; Rosch and Mervis, 1975). Rosch and her co-workers also worked with birds both as a category and group of sub-category. Using a series of questionnaires, she found that most people think of certain birds, like robins, as prototypical members of the bird family, while chickens, although still classified as birds, were more peripheral members. Natural categories are also open-ended. Rosch found disagreement over whether pumpkins, for example, ought to be classified as fruits or leeches as insects. In different cultures there will be different 'natural' distinctions. It is well known that eskimos recognize about fifteen different varieties of what we simply call 'snow'. What is universal, however, is the fact that categories are a basic form of cognitive organization, or schema!

The point Kühn wanted to make was that 'exemplars', the basic building blocks of tacit knowledge, are concrete categories directly applicable to the real world. Explicit knowledge is not like this. It involves formal rules and definitions. These rules and definitions are needed so that knowledge can be shared and communicated but they are not the way we actually know the world. Tacit knowledge is organized in 'open-textured' natural categories which are not firmly bounded by explicit definitions but gradually and pragmatically built up by the accumulation of experience. To answer a teacher's question, 'What is a swan?', a child has to use explicit knowledge in which categories are defined by rules: a swan is a bird, a water-bird, white and so on. To answer the same question for herself she consults the categories of her internal world and says to herself, 'That is a swan.' Explicit knowledge is like the dictionary definition of a word but our tacit knowledge of the same word includes the infinite shades of meaning, nuances and personal associations derived from our total experience of the use of that word. You and I may agree about what a swan is but the way we actually know swans is personal to us.

Intuitive Fit

Judgement

Whereas explicit knowledge is built up by learning to apply rules and definitions, tacit knowledge is built up by the recognition of similarities. The young child learns to recognize ducks as like swans in some ways, different in others. Students learn how to solve a new problem by recognizing the similarity between it and a familiar one. In both everyday life and scientific training, people are learning to 'see as', to recognize the objects of experience as variations on the patterns of previous experience, building up their stock of knowledge through the recognition of similarity relationships. But this means that there must be in human make-up some kind of 'analogical sensitivity', an ability to recognize patterns and discern similarities.

Analogical sensitivity is the key to schema selection. One of the skills of understanding is the ability to select, more or less unconsciously, the appropriate schemata for a given situation. In familiar situations this presents few problems. On the journey to work, the need to make use of the full range of driving skills, a mental map and the ability to understand whatever might be on the car radio is a matter of habit. A more interesting question concerns how schema selection works in *unfamiliar* situations in which we find ourselves momentarily 'stumped', unable to make sense of our surroundings or a given task. What enables Kühn's students for example to discover and apply an appropriate exemplar from their existing knowledge in order to solve an unfamiliar problem? If students learn science by spotting resemblances between new problems and familiar ones, how did they learn to see resemblances in the first place? What is it that tells them that 'this' is similar to 'that'? Dreyfus (1992) quotes the example of the US military's failed attempt to train a computer to distinguish a picture of a forest without tanks from one of a forest with tanks. At first the experiment appeared to be successful as the computer successfully 'recognized' the first few pictures with tanks. Only when it subsequently began to make mistakes did the researchers realize that some of the pictures had been taken on cloudy days and others on bright days. What the computer was distinguishing was forests with or without shadows! Human beings have something that computers do not that makes us successful at schema selection most of the time. However, as Kühn pointed out, the faculty of 'analogical sensitivity', the ability to spot similar patterns, exists without the help of any explicit rules specifying where the similarity lies. What then is the explanation for the ability to recognize 'analogical fit'?

There is an interesting passage in Immanuel Kant's *Critique of Pure Reason*, in which he points to the difference between the ability to manipulate abstract formal rules and that of recognizing how to apply the rules to particular cases:

> If understanding in general is to be viewed as the faculty of rules, judgement will be the faculty of subsuming under rules; that is, of distinguishing whether something does or does not stand under a given rule. General logic contains, and can contain, no rules for judgement. For since general logic abstracts from all content of knowledge; the sole task that remains to it is to give an analytical exposition of the form of knowledge [as expressed] in concepts, in judgements and in inferences, and so to obtain formal rules for all employment of understanding ... And thus it appears that, though under-standing is capable of being instructed, and of being equipped with rules, judgement is a peculiar talent which can be practised only, and cannot be taught. It is the specific quality of so-called mother-wit and its lack no school can make good ...
> A physician, a judge or a ruler may have at command many excellent pathological, legal or political rules, even to the degree that he may become a profound teacher of them, and yet, none the less, may easily stumble in their application. For although admirable in understanding, he may be wanting in natural power of judgement. He may comprehend the universal *in abstracto*, and yet not be able to distinguish whether a case *in concreto* comes under it. Or the error may be due to his not having received, through examples and actual practice, adequate training for this particular act of judgement. Sharpening of the judgement is indeed the one great benefit of examples. Correctness and precision of intellectual insight, on the other hand, they more usually somewhat impair ... Examples are thus the go-cart of judgement; and those who are lacking in the natural talent can never dispense with them.
>
> (1787, pp. 177–8)

Insight

The last two sentences point up the difference between what we might call 'wisdom', based on experience, and training or book-learning. For Kant the goal of philosophy was the establishment of universally binding rules of thought. Too much concentration on concrete examples could get in the way of the logical precision required to accomplish this. But, as Kühn observed, knowledge is only useful and can only be said to be understood when it can be correctly applied. The philosopher may deal in abstractions but 'wisdom' grows from familiarity with living examples. Kant clearly recognized the importance of our ability to perceive similarity relationships, but since he was unable to account for it in terms of logically governed rules, he concluded that it lay outside the province of the philosopher. It is, he concluded, 'an art concealed in the depths of the human soul, whose real modes of activity nature is hardly likely ever to allow us to discover, and to have open to our gaze' (1787, p. 183).

Yet without insight there is no discovery. 'Thought', the mathematician Poincaré is supposed to have said, 'is only a flash between two long nights – but the flash is everything.' The importance Poincaré attributed to the moment of inspiration owed much to his own experience, especially in his search for what he called the 'Fuchsian functions' as a young man in the 1880s. Hours of intense concentration had left him no nearer to a solution when he had to leave his work to go on a geological excursion. Just as he was about to climb on to the bus to leave on the expedition, the solution occurred to him. In the hours that followed, there was no opportunity to verify the conclusion but he had no doubt that it was right. All he needed, when he finally returned home, was time to work from the solution to the reasoning which supported it. 'Eureka' moments of sudden fresh insight like Poincaré's are a common experience in both scientific investigation and everyday life.

In his book *The Transforming Moment*, James Loder (1981) describes five stages through which a person travels on the road to a new discovery. The first is 'conflict', the sense of a problem important enough to demand attention and require resolution. But because the source of the solution is unknown, the next stage is an interlude for scanning, waiting, wondering, perhaps following various hunches. Sometimes the searching stage goes on for a long time. According to Einstein the formulation of the theory of relativity began with a sense of paradox which first occurred to him at the age of 16. It was ten years before the solution to the paradox emerged. The searching stage ends with a constructive act of the imagination in which the 'penny drops', everything falls into place and a problematic situation or puzzling set of facts finally begin to make sense.

What has happened is that a new schema has been formed, giving that problem or puzzle a context and placing it in a relation to the rest of our experience. With the formation of the new schema comes a sense of release from the constraint of the problem situation and often a strong intuitive sense of 'rightness' about the newly discovered solution. The final stage is the exploration of the new solution for its wider implications, perhaps in areas which were not previously thought to be part of the original problem. The question at the heart of this process is what enables the intuitive leap by which the new schema is formed. According to Kant the factors which lead to the choice of one schema over another guide the search for a solution to a problem and enable the imaginative leap by which a new schema comes into being are 'concealed in the depths of the human soul'. Nevertheless there are clues to be gleaned from both the process of scientific discovery and experiments into everyday reasoning and these have important implications for the structure of tacit knowledge.

Sometimes a situation occurs when schema selection takes place 'on the surface' in the full light of day. One is the need to choose between competing paradigms, which occurs regularly not only in science but also in other disciplines. Kühn suggested that when two possible paradigms compete for the allegiance of a particular group of scientists the choice of one over the other will be affected by the *values* the scientific community shares. The criteria for a 'good' theory include such things as accuracy, simplicity, fruitfulness for future research and elegance, even beauty. Kühn calls these the 'values' of the scientific community. In their search for the structure of DNA, Watson and Crick were guided by the belief that the solution would turn out to be beautiful. 'Ugly', Watson is supposed to have remarked, 'doesn't deserve to be true!' Paul Dirac claimed that it was his keen sense of beauty which led him to the wave equation for the behaviour of electrons. Two scientists discussing the merits of rival paradigms may differ about the relative fruitfulness of their theories or they may differ about the relative importance of fruitfulness, beauty or simplicity. In this dispute there is no neutral standpoint from which their argument may be decided. It is a question of how much *importance* the individual scientist or the scientific community as a whole gives to the value in question. Another situation of the same kind occurs regularly in a court of law. There may be no disagreement at all about the evidence presented. Some of it suggests that the accused is guilty, some of it throws doubt on his guilt. The final decision will rest on the *importance* to be given to each separate piece of evidence.

Salience

All this suggests that schema choice is guided by 'value', 'importance' or, to use a more technical term, 'salience'. There are in fact a whole series of experiments which illustrate the importance of 'salience' on perceptual judgements and other aspects of thinking. Some of the clearest were conducted with children by the American researcher Richard Odom in the 1970s (Odom and Guzman, 1970; Odom and Corbin, 1973; Odom, Astor and Cunningham, 1975). In a typical experiment Odom used a set of cards with a variety of designs each of which had four key variables, the number, form and colour of the designs and the position of each design on the cards. First, he carried out a number of tests to discover the relative salience of each of the variables for each of the children. Some responded more readily to the colour of the cards, others to the shape of the design and so on. He then set them a number of logical tasks using the same or similar cards. The logical form of each of the tasks was completely independent of colour, shape and so on. Nevertheless Odom found that the children tended to make fewer mistakes when the information they needed for a particular task involved variables that were more salient for them. After the logical problems the influence of salience was tested in a different way. The children were asked to say what they could remember about them. Again most of them remembered the salient variables better than those which had led to the correct solutions.

Odom's experiments suggest not only that salience or lack of it obscures the pure logical form of a situation but even that it may get in the way of finding a correct solution. To demonstrate this he ran an experiment in which an identical problem was given to 20 adults and 20 children. The problem is written down here but in the experiment it was given verbally and both children and adults were asked to solve it in their heads:

> Imagine that I have two cans. One has red beads in it and it is called the red-bead can. The other has blue beads in it and is called the blue-bead can. There are the same number of red beads in the red-bead can as there are blue beads in the blue-bead can. Let me repeat that. There are the same number of red beads in the red-bead can as there are blue beads in the blue-bead can. Now imagine that I dip a cup into the red-bead can and take out five beads. I pour them into the blue-bead can. Then I mix up all the beads in the blue-bead can. I then dip the cup into the blue-bead can and take out five beads and pour them into the red-bead can. Will the number of red beads in the red-bead can and the number of blue beads in the blue-bead can be the same or different?
>
> (Odom, Cunningham and Astor, 1975)

Try doing the problem yourself and see what answer you come up with, 'the same' or 'different'. Seventeen out of the twenty adults gave the answer 'different'. Nineteen out of the twenty children said 'the same'. In fact the 17 adults were wrong and the 19 children right; the correct answer is 'the same'. The sentence, 'Then I mix up all the beads in the blue-bead can', is irrelevant to the problem. What it does is to suggest that the correct solution depends on a judgement of probability. This suggests why so many adults got the problem wrong. For them probability is a salient concept. They accepted the suggestion in the irrelevant sentence, which led them to estimate the probability of all the red beads returning to the red-bead can. Since this is very low they gave the answer 'different'. The children had not been misled by the sentence suggesting a probability solution. They presumably focused on the fact that for every red bead transferred to the blue-bead can a blue bead goes the other way. But this could have been because they did not understand probability rather than because probability was not salient for them. So Odom carried out a further test with 10 more children. He increased the salience of the probability information by rephrasing the irrelevant part of the problem. This time 9 of the 10 gave the wrong answer, showing that it was not because the children did not *understand* probability that they avoided paying attention to the irrelevant sentence. It was because the concept of probability was not as *salient* for them as it was for the adults.

Dissonance: A Cognitive Theory of Emotion

If the value or salience of each piece of information is an important element in tacit knowledge, it must have a considerable effect on the way we understand and experience the world. But value and importance belong to the *affective* domain of psychology, that concerned with the influence of emotion on judgement. Conventionally emotions have been seen as a distorting factor in our thinking. It has been assumed that correct judgements are much less likely when we are influenced by our emotions. In fact when Thomas Kühn suggested that paradigm choice might be influenced by the values scientists hold in common, it led to a storm of protest and ridicule, with philosophers of science declaring that Kühn had reduced science to arbitrariness and irrationality. Even though the furore has died down and paradigm theory largely accepted, the implications of his position are still virtually unrecognized: that the key to understanding the logical jump involved in our ability to perceive 'analogical fit' lies in the domain of value and is vitally affected by our emotions and relationships.

To explain why this is so, we begin with a venerable but extremely influential line of enquiry: the theory of *cognitive dissonance*. First outlined by Leon Festinger (1957), in its first twenty years the theory stimulated several fruitful lines of research, then entered a 'doldrums' period before re-emerging in the 1990s as 'a powerful means of predicting and changing human behaviour' (Aronson, 1999, p. 103). Cognitive dissonance theory is an attempt to explain some at least of the affective or emotional factors involved in judgement and decision-making in cognitive terms. Festinger called any item of knowledge a 'cognition'. But cognitions include not only facts and concepts but also such things as beliefs, hopes, attitudes, likes and dislikes. Thus if I happen to like animals, this knowledge is expressed in the cognition 'I like animals'. Cognitions are related to one another in three possible ways:

1   They may be *irrelevant*, which is another way of saying they are not related at all, for example, 'I like animals' and 'My wife is wearing a blue dress'.
2   They may be *consonant*, for example, 'I like animals' and 'We own a cat'.
3   Or they may be *dissonant*, for example, 'I like animals' and 'I believe that dogs are dirty'.

A relation of dissonance is said to exist between cognitions when the converse of one follows from the other. But dissonance is not the same as logical contradiction. 'I dislike animals' would not only be dissonant with 'I like cats' but logically contradictory. But there is no necessary logical contradiction between 'I like animals' and 'I believe dogs are dirty'. The dissonance is not logical but psychological, something much more flexible and difficult to define but which leaves room for the influence of the emotions. Moreover dissonance theory is implicitly interactionist. Dissonance arises as a result of the interaction between a person's view of the world, based on past experience, and his or her present situation. If as a result of past experience a person has come to dislike dogs, then the experience of being asked to look after a friend's dog is likely to arouse dissonance. It is not the request itself which gives rise to the dissonance but the schema which says 'Dogs are dirty, potentially fierce and a nuisance'.

Most important of all the 'magnitude' of the dissonance experienced is a function of the salience of the cognitions involved. Take for example a man who supports the Labour party but whose wife votes Conservative. The cognitions 'I vote Labour' and 'My wife votes Conservative' are dissonant.

The amount or 'magnitude' of dissonance will depend very largely on the importance of politics in the man's life. If politics is not important to him the dissonance, though present, may be very small, though rising perhaps at election times. If it is important, however, and assuming his wife's beliefs are also important to him, he has a problem, and there are various ways in which he could attempt to reduce the dissonance. He could change his behaviour by becoming a Conservative. Not only will the fact that his wife, someone of value to him, is already a Conservative make this course of action seem a possible one but the presence of dissonance will give him a powerful motivation to consider it. Alternatively he may try to persuade his wife to vote Labour. If neither of these seems possible he could attempt to minimize the dissonance by avoiding the whole area. He and his wife could agree to differ and not to discuss politics. Or he might find reasons for downgrading the importance of politics in his life generally.

Festinger also carried out experiments in which participants were asked to take part in 'dissonant behaviour'. They had to write an essay justifying a point of view with which they disagreed. After the essay the experimenters discovered that many of the participants had changed their point of view. There were two possible causes for this unexpected result. Either the participants who changed had convinced themselves of the merits of the opposite point of view or the dissonance aroused by the experiment had been great enough to make them want to change their attitudes. So to find out which was the true reason some of the participants in subsequent experiments were offered money for writing the essays and follow-up tests found that these people had changed their points of view much less, if at all. To engage in 'dissonant behaviour' with the excuse of making money did not seem to arouse feelings of dissonance to the same extent. These subjects were able to write their essays 'with fingers crossed'. This strongly suggests that for the others it was the dissonance aroused by the experiment rather than the arguments in the essay which produced the need to change their minds.

Dissonance, Festinger argues, is not an isolated occurrence but a regular feature of everyday life and much of our behaviour can be explained by the attempt to reduce the dissonance between cognitions. Making a decision, for example, involves balancing pros and cons on both sides. We may have to choose between a powerful and stylish car and a less attractive but cheaper model. Whichever decision we make will mean rejecting the good features of the opposite choice and this will arouse dissonance. If we choose the cheaper car, we need to minimize the dissonance caused by passing up the good features of the more expensive one. One way would be to look for extra reasons why it was important not to spend too much money on a new car at this particular time. We may also subconsciously seek out other people who are likely to agree with our choice and talk it over with them as a way of gaining psychological support.

What dissonance theory does not explain is *why* we dislike and avoid the experience of dissonance. The theory itself does not attempt to explain it; it simply observes that the motivation exists. This means that some broader, more comprehensive motivational theory is needed. To find out what kind of theory this must be, we can examine dissonance theory more closely. One of Festinger's examples of dissonant cognitions is 'I am a smoker' and 'Smoking damages your health'. But why are these cognitions so 'obviously' dissonant? To explain it we need another cognition, something like 'I am a rational person and want to maximize my own health.' In other words the existence of dissonance depends on certain beliefs *about oneself.* The broader context required by dissonance theory is a theory about self-perception and self-image. Dissonance occurs when a situation presents us with a threat to our self-image or self-esteem. People asked to tell lies in experiments or to express support for a point of view opposed to their own often reduce dissonance by changing their attitudes afterwards. But this only takes place when they perceive their behaviour as freely motivated. When the participants in the experiments were able to attribute their behaviour to some other factor, for example where they were offered money, much less change took place. The dissonance caused to a Labour supporter whose wife votes Conservative arises not only from the possibility of conflict in the home but, perhaps even worse, the possibility of being thought to be wrong in political matters! Dissonance theory points to the importance of 'self' in our knowledge of the world (Greenwald and Ronis, 1978, pp. 53–7).

More important still, several researchers believe that the magnitude of a person's dissonance in a given situation is crucially affected by their degree of *self-affirmation.* In other words, most people want to see themselves as competent, moral and able to predict their own behaviour and moreover do see themselves in this way for much of the time. Dissonance experiments place them in situations where these aspects of self-perception are threatened. One interesting finding is that when participants' self-esteem is boosted prior to the experiment, such as through a questionnaire inviting them to focus on their better qualities, their tolerance of dissonance increases. This suggests that while the dissonance experiment itself may threaten their self-esteem, the pre-activity offered a counterbalancing positive view of themselves, which made the poor self-reflection given by the experimental situation less salient. Another experiment suggested that boosting self-esteem made cheating behaviour less likely; higher self-esteem appeared to make anticipation of an immoral action more dissonant than otherwise it might have been and as a result participants displayed higher resistance to being asked to engage in doubtful behaviour. Thus dissonance theory suggests the powerful influence of self-perception and self-esteem in the way we understand both the world and our own behaviour (Aronson, 1999, pp. 109–12; Aronson et al., 1999, pp. 128–30).

Attitudes and Affective Processing

Our studies of perception, paradigm choice and cognitive dissonance suggest that it is value or salience that lies behind the analogical jump by which people learn to 'see' one thing as like another and so choose the kind of schema by which to interpret them. More important still, they suggest that the salience of an experience or item of knowledge is actually recorded as part of the information in a given schema. Finally they suggest that the emotions expressed by the drive to reduce dissonance are aroused by threats to our value system and what lies behind it – the perception of ourselves.

These conclusions draw further support from the study of attitudes. One of the earliest textbook definitions of an attitude clearly suggests that attitudes work in the same way as schemata. There Gordon Allport described an attitude as 'a mental and neural state of readiness to respond, organised through experience, and exerting a directive and/or dynamic influence on behaviour' (1935, p. 798). It is interesting to compare this definition with those we have applied to schemata: an 'active organization of past reactions', a means of simplifying or stereotyping experience for easier comprehension. Current researchers in the field define attitudes more broadly as 'a psychological tendency expressed by evaluating a particular entity with some degree of favour or disfavour' (Eagly and Chaiken, 1998, p. 269). Even on this vaguer definition, it seems clear that an attitude is a synthesis of beliefs based on past experience. It is moreover a large-scale or 'dominating' schema, one which itself organizes a number of other subsidiary schemata and, most important, the distinctive feature of attitudes is that they are structured by salience or evaluation.

The fact that attitudes unify large areas of experience by gathering up all the knowledge and beliefs relative to a situation and giving them a common evaluative 'gestalt' or overall pattern suggests that values and the emotions associated with them play a much greater part in the way we experience and perceive the world than simple logical or factual connections. Take for example a person's attitude to their daily work. The schema for a given work situation will include a number of beliefs and items of information, each of which will have varying degrees of salience or importance. Whether or not the job is well paid, whether it is particularly difficult and the amount of status it carries are all likely to be salient items. Flexible working hours or congenial colleagues may be more or less salient. Other items, such as the form of the works football team, may not figure as important at all. A person's overall attitude will be based on the way they respond to the most important aspects of the situation. They may either resent the difficulty of the job or value it highly for the self-esteem it gives. As long as the evaluation of the most salient aspects of the situation is favourable they may be able to take the less desirable elements of the work in their stride. But some change in the situation, a difficult new boss for example, might jump quickly to the top of the salience league. This in turn might have the effect of overshadowing the more positive aspects of the job and giving greater significance to the negative aspects, previously overlooked.

Attitudes gather up a variety of cognitive material, including facts and beliefs, within an overall affective framework. They act as dominating schemata within which a large number of subsidiary schemata, such as the length of the journey to work, relationships with colleagues and the hours required, relate to each other. The way we *feel* about a situation is not to be understood merely as an extraneous biasing factor but as a vital part of the way we construct that situation as part of our internal world. John Hull offers another example when he writes:

> The emotional value which is placed upon a construct must not be thought of as a mere feeling which is so to speak painted on the surface of an idea and which remains the same whatever colour it has ... If I disapprove of fox hunting, I will place the construct in a constellation together with bull fighting, bear baiting, gladiatorial contests and other forms of inflicting cruelty for entertainment. If I approve of fox hunting, I will associate it with healthy outdoor life, the love of the countryside, the old English traditional values and so on ... The fox hunting of which somebody approves is actually known in quite different a manner from the fox hunting of which somebody else disapproves.

> (1985, p. 106)

To conclude: we have seen that schemata are flexible, open-ended data structures, based on concrete experience rather than formal or logical rules. We have seen that along with purely factual information, they also record the *value* we place on that particular piece of information or area of experience. When new schemata are created they tend to echo the patterns of previous schemata; we interpret new information as similar to some aspect of our previous experience. In schema selection as in paradigm choice the answer to the question 'Similar with regard to what?' depends on values and emotional commitments to beliefs and ways of seeing the world. Cognitive dissonance theory offers a clue to the reason this is so. 'Cognitions' or items of knowledge derive their consonance or dissonance from their relation to something we know and believe *about ourselves*. The magnitude of dissonance varies according to how important the particular cognitions are *to us*. In fact the emotional upheaval that is dissonance appears to be a by-product of the need to maintain a coherent self-image and a reasonable level of self-esteem.

If revelation is a process of learning, some important observations follow. First we should be able to notice in the content of revelation a pattern which is already familiar from our previous experience. In order to grasp it we will see it as 'like' something we already know. Moreover this 'likeness' will have evaluative content. We should not expect revelation to consist of a set of abstract or objective facts but rather of something with value content, something of potential relevance and importance to us. The 'cognitions' of which revelation consists may well cause dissonance. They may be threatening or, alternatively, appealing. In particular they may have something to say to our self-image and self-esteem.

Our study of learning is not complete therefore without a look at the way self-image and self-esteem are formed and maintained – the field of relationships and the part they play in learning. Learning is an inherently relational activity; we learn from other people. But deeper still, what we learn about in relation to others is not simply the world around us. We learn too about ourselves. Moreover in turning to the formation of identity, we will discover not only the key to learning but the crucial factor linking learning to revelation.

Chapter 4
Knowing the Self

The Development of Identity

The emotional content of our concepts is not an extraneous extra 'painted on the surface of an idea' but an integral part of the way we know. The importance of emotions in the way we understand and respond to the world is due to the influence of the 'self' in all our knowing. The reason for the relative inflexibility of attitudes is that they mediate between the self and specific areas of experience such as work, family, members of the opposite sex, politics, religion, foreigners, animals, sport and so on. Just as the underlying factor creating cognitive dissonance is a particular self-image, an attitude also reflects an implicit self-evaluation. A person discontented with their job may consider themselves capable of achieving more in the way of satisfaction or financial reward. Someone who dislikes foreigners considers himself threatened in some way by their obvious difference from himself. Changing our attitudes is difficult because it requires a change in our underlying self-understanding, which, knowingly or unknowingly, we may be strenuously defending. The place of self in our knowing reflects the important fact that learning takes place in relationships, and relationships are pre-eminently the sphere of the affective – of value and emotion.

The Boundary of Self

The most important relationships within which the concept of the self takes shape are those between the child and other members of her family, especially with her mother. On this relationship largely depends the child's sense of the regularity or trustworthiness of the world in general and security about her own place within it. Until the moment of birth the child's mother provides her total environment. From birth onwards the mother is only a part of a much more complex world but the child remains totally dependent on her parents. She is exposed to light, louder and more varied sounds, heat and cold. More important still, she begins to experience states of physical need such as hunger and discomfort and inevitable delay before these needs are met, leading to anxiety, fear and anger. In the ideal situation, mother and child adapt to each other successfully and happily and the child develops a lasting sense of security which the psychologist Erik Erikson (1959) called *basic trust*. The worst possible situation is where the child is neglected to such an extent that she dies. In between these extremes is a continuum of possible outcomes depending on the ability of her parents to provide a secure atmosphere. A sense of 'basic trust' acquired in infancy provides a firm foundation from which the child is able to tackle future stages of development. If a less than satisfactory early upbringing leaves the child with a lasting sense of anxiety or insecurity, these fears can affect the whole of the rest of her life. The person who misses out on basic trust in early life finds it very difficult to restore the loss in later life.

In the earliest months of life it is likely that the child has no clear sense of a boundary between what is 'me' and what is 'not me'. She has, after all, been used to being part of her mother. Hands and feet will drift in and out of her field of vision without her being aware that they are her own. But after a few weeks she will begin not simply to see but actively to look at the objects of her environment. She will pay attention to certain sounds and reach out and grasp certain objects. The process of establishing a boundary between self and others has begun. When the child learns to move and in particular to walk, the possibilities for independence and decision-making expand enormously. Equally, so do the possibilities for disobedience and for innocently disrupting the world of the adults who care for her. If it were not already so, the love the toddler receives from her parents becomes increasingly conditional on her behaviour.

What the child needs at this stage is *autonomy* and *self-esteem*. She needs to be able to exercise enough autonomy to establish a sense of being in control and the self-esteem that goes with it without undermining that self-esteem by incurring the wrath of those in charge. This is why the characteristic of this stage is constant testing of the boundaries. It is the period of the 'terrible twos', in which the most commonly used word seems to be 'No!'. She must also learn to control and express her emotions in an acceptable way. The fear of the big world and the big people who run it, as well as anger and frustration at the limits imposed by the control of others, mean frequent swings of mood. The little girl who 'when she was good was very very good and when she was bad she was horrid' was probably two or three years old. If the child's parents are able to be both firm and tolerant, to set clear and consistent boundaries and to discipline without undermining self-confidence, it is likely that the child will develop the autonomy and self-esteem she needs. Affirmation within clear boundaries will give the child a sense of being loved and valued. Consistency of nurture will enable the sense of 'I am loved' to take root as 'I am lovable'. Not all parents are able to provide this. Either because of deficiencies in their own upbringing or because of increasingly complex and demanding life demands, they may fail to provide the nurturing environment the child needs. The result for the child will be a sense of shame and doubt about her acceptability which may persist into adult life, especially in situations where she is called on to exercise independence or challenge other people.

The establishment of autonomy and self-esteem is also the crucial stage at which the boundary between self and the world begins to be defined. 'What creates in me a consciousness of self', writes psychologist Paul Tournier,

> is the consciousness I have of a not-self, of an external world from which I firstly distinguish myself, which next I observe objectively from without, and with which I enter into relationship ... There is a double movement, first of separation and then of relation, between the self and things.
>
> Next, what creates in me consciousness of being a person is entering into a relationship with another person, the 'thou'. Here again, we find the double movement: the consciousness of being distinct from another person, and the possibility of entering into personal relationship with him.
>
> (1973, p. 123)

The security of the boundary created at the stage of autonomy may be the single most important factor in our ability to relate satisfactorily to others. The toddler who can choose whether to play, when to go to the toilet and whether to eat when meal-time comes is defining herself over against the other people in her life, creating a boundary between herself and others, especially her mother. With the boundary comes a distinction between what is 'me' and what is 'others', the ability to think about 'oneself'. However, a boundary like this is only tolerable as long as the child can maintain satisfactory relationships across it. The very definition of a boundary creates both the awareness of separateness and also the possibility of invasion, which can lead to fears of exposure, sometimes expressed in adult life in dreams of being found naked. Good relationships are the foundation to the creation of a sense of self and its maintenance throughout our lives.

The Crystallization of Self

Within the boundary thus created in early childhood grows a sense of 'who I am' based on the continuity of experience. Psychologically, this sense of 'identity' grows out of a continuing story in which it is possible to identify memories of different periods of our lives as belonging to 'me' and recognize 'the person I am now' as the successor of 'the person I was then'. The critical period for the crystallization of this sense of identity comes with adolescence, at the boundary between childhood and adulthood. The fact that adolescence has only been recognized as a distinct phase of life in relatively recent years reflects the important role of society in a person's psychological formation. In Victorian times teenagers were treated either as older children or young adults. In stable societies the choice of adult roles is limited and largely determined by education, wealth and status and most children grow up knowing within fairly narrow limits 'what they are going to be'. One of the characteristics of modern western society is that the choice of adult role has grown to the point where it has become positively bewildering, making the transition from childhood dependence to adult responsibility much more complex and requiring an extended period for its completion.

The onset of adolescence is brought about by the disruption of the samenesses and stability of childhood. Young people begin another stage of rapid growth. The muscles of boys double in size between the ages of 12 and 16, resulting in alternating periods of lethargy and boundless energy. Physical growth is accompanied by profound sexual and emotional changes. Socially the relationship with the adult world begins to change as young people step out of the dependent roles of childhood. Nothing will ever be the same again and it is far from clear whether the sense of sameness will ever be recovered. In the words of Erik Erikson,

> Deep down you are not sure that you are a man (or a woman), that you will ever grow together again and be attractive, that you will ever master your drives, that you really know who you are, that you know what you want to be, that you know what you look like to others, and that you will know how to make the right decision without once and for all committing yourself to the wrong friend, sexual partner, leader or career.

> (1968, p. 200)

Another way of expressing the tension of this time is in the words of the cowboy motto, displayed in a bar in the old West: 'I ain't what I ought to be, I ain't what I'm going to be, but I ain't what I was.' In fact, in nineteenth-century America, the West offered a prospect psychologically similar to the dreams of adolescence: freedom from the ready-made roles of authoritative elders and wide open space in which to explore the possibilities of a new identity. The question for young men and women embarking on the risky journey to adulthood is, 'Who am I really?' One way of exploring this question is to ask, 'Who could I be?' The outcome is identification with high-profile personalities such as pop stars or sporting heroes. Another is falling in love, in which the good qualities we would like to see in ourselves are projected on to the object of infatuation. Another important question is, 'What do others think of me?' The ways this question is explored include banding together in groups, sharing the same social norms and dressing alike, talking endlessly (especially for girls) around issues of identity, exploring the adult world and criticizing the mess adults are making of it.

The goal of adolescence is to regain confidence in that inner sameness and continuity, supported now not by the authority figures of childhood but by society as a whole represented by one's peers. The sense of continuing identity will both enable and be further supported by a smooth transition to the world of work, giving a sense of one's value to the community. It also forms the foundation for the ability to enter stable and committed relationships, especially sexual ones. The danger is role confusion, in which the young person never quite achieves a secure sense of 'Who I am' and as a result enters jobs and relationships in adult years still looking for the social support he needs to achieve a stable identity.

Although identity, once achieved, remains relatively stable in adulthood, it is far from being fixed or static. Having successfully entered the world of work and formed relationships of mutual responsibility, there comes a time when adults need to be able to assess what they have achieved, either through a job or in helping to bring up the next generation. A stage is reached for most of us when it becomes clear that in the time left we will only be able to realize a limited number of the goals and aspirations with which we set out in adult life. Later still, the fact of our own death asks us to look back on the course of lives and judge them either with satisfaction or regret. All these important developmental stages involve a further re-examination and reintegration of identity. Nor are they the only possible turning points for the realization of new aspects of the self. Experiences such as the meeting of a particular challenge requiring the discovery of new talents or resources; the possibility or actuality of failure; the need for commitment, in marriage for example; the performance of a new role; divorce; bereavement; or betrayal are all self-involving. They call for reflection, self-evaluation and a change in our sense of who we are. Even without the effects of unexpected or decisive events, many lives follow a pattern of predictable status passage involving the gradual development of identity. A person in employment may progress from raw recruit to employee with potential, through promotion, the realization of having reached the limit of one's achievement to eventual retirement and reorientation away from work. Parents progress from the care of young children, to that of teenagers, through the time the children leave home to the role of grandparents.

Two important conclusions flow from this account of identity formation and development. First the knowledge of ourselves is a developmental achievement; it is we ourselves who create and maintain our sense of 'me' or 'the person I am' throughout our lives. Secondly the ability to do so is dependent on society as a whole; we cannot become coherent persons except in society. In the development of identity, inner psychological development and outward social integration take place together. The 'right time' for each successive stage of growth is determined both by physical and psychological development and by social expectations. Psychologically the formation of the boundary between self and the world in early childhood enables the child to create a schema for 'myself'. The importance of the 'self-schema' cannot be underestimated. Once formed it continues to develop throughout the rest of our lives. It forms the dominating schema for interaction and learning, imposing coherence and direction on experience, establishing a relationship between past, present and future and between separate areas of experience.

Primary Socialization

The role of society in the development of identity emphasizes the importance of relationships in learning of all kinds. Learning is a social activity, not just in the trivial sense that we tend to learn in groups alongside other people but because we derive the schemata through which we interpret the world *from other people*. In the present climate it is important to stress this point to counteract undue emphasis on the growth and development of hypothetical internal structures. Recent advances in genetics added to the high profile of computer science and the legacy of mid-twentieth-century structuralism have created a climate in which the emphasis is placed on the innate capacity of individuals rather than the resources for learning to be found in social interaction.

Learning to Speak

A comparison of two alternative explanations of language learning serves as a good illustration of these opposing points of view. The ability to speak a language is one of the most complex tasks we ever perform, yet most children master it at an early age. To explain this outstanding achievement, structuralist Noam Chomsky advanced the theory of an innate genetically given structure in the brain which generates the ability to understand and speak a language. This left Chomsky and his followers with the formidable task of working out what kind of pre-linguistic structure could actually serve as the source and foundation for any and all of the varieties of languages and dialects found in the real world. As in the case of strong AI, early confidence based on commitment to the paradigm has given way to disappointment.

In fact the problem is easily solved by taking an opposite standpoint, restoring in the process that aspect of language all too easily forgotten in the structuralist tradition – its function as a *means of communication*. In an article with the imposing title 'The ontogenesis of speech acts', Jerome Bruner (1975) records the results of observations of the interactions of mothers as they fed, bathed and played games with their children. What he noticed was that the mothers continually interpreted the movements of the children as intentions to perform certain actions or to pay attention to particular objects. If a child looked at a particular object the mothers would name it, perhaps holding it steady to allow the child to grasp it or play with it. They would mark a child's completed action with words like 'There' or 'Good boy'.

What comes before language, Bruner insisted, is not a genetic structure but rather the structures of human interaction. Moreover it is these that come to be reflected in the structures of language. The origin of case-grammar, for example, is to be found in the standard features of a typical action: the agent, the action itself, the object of the action, the recipient, the location and so on. The child first grasps this pre-linguistically as a standard human interaction. Then she learns to describe it in language. At first she uses non-standard forms which require a knowledge of the context to be understood. Gradually she learns the proper grammatical forms. As she learns how to speak, the learning of meaning and language begin to go hand in hand. Grasping the meaning of a situation acts as a clue to the meaning of the words adults use to express it. In turn the ability to describe a situation in language opens up new possibilities for meaning within it. From this point of view, what is innate is not a genetic structure but the features of human action and intention we all learn to communicate in language.

The 'Zone of Proximal Development'

Another theorist who stressed the interaction between psychological and social development was the Soviet psychologist, Lev Vygotsky. In the 1960s the field of developmental psychology was dominated by the controversy between Vygotsky and the structuralist Jean Piaget. Whereas Piaget emphasized a child's 'readiness' to learn, dependent on the development of the necessary structures in the brain, Vygotsky developed the idea of the 'zone of proximal development', by which he meant what a child is capable of learning *from another*, usually an adult. At any given age there are some things a child has mastered and can do for herself, others she has no chance of mastering because they are just too difficult. In between lies the 'zone of proximal development', the things she is ready to learn with help from another. Vygotsky suggested that the most effective teaching is that pitched in the zone of proximal development. It should aim at capacities the child has not yet developed but could develop with appropriate help.

Following Vygotsky's lead, American psychologist James Wertsch (1979) set up an experiment which involved mothers and their children working on a task together in order to observe the way children learn from a trusted adult. He gave each mother and child a model of a truck and its cargo and a set of separate pieces which when put together made up the same model. The object was to find out what help children of different ages needed from their mothers in order to accomplish the task. The children were aged 2½, 3½ and 4½. As a result of his observations, Wertsch described the following four stages:

1   The youngest and least able children could not manage the task even with their mothers' help. They could not understand what they had to do. These children had no definition of the situation so there was no way of interpreting their mothers' instructions.

2   Slightly older or more able children were able to respond to specific instructions such as 'Fit that piece here', or 'Put the green one next to the red one.' They had got as far as realizing that they and their mothers were engaged in a common task but had no understanding of the task itself. They were simply carrying out the mother's instructions one by one.

3   At the next stage mother and child began to share an understanding of the task, though the child's understanding was still limited. The children were able to respond to non-specific instructions such as 'What do we do next?' (an implicit direction to look for the next part of the task). These children had the capacity to begin to form their own schema for the shared task. The transition from other-regulation to self-regulation had begun.

4   The older children could usually carry out the task but frequently repeated their moves out loud, asking and answering their own

questions. By this stage they had taken over the mother's definition of the situation and were working out the required moves for themselves. What had begun as an interpersonal, shared task – something the mother had to show the child how to do – had become an intra-psychological, internalized definition of the situation – something the child could now do for herself.

Wertsch's experiment illustrates a process by which children *take over schemata from others*, usually the adults closest to them. As they learned from their mothers how to build a truck from a kit, the children were taking over from their mothers a schema for handling the situation. At first only the mothers understood the situation; by the fourth stage the children had learned to see it as their mothers did. The significance of this small-scale experiment is that it clearly points to a larger-scale process in which children learn, not simply by formal education but also in a great deal of informal learning, to structure their own world in the same way as that of their parents and elders in general. 'Give me a child until the age of seven', Ignatius Loyola is reported to have said, 'and he is mine for life.' The young child grows up in a world already structured by others, which he experiences as *given*. This is the main feature of *primary socialization*. The child learns by taking over schemata or frameworks of comprehension from other people, learning to make them her own and to 'indwell' them. This is the way culture is passed from one generation to the next.

Self and Others

Responding to Others

The social dimension of learning is not limited to the passive reception of schemata from parents, significant others (such as teachers or grandparents) and society as a whole. From a relatively early age, we not only take over schemata from others but also *make* schemata in response to others. This applies to both the knowledge of the world and the knowledge of ourselves. In the earliest experiences by which identity is formed we are largely passive. We rely very largely on the quality of our parents' nurturing for the establishment of basic trust. But the older we become, the more active the part we play in the development of identity. The family unit as the original matrix of socialization very quickly becomes part of the child's wider experience. In modern society, where children are exposed to institutional and peer group influences from an early age, not to mention those of the media of mass communication, the family is much less of a 'total' institution than it might once have been. Peer-group influence begins virtually as soon as the child meets others of her own age but reaches its greatest importance during adolescence. School teachers become significant others with powers of reinforcement and personal influence. The school itself imposes a particular set of values by institutional means rather than by direct personal influence. Television provides a wide variety of possible adult or peer-group models.

The wide variety of relationships in which young people are involved presents a problem of inconsistent socialization. Often the standards and values expected at home differ from those at school or among friends. The tactics a young person uses to cope with inconsistent socialization may have a considerable effect on the development of her personality. Some will choose one pervasive loyalty, often to the values of home but sometimes to those of her peer group. Alternatively she may compartmentalize her loyalties, taking on different value systems in different situations. A relatively minor example of this is the child who takes care to mind her language at home to conceal from her parents that she regularly uses bad language when among her friends. She may attempt to balance the various roles and loyalties demanded, not identifying too closely with any particular one, or she may begin positively to reject the authority often of the school but sometimes of the home as well. The ideal adult solution is the integration of the various roles demanded into a secure and stable identity, enabling her to influence the expectations of most if not all of the groups of which she is a part, but this solution is rarely available before adolescence and is by no means uniformly successful even in adulthood (Lippitt, 1968).

As they grow up, children learn very quickly to step into the roles of others and try out for themselves the values and expectations demanded. One of the most important ways in which they do this is through play. In play, the children are able to try out the roles of parents, friends, teachers or some other model, as far as they can grasp them, vicariously expanding their experience of life. Before long they take an important step forward in the transition from 'play' to 'the game'. Whereas in 'play' the child takes on or interacts with one role at a time, in 'the game' the participant must construct the role of all the players simultaneously. She must respond to the game as such rather than to any one player individually. To achieve this requires the construction of a *generalized other*, which embodies both the rules and the purpose of the game (Mead, 1934, pp. 149–60).

Reference Groups

Ability to engage in 'the game' governed by a corporate role is the foundation for one of the most important features of adult life, membership of a variety of 'reference groups' (Shibutani, 1962). Reference groups may be large or small, temporary or permanent. They include the family and the state, regular workmates or the occupants of a railway compartment. Some reference groups, such as history or 'posterity', may not even exist in the present. A reference group is formed and maintained by channels of communication, be it direct personal communication, a newsletter or journal, the mass media, even perhaps through the Internet. Each role a given individual plays takes place within a particular reference group. He may be husband and father, employee, committee member, club or church member, citizen or sports enthusiast. In taking each role, the group member responds to the generalized other, the expectations and values the group hold in common, the 'rules of the game' which maintain the group in being. But within these expectations there is also scope to *take* the role, defining it according to one's own personality and preferences. A waiter, for example, has a job to do, but the relationship he attempts to cultivate with the patrons may be less tightly defined. Similarly the role of a committee chairman is made up partly of mandatory expectations, partly of a range of options. He may be easy-going or a stickler for procedure, authoritarian or democratic.

A reference group has two components: *the people who belong to the group* and *the perspectives which they share in common*. Membership of a particular reference group involves sharing a definition of the relevant situation, at least to the extent necessary for participation in the group. This definition forms the foundation for any personal relationships which develop within the frame of reference thus provided. Readers of *The Times* either share a certain social and political outlook or are content to respond habitually to that outlook when thinking about society and politics. Members of a local rugby team share a commitment not only to the game but usually to certain norms of behaviour before and after matches. A committee must share a definition of its task, a club exists for the benefit of those who share the same interests and the stability of a state requires a degree of consensus. Through the provision of a shared perspective to which all the members can relate, reference groups contribute to the formation of individual identity. A person may express his knowledge of himself as 'The best 400 metre runner in my athletics club', 'A valued member of the church choir', or 'An up-and-coming young executive'.

In traditional societies there were relatively few reference groups. Most people lived in small communities where everyone knew everyone else and most had prescribed roles. Modern pluralist society allows many more people to belong to a variety of reference groups of their own choice. Almost no one has all the same friends, contacts and interests as someone else, even their own wife or husband. Each individual is the unique intersection of a number of reference groups. Although this allows the possibility of social mobility and relative independence from all-pervasive social norms, it also brings with it the possibility of role conflict, similar to the problem of inconsistent socialization in childhood but here a potentially disruptive factor for adult identity. It is part of the condition of post-modern society that people live their lives as members of a variety of potentially competing social groups. Rarely does one group claim exclusive or overriding loyalty. Instead we 'play off' loyalty to one group against the others. We may miss a play rehearsal or choir practice because of a family problem one day, cancel an evening out with the family because of the pressure of work on another and decide to leave work early in order to get to a football match on time on a third. The problem of postmodernity is that without an overriding commitment to any particular group or set of values it is hard to maintain a coherent and stable identity.

The Christian Learning Community

The Church, both in its universal and local manifestation, is also a reference group. As such it involves the same two components: the particular members who make it up and the perspectives which they share. Belonging to the Church means both sharing fellowship with a particular group of people and sharing the perspective of Christian commitment. In traditional societies, where there is often one overriding reference group, Church and community could easily come to be virtually interchangeable. The values of Christianity might influence community life profoundly, but might equally be distorted or overshadowed by those of the community. In pluralist societies the Church faces the problem of competing loyalties. Jesus called his followers to a single overriding loyalty to him and the extension of God's kingdom, but work, family and other interests continue to take a higher priority in the lives of many church members. Church membership is often seen as a leisure-time pursuit and is expected to take its place alongside all the other demands of increasingly crowded lives.

Nevertheless the task of the Church is to be a learning community in which the distinctive perspectives of Christian commitment are both modelled and passed on. Teaching and learning will take place explicitly in Sunday schools and other children's groups, through sermons, in home groups and in a variety of training activities from occasional Lent courses to full-scale theological training. It also takes place implicitly through the day-to-day life and regular worship of the community. The welcome offered to strangers and occasional worshippers; the demeanour of the worship leader; the content of the liturgy; the scope of the prayers; the relationships in evidence between the worshippers; even the state of the building – all these convey, often in a far more effective way than any sermon or deliberate teaching event, what the members of a particular local church really believe and value. The Christian perspective consists not only of doctrines but of attitudes, such as the love of self and others, and these tend to be 'caught' rather than 'taught'. There is, in Christian conversion and discipleship, a strong element of *resocialization*, in which people both unlearn and relearn the attitudes and values they first developed in the earliest stages of their lives. Often this means the healing of the damaged child, as people learn to value themselves for the first time and grow in their capacity both to love and be loved. Learning and change of this kind of depth and extent requires a high level of community support. The attitudes we learned in childhood we learned in the context of the family, a situation of high power and high emotional intensity. In resocialization, a similar level of non-manipulative emotional support is needed. The idea of the Church as a family in which Christians relate to one another as brothers and sisters is not merely an abstract doctrinal truth. It plays a vital role in enabling the kind of learning required of disciples, the change of attitudes necessary to become like Jesus.

Churches, and their leaders in particular, also have to ask themselves whether, in the pattern of their common life, they are being faithful to the perspective they profess to share. We may talk idly of the Christian family and sometimes 'family' worship, but the level at which most people actually relate may be adequately expressed by a perfunctory handshake, at least in churches where the 'peace' is shared. Evangelism and social concern may be preached from the pulpit but absent from the agenda of the PCC or elders' meeting. The words of the liturgy may invoke the presence of God through his Holy Spirit but the actual performance may be dry and empty of his life and power. In the community that is consciously endeavouring to be faithful to its calling together, each individual member, as they take their role within it, will find themselves growing in personal discipleship. Where the community has lost sight of some or all of the distinctive perspectives of Christian faith, individual members may be confused or misled about the role they are to play and the way they are to play it.

Identity and Learning

We learn about the world through relationships and many of the schemata which make up our mental world models are derived from others. We learn about ourselves in the same way. A self-schema, and with it a sense of continuing stable identity, develops in relationships – with family, peer group, institutions, especially schools, and the wider society as a whole. The self-schema is the source of continuity and coherence, binding the disparate areas of experience together as 'our' experience and forming the dominating schema for the attitudes by which we relate to particular areas of our world. Learning about the world and learning about the self are two sides of the same coin. Almost every new piece of learning about the world contributes to, and sometimes challenges or calls into question, our understanding of ourselves. Of the two *it is the search for identity and the need to maintain a coherent sense of identity which is the principal motivating factor in learning.*

Adults' and Children's Learning

One of the ways the influence of identity formation on learning is clearly seen is in the difference between adults and children in regard to learning. Researchers have often been puzzled by the fact that children learn much faster and more efficiently than adults. The ability to speak a language is so complex that it defies analysis, yet most children acquire their first language quickly and naturally at a very early age. Throughout their schooling children continue to learn quickly but with the arrival of adolescence many begin to display a marked reluctance and even cease learning altogether. Adults, especially those in occupations which require them to do so, may continue to learn throughout their lives, although many fail to do so. Their learning becomes predominantly task-related, limited to what is necessary to enable them to fulfil social roles and occupation.

These differences between adults, children and adolescents can be attributed to the difference in stages of identity formation. For children not only is there an overwhelming need to comprehend the environment in order to cope with it but the role of learner is part of the identity of a child. A child is willing to learn what parents and teachers tell her she needs to learn because she defines herself as an aspiring adult and her goal is to learn to be like them. In adolescence, questioning of adult authority and the rejection of the dependent relationships of childhood are necessary developments and these changes in identity can profoundly affect the progress of learning. The breakdown of the stabilities of childhood may also make it difficult for teenagers to relate new learning to a clear sense of who they are becoming. Finally, adults usually learn easily only those things required for the maintenance and extension of identity in those areas clearly seen to be relevant. Adult learning can be just as quick and efficient as a child's if the demands of a new job or a new social task, such as having a baby, make it necessary or where the desire for a new self-understanding stimulates the desire to learn. For adults, adolescents and children, ability to learn is dependent on the process of identity formation and maintenance.

A particularly good example of the relation between learning and identity formation is the case of bereavement. The bereaved person, particularly the bereaved spouse, has lost a part of his or her identity with the death of the partner. In the months which follow, a great deal of what Colin Murray Parkes (1986) calls 'grief-work' must take place, by means of which the bereaved person readjusts to life on their own by recovering those aspects of identity lost with bereavement. The bereaved wife may have to take on the role of breadwinner, learn to drive a car, fill in tax forms and provide as much as possible of what her children now lack in the absence of a father. All these learning tasks contribute to and arise from the need to discover a new identity, both socially, in regaining a satisfactory complex of roles in society, and psychologically, in learning to do without the support of friend, provider and sexual partner. The loss of a partner is moreover only one type of bereavement. Other kinds of loss, including the loss of a limb, the loss of a job and moving house, require similar responses. The learning of new skills, new roles and new identity is interwoven.

Motivation in Adult Education

The clearest evidence of all comes from studies of adults in further education talking and writing about their experiences and what motivates them. A recent survey of adult learners (Coare and Thomson, 1996) unearthed several overlapping factors leading people to take the plunge back into education. On the surface, the reason may be the need to learn new skills during a period of unemployment. The catalyst may be a change of life which itself requires a change of identity, such as bereavement or the last child leaving home. But underneath these there is often a desire to change oneself in some way, to become a different sort of person. As one adult learner put it:

> I had a feeling of emptiness that only intellectual growth would fulfil. I began to question my life, my choices, who I had become. I fitted the mould of wife and mother, but I wanted a new identity, with a sense of purpose, not the negative labels I had attached to myself along the way.

Others expressed a sense of lost opportunities, of something missing in their lives. Or they may have begun the course looking for the skills needed for new employment and discovered much more:

> Is adult learning for me? The answer has got to be 'yes' because only further education can put right the mistakes of the past ... I am hoping that this course will give me self-confidence ...

> As a child at school I was a distracted student, and now realise ... how much fun – and how absorbing and satisfying – learning actually is! ... I actually feel liberated!

Linden West summarizes the results of a series of in-depth interviews with adult learners over a period of several years:

> The learners used a variety of language and metaphor to describe how they felt and why they wished to change direction. They talked of emptiness at home, of personal inadequacy and dissatisfaction in relationships, of lost status through unemployment; or of being unable to cope with insecurities in their working lives and wanting to escape into a different career ... Many students talked of distressing gaps between who they felt they were and what they wanted to be...

> (West, 1996, p. 35)

One of the interviewees, 'Brenda', expressed particularly well the desire for a change in identity which drew her to adult learning:

> I was mindful of the fact that the family was growing up and there would come a point when they would start moving away ... I needed something I really could get to grips with but that would also be interesting but fulfilling as well ... it is important that I have my own little bit of identity down here again with studying ...

> ... he [her husband] has gone up several rungs of the ladder ... so maybe that is another motivation ... because at least I will be able to offer him a lively mind.

As the interviews went on, Brenda realized that taking an Access course answered another deeply rooted motive, the need to be allowed to take risks:

> There was that co-dependency from the point of view of, 'I shouldn't do that if I were you', and, 'be careful, you'll fall.' I was caught climbing trees when I was twelve and was severely punished ... So again, the Access course for me is risk-taking, and I am enjoying it ...

I've had people say, 'What do you want to go and do a degree course at your age?' and things like that but that doesn't worry me. I know that somewhere in my psyche it'll bring out the 'me' ...

(Coare and Thomson, 1996, pp. 48, 52, 54)

Even when seeking a change in identity was not one of the consciously expressed reasons for entering adult education, it was often the most important result for many of the participants: 'My life opened up. It was like a picture opening as I tried to do things I had never done before ... Starting to learn again after so many years changed my life, in some ways saved my life' (Coare and Thomson, 1996, pp. 193, 195)

We all learn most readily when what we are learning contributes to the development of our sense of identity, or knowledge of who we are. We learn far less efficiently when there is no discernible link with identity in the new knowledge we are being offered. And when the new information or the learning process itself threatens our sense of who we are or want to be we positively resist learning. It is moreover not simply the need to know ourselves which acts as the engine of learning but the need to *like* and *value* ourselves, to discover an identity which is 'more "me"' than the one we may be familiar with. But why should the formation of identity play such an important role in our lives? In order to answer this question we first need to consider a puzzling feature of identity which has been a staple problem of philosophers in all ages.

'I' and 'Me'

The 'self' we know is part of our mental world. It includes information about our appearance, capabilities, likes and dislikes, past history, achievements, social roles and much more. This is the information which would fill an essay about 'myself', the kind that schoolchildren are often asked to compose. The self we know develops during the course of our lives. About this self we could say truthfully that we not the same person today as we were some years ago. We have changed and our sense of identity has changed. But in another sense we believe that we *are* the same person. We have memories stretching back over most of our lives which bind our separate experiences together and we can tell a story about our lives which gives these memories meaning. The self which is the object of these memories is the self we know and can describe. But behind the self we call 'me' is another self, the person to whom the memories belong and the one who tells the story, an 'I' who is and has been the subject of all our experiences.

What is 'I'?

However, the recognition of 'I' immediately causes a problem because, although it is clear that 'I' must exist, it is far from clear exactly what this 'I' is. The self which others observe and which we can describe can be an object of knowledge but the 'I' or knowing subject cannot be known in the same way without itself becoming an object. Whatever 'I' is, is different from any description which could be given of it but, in the words of A. J. Ayer, 'It is a difference which defies description' (1956, p. 186). It is, wrote John Locke, 'something, we know not what' (1690, II.23). Some philosophers have claimed that the idea of a continuing subject is a mistake. The self is, in fact, no more than the sum of experiences. 'There are some philosophers', wrote David Hume, in a famous passage in his *Treatise of Human Nature*,

> who imagine we are every moment intimately conscious of what we call our SELF ... For my part, when I enter most intimately into what I call *myself*, I always stumble on some particular perception or other, of heat or cold, light or shade, love or hatred, pain or pleasure. I never can catch *myself* at any time without a perception, and never can observe anything but the perception ... If anyone upon serious and unprejudiced reflection, thinks he has a different notion of *himself*, I must confess I can no longer reason with him ... He may, perhaps, perceive something simple and continu'd which he calls himself; tho' I am certain there is no such principle in me. But setting aside such metaphysicians of this kind, I may venture to affirm of the rest of mankind, that they are *nothing but a bundle or collection of different perceptions*, which succeed each other with an inconceivable rapidity, and are in a perpetual flux and movement.
>
> (1739, pp. 251–2)

Yet even Hume, in an appendix to the *Treatise*, had to concede the 'feeling' of an ongoing personal subject as the form of the unity of our perceptions over time. Unless we are to conclude with Hume that the 'I' is non-existent – and there have been plenty of philosophers who have shared this conclusion – we need a coherent account of the status of the knowing, remembering and imagining subject.

George Herbert Mead was an American social psychologist who described in detail what he called the 'I–me' relationship.[1] 'Me' is the socially constructed 'self', which meant, for Mead, a complex of the attitudes of others assumed by the self in the process of self-definition. 'I' is the *response* of the individual to those attitudes (1934, pp. xxiv, 173–8, 200–213, 331–5).

---

[1] Mead's theory forms the basis of the symbolic interactionism in the social sciences, and is implicit in other approaches to social psychology.

Each person plays a variety of roles, for which the expectations or standards of performance are socially defined. He must accept, for the purposes of performing the role, the perspective of the particular reference group within which the role acquires its meaning. But a role is not necessarily a rigid set of expectations. More often there is a continuum of acceptable responses. The waiter may be friendly or formal, the committee chairman authoritarian or democratic, the teacher strict or easy-going, the father aloof or involved. By selecting a particular response, an individual not only *takes* but simultaneously *makes* a role. The decision as to how to play the role is that of the 'I'. Role-taking is a practical example of the response of the 'I' to the socially organized 'me'. A person is 'I' and 'me' in relationship.

However, in Mead's approach it is 'me' which gives rise to 'I'. First comes social interaction, organized by meaningful gestures which in human beings take the form of language. Social interaction creates the 'me' as each individual creates a self-schema in response to the attitudes of others. 'I' emerges only at the end of the chain as a response to 'me'. Interestingly, the philosopher Wittgenstein reached the same conclusion in his later philosophy. What is given, he hypothesized, is 'forms of life', by which he meant certain characteristically human interactions. According to Wittgenstein there is nothing deeper than 'forms of life'. Forms of life are on the surface and there is no inner 'I' either giving rise to or forming private interpretations of these forms. They 'just are' and as such are the only correct subject of philosophy. Stanley Cavell spells out the implications for the philosophy of the self:

> The extent to which we understand one another or ourselves is the same as the extent to which we share or understand forms of life, share and know, for example, what it is to take turns, or take chances, or know that some things we have lost we cannot look for but can nevertheless sometimes find or recover; share the sense of what is fun and what loss feels like, and take comfort from the same things or take confidence or offence in similar ways. That we do more or less share such forms rests upon nothing deeper; nothing *ensures* that we will, and there is no foundation, logical or philosophical, which explains the fact that we do, which provides the real forms of which our lives, and language, are distortions.
>
> (1984, pp. 223–4)

Forms of life, Wittgenstein believed, provided the most fundamental context of human life available for study, more basic than thought, speech or language. To pursue 'mental models' can only distort the real picture since the supposed 'I' or thinking self is not the origin of the forms of life but the outcome of them. Consequently his method was to examine in as much detail as possible what was on the surface: the forms of life themselves, describing and drawing inferences from as many facets of human behaviour as possible in order to build up a richly nuanced picture of experience. Eschewing definitions, Wittgenstein sought to paint his picture by the use of examples, selected and arranged to throw light on the characteristically human.

In the light of the argument to this point, we could say that Wittgenstein's method was the attempt to make tacit knowledge explicit. Tacit knowledge, as we have seen, is dependent on examples drawn from experience. The 'forms of life' – expressing anger or pity, taking chances and taking turns – form what Hubert Dreyfus calls the 'inarticulate, pre-conceptual background understanding of what it is like to be human' (1992, pp. xi–xii), that 'more than we can tell' which makes up tacit knowledge. But the 'more than we can tell' includes some things that give rise to forms of life even if they are not in themselves describable. The fact that language arises from communication, which is an action, the starting point of Wittgenstein's second philosophy, originates in the logically prior fact that people are agents, whatever that may mean. Nor could we express anger or pity, take chances or turns, without some prior *capacity to relate*. As Fergus Kerr puts it, 'To understand language as a form, or rather as a multiplicity of forms, of expressive activity, as Wittgenstein encourages us to do, is to rehabilitate the self as a responsive agent in vital connection with others of the same kind' (1986, p. 134). The idea of a capacity to relate is precisely what we will find expressed by the biblical image of mankind made 'in the image of God'. Thus although the 'outside-in' framework of Mead and Wittgenstein poses challenges which advocates of 'mental models' and believers in the knowing self must face, they do not entirely rule out the propriety of the investigation.

The Personal Subject

In fact there is a strong foundation in the history of both philosophy and social science for this position. Immanuel Kant found the idea of the knowing subject, which he called both the 'transcendental ego' and, in a more down-to-earth way, the 'I think', indispensable to his philosophy. Carl Jung spoke of the inner *person* behind the outward *persona*. But in order to put flesh on to the bones of this approach we turn to Christian theology, where there is a long history of speculation about the nature of persons originating with the exploration of the doctrine of the Trinity.

At the heart of the doctrinal debates of the early centuries of the Christian Church, in particular in the hard-fought battles over the correct way of understanding the Trinity and the Person of Christ, lay the need to preserve the concept of person from reduction to terms appropriate to the analysis of impersonal nature. Eventually these intense theological struggles led to the promulgation of the Nicene Creed of AD 325 with its definition of the relationship of Christ and the Holy Spirit to God the Father and the 'Definition' of the full human and divine natures of Jesus promulgated by the Council of Chalcedon in AD 451. The discussion turned on the meaning to be given to the Greek word *hypostasis* in relation to the term *ousia*. In secular usage these words had broadly the same meaning, namely 'being', but the term *hypostasis* was adopted by the early Church Fathers to stand for the distinct 'Persons' of the Trinity in contradistinction to the *ousia* or 'essence' which they share in common. Thus Gregory Nazianzus could write, 'The Son is not the Father, but he is what the Father is', and Basil of Caesarea:

> It is indispensable to have clear understanding that, as he who fails to confess the community of the essence (*ousia*) falls into polytheism so he who refuses to grant the distinction of the *hypostases* is carried away into Judaism ... For merely to enumerate the differences of Persons (*prosopa*) is insufficient; we must confess each Person (*prosopon*) to have an existence in real *hypostasis*.
> (Epistle ccx.5 in Stevenson, 1966, p. 112)

In other words Basil is saying that the distinction of persons in the Trinity is not simply a difference of mask (in Greek, *prosopon*, or 'face') but a difference in real being. In the Trinity three separate *hypostases* or 'realities' share the same *ousia* or essence. The effect of Basil's revolutionary definition is to make the idea of *hypostasis* or personal being an ontological category, a category of being. Personal being is not something which emerges from some non-personal essence which is more fundamental. Personal being 'really is'.

What Basil and Gregory have done is to give logical priority to the category of 'person' (Gunton, 1997, pp. 93–6). Having established that personal being has real existence, the next step is to work out what kind of existence it is. Here again the key is to recognize the uniqueness of personal existence over against the 'nature' or 'essence' that things, or people, of the same type share in common. To maintain that the *hypostasis* – personal being – does not emerge from *ousia* or essence is to say that God the Holy Trinity is not first 'God' and then 'Father', 'Son' and 'Holy Spirit'. The persons of the Trinity are not different individual expressions of their common 'Godness'. Rather God's nature or essence comes to be only as it is 'hypostatized' or given personal being as Father, Son and Spirit. Without the persons of Father, Son and Spirit there would not be any 'Godness'. The origin of God is not the nature which Father, Son and Spirit share in common but the person of the Father who brings forth the Son and the Spirit. The nature of God is to exist as Father, Son and Spirit. To take a further step, this means that God's nature is to exist in relationship. Father, Son and Spirit are not separable entities; they not only work together but have their very existence in relationship. The essence or being of God is communion or relationship. The nature of persons is to exist in relationship; without relationship they could not exist (Zizioulas, 1985, pp. 27–65).

Despite having been lost in the western Church, the importance of the Fathers' approach is increasingly recognized. This is precisely because it offers a way of restoring the importance of the idea of 'persons' in a world in which much secular social science comes close to abolishing it (Gunton, 1997, pp. 110–14). John Zizioulas, for example, sees the potential of relating the doctrine of the Trinity to the idea of human persons as a way of commending both to a Christian audience (1991, p. 21). But is the idea of *hypostasis* as an ontological category denoting personal existence applicable to human beings as well as God? Is the state of being a person really the essence of human existence? If the early Church fathers failed to make this connection it was because of their reluctance to be drawn into definitions of either *ousia* or *hypostasis*. However the analogy was certainly developed in the twelfth century by Richard of St Victor, who appealed to the human experience of subjectivity as an analogy for our understanding of the Trinity. 'Person' he defined as *divinae naturae incommunicabilis existentia* or the incommunicable 'standing forth' of the divine nature. The substance of the individual, he maintained, tells you the What?, the nature or *ousia* of that individual. But the person tells you the Who?, the only 'definition' of which is a proper name, an incommunicable and irreducible individual (1959, iv. 6–7).

Thus, as Colin Gunton sees it (1997, pp. 84–96), the idea of 'personhood' as a logically prior category has the potential to restore the 'middle term' in the debate about the self. The quotation from David Hume given above illustrates the way the self virtually disappears in the individualism of the Enlightenment outside of Kant. On the other hand, in the collectivism of Marx the individual similarly loses his significance to be swallowed up in the collective. The tradition of Basil, Gregory and Richard of St Victor, which also surfaces in the thought of the English philosopher and poet Samuel Taylor Coleridge and Scottish philosopher John Macmurray, places between these extremes the 'person in relationship', an individual for whom life and meaning is impossible apart from community, who cannot develop a concept of self or the world apart from interaction with others. If the sceptical social scientist were to ask what empirical support there might be for such a concept, we could answer, on the basis of the argument I have developed so far, that vast amounts of psychological and sociological research – the perceiver's 'effort after meaning', the nature of schemata, the role of value and salience in perception, the effect of the self-concept on cognitive dissonance, the role of joint attention in language learning, the interaction of psychological and sociological stages in the development of identity – all point to the vital importance of social interaction in the development of the self. Moreover in the next chapter I shall try to show how this very conclusion is further reinforced by the way the separate disciplines cohere.

Who Am 'I'?

There is a mystery about human persons. Beneath the what? of human life is something different, a unique and irreducible subject, a who? The knowable 'self' is a mask, a social construct, fashioned by the circumstances of a person's life. But, as some of the adult education diarists dimly recognized, behind the socially constructed self was a real and more authentic identity waiting to emerge. In the words of psychologist Paul Tournier, behind the *personage* is the real *person* and it is the 'I' or person rather than the social self whom God deals with. As V. Baillie Gillespie writes,

> Who people really are becomes the biblical identity question. Exodus 34:33–4 suggests that Moses put a veil over his face, a mask, so to speak, when communicating with the people, but when in direct contact with God he took it (the mask) off. What is implied is that in the direct confrontation of the Creator God all false roles and non-me identities must be shunned ... In God, or 'in Christ' in the Christian tradition or Pauline sense, we find the real 'knowing-who-I-am me'.
>
> (1979, p. 127)

But how do we know the real person behind the mask when that real person is in principle unknowable? Our analysis of God's Trinitarian existence suggested that it is of the essence of persons to exist in relationship. This is the ground for what we actually do experience, the indispensability of relationships to our becoming fully human, the reason why we learn from one another and why the social self emerges only in the course of social interaction. But the 'real me' on the inside, the question 'Who am I really?' remains unanswerable. We ourselves do not know the answer nor do the people with whom and from whom we learn about the world. As a result the 'me' or 'self-schema' which guides our learning and social interaction is inauthentic, inadequate and out of harmony with the 'I' or real self within. We could only come to a true knowledge of the people we really are in relation with a person who actually knew.

At the end of the last chapter we concluded that revelation must convey something of relevance and importance to us. Now we can go further to say that revelation must convey something about *who we are*. If learning about the world and the growth of identity go hand in hand as opposite sides of the same coin, learning about God in revelation must involve a consequent change in identity. As we learn about God our identity will change to reflect that new learning. We have also discovered that it is the search for identity which is the primary motivation in learning – people learn what they need in order to create and maintain self-image and self-esteem. This implies that the search for identity is the key which opens people to revelation. The door through which revelation enters human experience is the question, 'Who am I?' We shall discover that revelation flows from a relationship with the person who knows the answer.

Chapter 5

Theology Among the Sciences

Separate Perspectives?

The problem of the 'I' – the true nature of our sense of subjectivity – arose from the sociological and psychological study of the development of identity, but at its root it is a philosophical question, which goes to the heart of the question of human nature. The contribution of the Nicene fathers takes us into a third field, the field of theology. We have in effect superimposed the resources available in separate disciplines one upon another like overhead projector transparencies in pursuit of an answer to a question which is fundamental to all. Having drawn on psychology, sociology and philosophy in the first four chapters of the book to explore human learning, the final two chapters will draw on theology to ask and answer questions about divine revelation. A practical theology, anchored in experience and moving between theory and practice, demands an interdisciplinary approach. But is this procedure justified? Is it allowable to cross the boundaries between disciplines, choosing from among the extensive resources of each those which seem relevant and perhaps congenial?

To use the resources of one discipline (theology) to propose a solution to a question which arises in another (the human sciences) is not only an unconventional method of operation but one which would be roundly condemned by many practitioners in the different fields concerned. Its justification from the point of view of the human sciences is that, as we have seen in the second chapter, they can hardly avoid the basic philosophical questions of human existence. From the theological point of view, the question is whether, without relating it to the scientific investigation of human life, it is possible to apply our thinking about God to the world in which we live.

What I am attempting to show is that an understanding of human learning provides the key to the understanding of revelation. But can the social sciences be used in this way? Can they be appropriated and become part of the raw material of theological enquiry? Is the question of human identity thrown up by the psychology of the self actually the same as the question of human identity as it occurs in theology? Is the question of the relation of hardware and software in artificial intelligence the same as the mind–brain problem or the place of the body in human interaction as it occurs, for example, in Wittgenstein's later philosophy? Can the theory of knowledge I have put forward be used to construct a theory of revelation and thus help to explain how it is possible to know God?

Historically, theologians have been open to the impact of philosophy. Examples abound. In the thirteenth century, Thomas Aquinas drew on the writings of Aristotle. In the eighteenth, central to Immanuel Kant's philosophy, was a 'turn to the subject' which appeared to make the search for a knowledge of God 'out there' through revelation illegitimate and sent theologians like Friedrich Schleiermacher in search of a knowledge of God in internal experience. In the twentieth century, theologians have had to respond to the impact of both logical positivism and Ludwig Wittgenstein's explorations of meaning and selfhood on the way in which the sense of theological and metaphysical statements are perceived. More recently, developments in science have also claimed attention; Thomas Torrance is among those who have argued from the kind of world that modern physics reveals ours to be to the kind of God we must conceive and the kind of knowledge we can have of him. These examples suggest that the social sciences might also have a role to play not only in supplying resources for theology but in influencing the form of the questions theologians must face and the way in which they come up with the answers.

In the present chapter I will attempt to provide a coherent picture of the way the separate disciplines of theology, philosophy, social science and indeed the natural sciences relate to one another. My aim is to justify the assertions that the social sciences do indeed furnish raw material for theology and that the theory of human learning I have presented can play a key part in developing the theological doctrine of revelation. But further, the possibility of our knowing God supplies the foundation for theology itself. If it is possible to develop a theory of revelation on the basis of these investigations in psychology and philosophy, this same theory will tell us something about the way theology needs to be done, about how and where we can expect to find the knowledge of God and what are its limits and constraints. Accordingly our attention will also turn to what our theory of knowledge can suggest about the methodology of theology itself.

In the view of many engaged in the natural or social sciences, philosophy or theology, each of these is a distinct discipline with its own particular methods and criteria of accuracy. The attempt to cross disciplinary boundaries – to attempt to use theological doctrines to solve the problems of social science or to import the disciplines of the social scientist into the field of theology – involves a category error. Just as an electrician's explanation of the way an electric signboard works bears no necessary relation to the message which it spells out, or an accountant's report on a school or church might cover everything from the strictly financial point of view but leave many questions to be asked about the purpose and methods of the institution, science is one way of looking at the world or mankind, theology another. They offer not only different but strictly incommensurate perspectives. To put it in a nutshell, science explains the 'How?' of the universe, theology the 'Why?'

However, the 'separate perspectives' view has to answer at least two questions, one practical and the other theoretical. The practical question arises from the use of the social sciences in practical theology and in particular in the way people are trained for Christian ministry. Students training for ministry with young people, for example, can draw on the social sciences for an account of the psychological developments characteristic of adolescence and on theology for a variety of views on Christian nurture and initiation. Others, training as Christian counsellors, may be offered the insights of Freud or Jung alongside some theologically derived principles of counselling. The use of a 'secular' discipline such as psychology implies that a judgement has been made about the appropriateness of including it in the course. That judgement requires a view of how Freudian or Jungian analysis relates to the theological stance of the course as a whole. But what is the relation between these particular branches of psychology and theology? Is there some theological basis on which they are to be judged appropriate or inappropriate? What criteria are there capable of comprehending two separate and incommensurable perspectives and how are they derived (Polkinghorne, 1998, p. 21)?

The theoretical problem for the 'separate perspectives' approach is how to avoid the kind of relativism in which none of the perspectives, including theology, is capable of advancing a claim to be *true*. When Malcolm Jeeves, for example, writes, 'It is a category error to oppose what is asserted in two different language domains' (quoted in Evans, 1979, p. 10), he is drawing on the philosophy of Wittgenstein, in which the meaning of any given statement is governed not by its reference to any external state of affairs but by its use within a shared set of linguistic conventions. He implies that each of the disciplines is a separate 'language game' with its own distinctive criteria of truth. The explanation of human behaviour given from the perspective of any particular 'language domain' – be it Freudian psychology, monetarist economics or Christian theology – is entirely dependent on the presuppositions of that domain. However, none of the disciplines can demonstrate the truth of its own presuppositions. There is no place at which language can conclusively be shown to link up with the real world. To adopt the separate perspectives approach is to risk being forced to accept that there is no way of establishing whether what is being said either by the scientist or by the theologian is actually true.

The first step in bringing the psychology of learning and theology of revelation together will be to construct an argument for the relationship of theology to the human sciences. This will involve further development of the relationship of science and theology previously dealt with in the second chapter. The key to this relationship, as Peacocke points out (1993, p. 20), lies in the epistemology or theory of knowledge which underlies each field of endeavour.

Paradigm Theory

Theory and Observation

In Bruner and Postman's playing-card experiment a number of university students had great difficulty deciding what they were actually seeing. They all had a schema for playing cards which told them what they *should* have been seeing and, in the cases of the normal playing cards, enabled them to recognize these very quickly. But these same schemata actually prevented them from recognizing the trick cards without a process of readjustment and even led some of them to report seeing things that were not there! Eventually, however, virtually all were able to modify their expectations so as to be able to recognize the trick cards without too much difficulty.

The playing-card experiment provides an excellent analogy to the situation of the trainee scientist. As a novice in a new world, he or she must learn to 'see' the objects of that world. For this the scientist needs a schema – a theory. Observation, the search for new facts, requires a framework of concepts. The doctor examining an X-ray photograph, the biologist looking into a microscope, the astronomer through a telescope, are using not only their eyes and their technological aids but also the knowledge they have acquired as a result of their scientific training to interpret what they see. In the words of N. R. Hanson, all data is 'theory-laden'. 'The construing', he writes, 'is in the seeing' (1958, p. 23). There is no neutral standpoint from which all the facts appear 'value-free', no privileged level of observation 'uncontaminated' by a given theoretical framework. Not only does empirical work take place within a framework of theory but it is the theory which suggests which of the possible research problems is likely to be most fruitful, influences the design of the research and tends to control the way the results are interpreted (Polkinghorne, 1998, pp. 9–11).

Stephen Toulmin gives the following examples of the importance of conceptual revision for the advance of the physical sciences:

> The arguments by which Galileo, Descartes and Newton launched the science we know as 'mechanics' were certainly as much conceptual – and even philosophical – as they were empirical ... Nor could the basic conceptions of modern dynamics – *matter, force, momentum* and the rest – ever have been established by empirical investigations alone; in actual fact they were quite as much the result of careful conceptual analyses.
>
> Einstein's initial work on the theory of relativity rested, likewise, at least as much on a refined reanalysis of our concepts of *space, time* and *simultaneity* as it did on empirical observations ... As Einstein emphasised himself, he was led to his ideas about relativity, not least by philosophical considerations derived from Hume and Mach.
>
> (1971, p. 28)

To accept a given fact as significant involves the acceptance of a framework of theory within which its significance is explained and by which it is related to all the other relevant facts. But the theoretical or conceptual framework is not to be seen as a straitjacket, incapable of modification. In the playing-card experiment, continual failure to recognize the trick cards eventually forced the students to modify their expectations so as to be able to recognize them. In the same way it is possible for empirical observation to throw up 'anomalies', findings the theory is incapable of explaining. If enough of these anomalies accumulate, the adequacy of the theory may be called in question and the search for a new theory, which can explain not only the accepted facts but also the anomalous observations, begins.

Shared Frameworks

The framework of theory by which the scientist makes sense of her observations is what Thomas Kühn (1969) called a 'paradigm'. A 'scientific revolution' is what happens when the gradual accretion of anomalies forces a change in the paradigm. To illustrate his theory Kühn pointed to outstanding examples of paradigm change which grabbed the historical headlines such as the 'Copernican revolution' in astronomy, in which the prevailing belief that the sun orbited the earth was replaced by a new picture in which the earth orbits the sun, or the way Newton's gravitational theory, which had dominated physics for over two hundred years, was superseded by Einstein's theory of relativity. The use of these high-profile examples caused a good deal of misunderstanding, particularly in the early days of paradigm theory. It suggested that scientific revolutions only occurred very infrequently and caused a good deal of conflict. In fact minor conceptual revision is taking place all the time in science as current paradigms are continually modified to take account of new discoveries (Toulmin, 1970; Kühn, 1977).

The value of Kühn's theory is that it helps to explain the impressive unity of the scientific community despite the dependence of observation on theory. Science is not a field in which 'anything goes', in which one person's interpretation is as good as any other's. On the contrary the point about a scientific paradigm is that it is *shared* by all the practitioners in a given field. This ensures that scientific data are public and scientific observations replicable and quantifiable. One scientist can request the results of another's experiments for independent analysis. One scientist can build upon another's results. Science progresses by taking as certain the results of previous series of experiments by establishing reliably tested laws and axioms. All this is achieved by *taking the paradigm for granted for everyday purposes*. Once he has learned the theory, the scientist can forget that it is there and get on with the job of exploration. Only when those explorations throw up results which are 'anomalous' does he have to think about the theory in order to decide whether it needs modifying.

The shared paradigm specifies the precise meaning of all the terms which fall within it. For scientists who share the paradigm every term and every observation has a definable, public, quantifiable meaning. When Einstein put forward his theory of relativity, part of what he was proposing was that many of the most important terms in physics, such as *force*, *mass* and *velocity*, should be understood in a different way. For this theory to be accepted it had to cease to be simply Einstein's theory and become the generally accepted 'language' of physicists. The acceptance of a scientific paradigm is in fact a more thoroughgoing and methodologically demanding example of what we all do all the time in order to communicate with one another. No one can be a Humpty Dumpty, for whom words mean whatever he wants them to mean. We all share a common framework of agreement about meaning, a framework within which we understand one another.

Basic Presuppositions

However, the foundation of every scientific paradigm always includes something that cannot be proved. Because scientists are used to taking the paradigm for granted in order to work within it, it is possible to ignore this or even be unaware of it. Nevertheless according to Sir Karl Popper (1959, pp. 110–11), the investigation of a scientific theory always terminates in a collective decision to accept some 'basic statement' as a valid description of reality. These basic statements, which depend on scientific consensus, are like 'piles driven into a swamp'. They never reach the solid bottom of indisputable fact but are sufficient for the time being to support the structure. One example of such a 'basic statement' might be that the laws of nature are always regular and predictable. The fact that science has had such a degree of success both in comprehending the physical world and predicting the way it will behave suggests that this may be true. But that is not the same as proving it! In fact this statement could never be proved because it is the presupposition of the whole scientific enterprise.

What this means is that there is no objective foundation to knowledge even in the natural sciences. The scientist can never arrive at the solid rock bottom of indisputable truth. All she can do is to propose the present paradigm as a 'model' of the world – or that part of it under investigation – just as our mental framework of tacit knowledge is a 'model' of the world we know. She knows that the history of science contains innumerable examples of models which appeared perfectly adequate in their time and have since been superseded. She recognizes, as Stephen Toulmin points out in the quotation given above, that science progresses as least as much by conceptual revision as by observation. She acknowledges that the current model is no more than a best approximation to the truth of nature. In short, the scientist acknowledges that she needs the philosopher as a partner.

Far from being two separate 'language domains', the work of observation and analysis, science and philosophy, go hand in hand. Science is primarily the work of empirical investigation; it is what takes place *within* a given paradigm or conceptual framework. Philosophy is primarily the work of conceptual analysis. It is what takes place when the theoretical framework is in the process of *revision*. On their own neither can hope to present an account of 'truth' or 'reality'. The scientist must work within a conceptual framework, which it is the philosopher's task to examine for coherence and logical implication. But the philosopher, if he is to say anything of relevance to the world we know, must from time to time make empirical statements and it is the work of the scientist to check these out by careful observation. Where these twin requirements go unrecognized or forgotten, science and philosophy suffer; scientists (of whom, as we shall see below, Marvin Minsky is one) confuse their working presuppositions with metaphysical fact, while philosophers (such as Ayer and Ryle) are content with anecdotal examples instead of properly researched empirical material. Science and philosophy should be seen as inter-related aspects of a single quest for understanding.

Interpreting People

When we turn from the natural to the social sciences the picture becomes more complicated. In the first place the social scientist is attempting to explain the behaviour not of the natural world but of people. Unlike the phenomena of the natural world, from electrons right through to animals, people are not simply the passive objects of observation. They have their own explanations for why they do things. People can answer back!

There are several extremely influential schools of social science in which people's own explanations for their behaviour are treated as unimportant. For example, at the turn of the century the sociologist Durkheim could write his major work, a study of suicide in French society, concentrating on the social forces that lead to the failure of a person to integrate into society and ignoring the subjective reasons which lead people to take their own lives. Durkheim belonged to the tradition of philosophers like Thomas Hobbes in the seventeenth century and John Stuart Mill in the nineteenth, a tradition for which an ideal 'scientific' approach to the study of human life requires a detached and objective enquiry into the causes of human behaviour. One of the effects of this tradition is that it leads the social scientist to investigate only one 'cause' at a time, ignoring all other possible influences. As a result social science is fragmented into a number of competing schools. Instead of one universally accepted paradigm, there is a huge variety. In psychology, for example, the Freudian tradition of analysis competes with the Jungian approach, humanistic psychology and a variety of others. Back in the 1960s one practitioner wryly observed,

> Psychoanalytic theories seem to suggest that man is basically a battlefield. He is a dark cellar in which a well-bred spinster lady and a sex-crazed monkey are forever engaged in mortal combat, the struggle being refereed by a rather nervous bank clerk. Alternatively, learning theory seems to suggest that man is basically a ping-pong ball with a memory. Along these lines, some types of information theory hint at the idea that man is basically a digital computer constructed by someone who had run out of insulating tape.
>
> (Bannister, 1966, p. 21)

Even in the natural sciences it is impossible to discover a level of observations and a language with which to describe them that is 'neutral' or 'value-free'. In the social sciences the fact that the objects of study are human beings makes it doubly misguided. The reason is that however great may be the effects of external causal factors, human beings also give reasons for their actions. We act on the basis of the beliefs and presuppositions which frame our understanding of the world. Even in the natural sciences *interpretation* is an indispensable part of theory construction. In the social sciences *the agent's point of view* – people's everyday explanations for what they do – cannot be ignored.

Nor do the complications end here. People's explanations and under-standings of their own behaviour arise in their own particular cultural context. Their reasons for what they do are influenced by the shared frameworks of understanding which are implicit in the institutions of the society in which they grew up. What people actually say and believe is only part of the story. Explicit beliefs rest on a deeper level, the implicit intersubjective agreement without which society itself could not exist. Theories based on a supposedly 'objective' point of view simply fail to take into account this vitally important element of the human situation.

All this means that the explanation of human behaviour is a *hermeneutical* exercise. It has to involve more than simply testing one given framework of explanation, that of the scientist, against observed events. It requires a process of interaction between the scientists' explanation and the various common-sense everyday explanations of the people under observation. He or she is more than simply an external observer but a member of a society whose own basic assumptions are in dialogue with those of the people under observation. What is required is an imaginative entering into the perspective of another person or group in order to explore it as an expression of the human condition which we all share, a willingness to try out a variety of general theories to see which are applicable to the case in question and which throw the most light on the particular situation. At the same time the scientist must allow the particulars of the situation to evaluate and correct the theories. He is required to do both science and philosophy at the same time, a combination which lies at the heart of a genuine hermeneutical method.

Images of Humanity

The Philosophical Foundation of Social Science

Behind the paradigm of any given school of social science lies a particular 'image of humanity'. The paradigm or governing model of cognitive science, for example, is the idea of people as 'information processors'; in social psychology it is people as 'actors'. Most of the paradigms of social science have yielded valuable insights, suggested many fruitful avenues for further research and added immeasurably to our understanding of human behaviour. From time to time, however, one of the practitioners in a particular field will push the governing model too far and make exaggerated claims. The claim of Marvin Minsky that people are simply 'computers made of meat' goes beyond the scope of scientific theory. The computational paradigm has ceased to be merely a working model or theoretical framework and has developed a metaphysical aspect. Minsky has confused the 'swamp' of agreed presupposition for the 'rock bottom' of solid, indisputable fact. In doing this he has advanced beyond the territory of science into that of philosophy. What Minsky's mistake shows clearly is that the paradigms of social science – its 'images of humanity' – do require a philosophical underpinning of some kind. We do really want to know what it means to be human. In fact that is the whole point of the enterprise.

It is not only the social scientists' theoretical framework that consists of an 'image of humanity'. The implicit foundation of intersubjective understanding which makes society possible is also a certain 'image of humanity'. It consists, in the words of Charles Taylor, of a particular definition of 'man, human motivation, the human condition', a particular 'vision of the agent and his society' (1971, pp. 182, 193). Comparison of different societies suggests wide divergence in their underlying shared beliefs about human nature. Contrast the aggressive individualism of the United States and many western societies for example with the equally aggressive collectivism of Marxism, the tribalism of many parts of Africa or the corporatism of Japan. Contrast the philosophy of self-fulfilment or self-realization typical of western society with the self-negation of eastern religion, in particular of Buddhism. The vision of the human condition and the goal of human striving undergirding a particular society may be explicitly expressed in such documents as the American Constitution or the works of Marx and Lenin or they may be implicitly present, expressed in the society's traditions or institutions.

Some sixty years ago the theologian Emil Brunner offered this description of the 'characteristic wisdom of the man in the street':

> It is aware of man's freedom and also of man's bondage; of the higher element in man and also of his pitiful need; of the unity of his personality and also of the contradiction it contains. It is aware of man's eternal destiny, and yet also that man dies, and that all his life is in some way determined by the fact of death, and

tends toward death … It is aware of the peculiar character of each individual, and also of the common element which binds all individuals together. This 'wisdom' knows all these things, but it cannot be grasped at any particular point. The more eagerly we try to seize it, the more elusive it becomes, this extraordinarily reflective, and yet at the same time superficial and incomplete kind of knowledge … Before and behind all scientific, philosophical and theological anthropology there lies this ordinary, universally human, naive, pre-reflective understanding of man, very variously interwoven, concealed, enriched and distorted by those other views, and yet independent of them.

(1939, pp. 46–7)

Had he been writing today Brunner may well have offered a slightly different assessment of the naive, pre-reflective understanding common to most people in his society. He might not have expressed such confidence in people's awareness of an eternal destiny; but might instead have added an awareness of the cultural variety of a world which is now a 'global village'. Yet in other ways we may not be very different from our grandparents. Like them we base our lives on a sense of what it means to be a human being, yet find it extraordinarily difficult to give that sense a full and coherent expression. We all struggle for an answer to the question 'What is it to be human?' and even more fundamentally 'Who am I?'

The Meeting Point

Science, social science, philosophy and theology, Brunner believed, all represent both a deepening and a distortion of this *sensus communis*. The scientist, the philosopher and the theologian are all doing the same thing. Each one, by means of systematic enquiry, draws out and gives explicit expression to a particular aspect of common human understanding. In other words the natural and human sciences, philosophy and theology are all, in their different ways, attempts to give a sense to what it means to be human. The point at which they all meet is philosophical anthropology, the theory of human nature.

Over two hundred years ago the philosopher David Hume introduced his *A Treatise of Human Nature* with the words:

It is evident that all the sciences have a relation, greater or less, to human nature; and that however wide any of them may seem to run from it, they still return back by one passage or another. Even *Mathematics*, *Natural Philosophy* and *Natural Religion* are in some measure dependent on the science of MAN; since they lie under the cognisance of men, and are judged by their powers and faculties. It is impossible to tell what changes and improvements we might make in these sciences were we thoroughly acquainted with the extent and force of human understanding, and could explain the nature of the ideas we employ, and of the operations we perform in our reasonings.

(1739, p. 4)

Hume hints at two reasons for the crucial role in all the sciences of the 'science of "man" '. The first has to do with the limits of human knowledge. Our knowledge of the world reflects the *way* we come to know it. Thus human capacity, human limitations and human interests are implicitly reflected in every piece of knowledge, whether it be in 'mathematics, natural philosophy or natural religion'. And secondly all our knowledge 'returns back to' the science of human nature because the study of any particular phenomenon, natural or social, is implicitly an attempt to understand ourselves. What is true of any science is true of theology. Like any discipline it is shaped by the limitations of human knowledge. And yet despite hundreds of years of discussion and investigation we are no nearer to the solution of this, the most fundamental problem of philosophy. 'The problem of indicating the character of the human species', concluded Immanuel Kant, 'is quite insoluble' (1974, p. 183). Or, as Reinhold Niebuhr memorably put it, 'Man is a problem to himself' (1941, p. 3).

The idea that theology and the social sciences occupy watertight compartments, each pursuing their own fields of enquiry and using their own particular methods, disables both theology and social science. It blinds theologians to the empirical and some of the philosophical dimensions of theology. In fact theology stands in the same relationship to the empirical work of social science as does philosophy. The point at which the disciplines overlap is anthropology – the study of human life and human nature. Like philosophy, theology contributes its own 'images of humanity'. One example is 'man in revolt', the title of Emil Brunner's book on the human condition. Others include men and women as *creatures* and made *in the image of God*. Unfortunately the evidence used to illustrate these theological generalizations is often merely anecdotal, consisting of the author's own observations or sometimes his acquaintance with one particular work or school of sociological or psychological research. If we are to be able to say what it means for human beings to be 'in revolt' or made in God's image, theological generalizations like these need to be 'cashed out' in terms of hard empirical evidence.

Equally the social scientist will want to know how these theological images of humanity are derived. If the models are to make sense to the contemporary world, a good deal of their authority will rest, as with any scientific generalization, on its evident success in providing a unifying and convincing explanation of all the available evidence. Yet questions will still remain to be asked about the process by which such models come to be proposed. And here theology is in a bind because of the state of ferment existing over its own methodology. Before proceeding to the theological part of the argument a word is in order therefore about theological method.

Access to God's Truth

Competing Paradigms in Theology

The title of this subsection is rather provocative, assuming as it does that the task of theology is to uncover and display divine truth. By no means every member of the theological fraternity would willingly sign up to such a definition, at least without copious qualification. The fundamental question of theology is whether divine truth is in fact available and, if so, how we can be confident of having discovered it. In order to apply the insights so far gained to the activities of theologians, two small books will serve as a starting point: George Lindbeck's *The Nature of Doctrine* and Charles M. Wood's *The Formation of Christian Understanding*. Wood's title focuses attention on the process by which theologians (and in fact the whole Christian community) grow in Christian understanding, while Lindbeck's expresses the result of that process in terms of actual doctrines. Both deal with the basic questions, what is the *source* of Christian understanding? and what *status* have Christian doctrines?; that is, what truth-claims are appropriate for them? Thus implicitly both ask about the *limits* on our possible knowledge of God. For both, the end result is a suggested paradigm for the way Christian understanding is derived; that is, a paradigm for the way theology is to be done.

Lindbeck begins by setting out three possible paradigms, which he will reject as inadequate. The first he call the 'cognitive' paradigm. In this paradigm doctrines function in the way most Christians and non-Christians expect them to: as truth claims or informative propositions about objective realities. In this way religions (and Lindbeck's book is a study of religion not just Christian theology) function in a similar way to philosophies. They provide more or less coherent orientations to life as a whole grounded on certain doctrines or propositions which are claimed to be true. The fact that in this chapter theology has been compared to philosophy in precisely this way – as supplying the possibility of an overarching theory of human life – suggests my approach to theology is closest to Lindbeck's first paradigm and this is, in fact, the case, though not without considerable modification of his analysis of it.

Versions of the cognitive type of theology include traditional Protestant orthodoxy, in which the Bible is held to supply propositional truths about God by means of a relatively straightforward process of interpretation within the compass of virtually every Christian believer. Similarly in traditional Roman Catholicism the teaching authority of the Church provides doctrines of a similar kind based on Scripture and tradition. The contemporary theological consensus, however, is that historical criticism of the Bible and the tradition of the Church have made this approach untenable except perhaps in very much more sophisticated versions. One such sophisticated version is that provided by Wood's book. Notwithstanding his debt to the philosophy of Wittgenstein, the key to *The Formation of Christian Understanding* is that Scripture retains the potential to be a vehicle of 'God's own definitive self-disclosure' (1993, p. 101). How Wood believes this to be the case, we shall examine in detail in due course.

Lindbeck's second theological type is what he calls 'experiential-expressive'. This type begins with the work of Friedrich Schleiermacher in the early nineteenth century and is especially congenial to liberal theology. In the 'experiential-expressive' understanding of theology, doctrines are essentially non-informative but rather 'symbols of inner feelings, attitudes or existential orientations'. They point to and seek to disclose an inner reality located in subjective experience but held to be part of a religious capacity of all humanity. In this theological orientation, doctrines may remain the same while their meaning varies, depending on the way the subjective experience they are held to symbolize is described. How this can be the case may become clearer as we examine Schleiermacher in greater detail.

Lindbeck mentions a hybrid type of theology, which he discerns in the Catholic theologians Rahner and Lonergan, but which, he claims, adds little to the overall adequacy of the situation. Instead he proposes his own third type, which he calls the 'cultural-linguistic'. This type takes religions as 'a kind of cultural and/or linguistic framework or medium that shapes the entirety of life and thought'. Lindbeck has drawn on cognitivist theories in the development of his own. He begins his book by mentioning the Bruner and Postman playing-card experiment but only as an example of the way the accumulation of anomalies can demand the replacement of an outdated or inadequate paradigm. The relevance of cognitivist theories is that, as we have seen, they postulate an all-embracing 'comprehensive scheme or story' which is 'used to structure all dimensions of existence'. However, unlike cognitive psychologists, Lindbeck does not see this all-embracing scheme as consisting basically of propositions but rather as 'the medium in which one moves, a set of skills that one employs for living one's life'. Rather than a set of doctrines or truth-claims about some external reality, a religion is much more like a language or culture in which one is simply immersed and which one needs to be able to live one's life. 'To become religious one learns how to feel, act and think in conformity with a religious tradition, that is, in its inner structure, far richer and more subtle than can be explicitly articulated' (1984, p. 35). In the cultural-linguistic paradigm, doctrines are not to be understood as supplying information about God or anything else but as a form of expression of what it means to live one's life as a practising member of a given religious community or as rules to regulate the way the community acts. A key criticism of this approach is that there is little sense of a real God standing over against the community; the paradigm is in danger of falling into a description of 'the way we do things' (Polkinghorne, 1998, p. 20).

The model Lindbeck proposes is 'part of an outlook that stresses the degree to which human experience is shaped, moulded and, in a sense, constituted by cultural and linguistic forms' (1984, p. 34). The outlook is that of cultural relativism, expressed in writers like Peter Winch, Peter Berger and Thomas Luckmann and, above all, as Lindbeck understands him, Ludwig Wittgenstein. The basic insight here is that knowledge is at its root not a 'knowing what' but a 'knowing how' – the skill of understanding how words and concepts are to be used. The culture or language in which words and concepts are used in a certain way is all-embracing and there is no appeal beyond it to some independently existing reality 'out there'. As Berger and Luckmann analyse it, 'rural Haitians *are* possessed and New York intellectuals *are* neurotic' (1966, p. 198).

Aside from the question of whether such a view of their own religious commitment is sustainable for anyone outside a university department, the most important question to be asked of Lindbeck is whether the cultural-linguistic paradigm is, in fact, an adequate expression of either cognitivist theory or Wittgenstein's thought. It is questionable whether Peter Winch's *Idea of a Social Science* in fact does justice to what Wittgenstein meant by 'language games' and 'forms of life'. Although Winch identified forms of life with the all-embracing contexts in which words and concepts make sense, it is far more likely that Wittgenstein was pointing to the characteristic forms of human interaction that make up life in all its diversity. Like the cultural relativism on which it is based, the cultural-linguistic paradigm is an example of what, in Marc de Mey's typology, is a third-stage, contextual model. As such it is itself relativized by the fourth-stage 'cognitive' context in which the focus is on the total experience of what it means to be a human being.

Universal Religious Experience?

This leads naturally to a consideration of Lindbeck's second type of theology, the 'experiential-expressive', where the emphasis is precisely on a supposed foundation of religion in universal human experience. In this type, rather than making truth claims about divine reality, doctrines are symbolic expressions of subjective religious experience. The earliest major example of this type of theology, and still one of the most instructive, is that of Friedrich Schleiermacher. Schleiermacher wrote in the shadow of the philosophy of Immanuel Kant, which appeared to place an insuperable barrier to any knowledge of God as an objective reality. At the heart of Kant's philosophy is the contribution of the knower. Just as in cognitive psychology, the knower supplies the framework with which to make sense of the data of experience. A major difference between Kant's thought and the argument developed here is that in Kant's philosophy the framework of knowledge (which he called the synthetic *a priori*) does not interact with the data of the senses and thus remains fixed and incorrigible. The possibility of the mind's 'world-model' being modified as a result of interaction with the data of experience significantly modifies the force of Kant's position.

As Kant pointed out, what is supplied subjectively by the knower cannot be shown to be objectively real. Included in the elements of the form of experience supplied by the knower, according to Kant, were space and time; in consequence, although we can presume our existence to be spatial and time-bound, we cannot know for certain what space and time might actually be in themselves. Similarly Kant also produced a proof, still widely accepted today, that the idea of God as the most real and perfect being was incapable of proof. It is rather a 'regulative principle of reason', belonging with those other concepts which it is necessary for us to have in order to form any knowledge of the world at all (1787, pp. 500–7).

Some two hundred years later many of the details of Kant's philosophy have been superseded. We may not be able to claim to know what space and time really are but we have good reason to believe that our theories about them bear some relation to a reality with independent existence, because the theory of relativity actually makes sense of scientific observations across a wide range of contexts from astronomy to atomic particles. In psychological terms this qualified confidence arises from the belief that our ideas do actually interact with our experience and are corrected by it so as to give a progressively more accurate picture of what 'reality' is really like. This is possible for space and time because scientists assume that in their observations they are in touch with the physical reality within which we live. God however is not an object of scientifically verifiable experience and thus not so easy to rescue from the synthetic *a priori*. Thus Schleiermacher's response to Kant still justifiably carries weight in contemporary theology.

Schleiermacher's aim was to provide a justification for believing that an awareness of God is an integral feature of normal human life. As he pointed out in the *Brief Outline of the Study of Theology*, 'Unless religious communities are to be regarded as mere aberrations, it must be possible to show that the existence of such associations is a necessary element for the development of the human spirit' (1811, p. 22). In making room for a transcendent possibility in ordinary human life Schleiermacher drew upon contemporary human studies. He proposed that the innate capacity of Kant's *knowing* subject be expanded to include not only knowing but also *feeling*. 'Feeling', as Schleiermacher defined it, is a feature of what he called 'immediate self-consciousness' (1821, pp. 5–12).[1] The 'immediacy' of self-consciousness characteristic of the realm of feeling may be compared with the 'immediacy' of the 'knowledge' of oneself as subject in the course of either knowing or acting. As Schleiermacher points out, in a comparison that reflects the difference between 'I' and 'me', joy or sorrow are immediate, as states of feeling directed wholly outward, in contrast to self-approval or self-reproach, in which the consciousness of an objective 'self' is present.

Piety, Schleiermacher went on to explain, is a particular modification of immediate self-consciousness (1821, pp. 12–18). It is distinguished from other states of feelings through being a consciousness of being in relation to God. Thus, rather than know God as an 'object' through our senses or understanding, God is known in the same 'immediate' way as one knows oneself as subject. Schleiermacher now adds a further stage in the argument. He defines this immediate consciousness of God that is piety as a consciousness of 'absolute dependence'. Drawing again on his knowledge of social theory, he defines all existence as existence 'along with another'. We cannot live except in relationships, nor can we be aware of ourselves

---

[1] In his letters to Dr Lucke, Schleiermacher described himself as a 'dilettante' in the field of human studies. Nevertheless, these occupy an important place in the foundation of his theology. Rather than base his theology on a position derived from human studies or interpret human studies from the point of view of a particular theological approach, his method was to attempt a new synthesis by using the insights of the two fields to interpret one another, a method comparable to the one I have attempted here.

except in some relationship or other. In every relationship there are degrees of freedom and dependence. Even the smallest child in relationship with her father has some degree of freedom. But with God there is no degree of freedom, only 'absolute dependence'. Thus the highest state of piety is the feeling in immediate self-consciousness of absolute dependence.

The idea that 'absolute dependence' should be the characteristic experience of human religious consciousness is the ground of the first set of criticisms to be brought against Schleiermacher. The fact that since his time several alternatives have been suggested, such as an 'abba' experience of God (Edward Schillebeeckx) or an 'agapeic way of being in the world' (David Tracy) calls into question whether a consciousness of 'absolute dependence' is in fact self-evidently the form of piety (Lindbeck, 1984, p. 120). The second set of criticisms are more far-reaching. Schleiermacher was writing under the shadow of Immanuel Kant's immense philosophical achievement. Two hundred years of further developments in philosophy have left that shadow still broad but not quite so apparently all-encompassing. In the light of these developments it is open to question whether the idea that our knowledge of God must be confined to subjective experience rather than derived from some objective source is still necessary. Nevertheless Schleiermacher's contribution is not to be summarily dismissed. His search for a credible alternative to an 'objective' knowledge of God in our understanding has yielded important results. In particular, he points to the important role of the subjective experience of being a knowing, feeling, acting 'I' in our knowledge of God. The idea that all existence is existence along with another, that we can never be without a consciousness of being in relationship, must also play a vital part in any relationship with God. In the following chapters I hope to emphasize the importance of precisely that element in human psychology, the agent who is a mystery to himself, and its role in revelation.

The Possibility of Revelation

In *The Formation of Christian Understanding*, Charles Wood gives full weight to the legacy of Wittgenstein. He is resolute in rejecting the idea that a prior theory of understanding (such as the one developed in this book!) can throw any light on Christian understanding. Understanding is not some 'mental state or process' to be experienced 'in the privacy of one's own mind'. Understanding is the use made of the knowledge in question and varies with the context. Thus a 'Christian' understanding is just that – the understanding relevant to the Christian context (1993, pp. 14–15). Rather than develop a theory of knowledge, Wood prefers to use carefully selected and apt examples in true Wittgensteinian manner. Finally, one of the key planks of his argument – the idea that there can be a 'canonical' sense to the Bible as a whole which acts as a criterion for the interpretation of any particular part – is not itself given as knowledge from some objective source but comes about as the result of a decision of the Christian community (1993, p. 66).

But despite his use of Wittgenstein, Wood's book is not simply another contextual approach of the same type as Lindbeck's. He is clear from the start that the aim of Christian understanding is 'the knowledge of God'. The canonical sense in which the Bible is taken as God's word of address may depend on a community decision, but Wood is clear that, with the decision made, Scripture is, in fact, the vehicle of God's 'definitive self-disclosure'. Both the community and the individual within it, if they are correctly disposed, are really and actually addressed by God. The biblical narrative becomes the story through which the community comes to understand who God is. He is not only its author but its chief character and through the intricacies of the story we become acquainted with the God who is 'behind this story and within it' (1993, p. 101). We may not know enough to grasp the complete concept, who is God, but we may come to know enough to understand what kind of a concept God is (1993, p. 34). This knowledge requires a wide range of skills and abilities, including many which are not specific to Christian life but required by a wider human maturity, but through the development of these abilities and skills we are enabled to grow in the knowledge of God, a knowledge which is impossible without a deeply personal response to a deeply personal address but nevertheless a real knowledge of a real God.

Having set out his position that the aim of Christian understanding is a real knowledge of God, Wood refers to Calvin's *Institutes of the Christian Religion*, whose opening sentence runs: 'Nearly all the wisdom we possess, that is to say, true and sound wisdom, consists of two parts: the knowledge of God and of ourselves' (1536, I.i.1). These two, writes Wood, are inseparably linked and interdependent. It is self-knowledge that prepares us to know God, yet without knowing God a clear knowledge of ourselves is impossible. We know ourselves clearly only in the light of God. Moreover knowing God and oneself properly entails 'knowing oneself precisely as a part of the whole of creation ... It is to have an effective sense of one's proper relatedness to all creatures and to their creator' (1993, p. 31). Knowledge of God thus arrives only as part of a life-shaping response. Knowledge of God and existential determination are bound up in such a way that 'It is *through* the existential determination that one comes to know God, and to know God is to have one's existence determined in certain ways ... One comes to know God by disposing oneself towards God in an appropriate fashion, which by the nature of the case also involves disposing oneself towards one's neighbour and the world in correspondingly appropriate ways' (1993, p. 32).

What Wood requires to draw out the significance of these quotations is, I would argue, precisely what he attempts to avoid, namely a prior theory of knowledge on which a theory of the knowledge of God could depend. Apart from this, his position anticipates the argument I shall be developing in the following chapters. The fact that we do not know ourselves, that humanity is a problem to its best thinkers and most creative minds, and that knowledge of ourselves and of God is inextricably linked constitutes the basis for the possibility of a revelation in which knowledge of the real nature and purpose of humanity and the real character of God are given together.

Every discipline of human investigation – the natural sciences, the social sciences, history, literature, philosophy, theology; even, according to David Hume, mathematics – is based on an image of human life. Yet no discipline possesses a definitive answer to the question of the 'character of the human species', an 'image of humanity' known to be true and sufficient. If this knowledge were available, if the nature and purpose of mankind could be known for certain, it would be of decisive and momentous importance. The quest for knowledge would still be hermeneutical but a firm foundation would be available on which the City of Truth could rise, built with analogy and imagination as well as logic and observation and measured by the plumb line of harmony with our knowledge of ourselves.

If there were to be a divine revelation it would tell us not only about the nature of God but also about who we are. Since learning about the world and the growth of identity go hand in hand as opposite sides of the same coin, learning about God in revelation will involve a change in identity. A revelation not only of God but also of the nature of humanity would provide a definitive hermeneutical baseline, a final solution to philosophy's fundamental problem. It would offer a fifth stage beyond de Mey's 'cognitive' paradigm, in which the context for all new knowledge is our total world-view. Instead the context for human learning and for the work of each academic discipline would be a standpoint not available within human experience but from which human experience might eventually be completely comprehended, an 'image of humanity' to serve as the governing paradigm for both the philosopher and the social scientist.

Since we have no final and compelling answer to the question of human nature, this line of reasoning suggests that no such revelation exists. It is certainly not the case that God has made himself obvious to the light of human reason. However, a simple dismissal of revelation on these grounds fails to consider the question of how any revelation, if given, would have to be received. In the words of T. F. Torrance, the knowledge of God has to be appropriated within the 'complex situation involving our cognition of the world around us and of ourselves along with it' (1969, p. 32). Revelation is not itself theology. In order to be understood and communicated it has to be expressed in concepts and thus *give rise to* theology. However, theology takes place within a social and conceptual framework, which includes as a basic component a shared vision of men and women in community, their character, significance and destiny. As David Brown writes,

> God's communication with man takes place in very specific contexts with certain things already assumed at each stage, an already existing canon of assumptions, as it were – a canon that has shaped the community's conception of God, and thus inevitably shapes both the present experient's response to a particular experience and also what it is possible for God to put into that particular experience by way of content.
>
> (1985, p. 70)

The reception of revelation will therefore involve a hermeneutical process in which the knowledge of God and ourselves given in revelation will be shaped and adapted to the culture and presuppositions of the receivers. The more widely the shared vision of human nature underlying any given culture differs from the image of humanity given in revelation, the more difficult it will be for the people of that culture to understand the revelation given and the more mistakes they are likely to make in interpreting it. Even the Jewish nation, trained by hundreds of years of life according to God's Law, failed to recognize the Word when it was given. How much more difficult will it be for those of other cultures? (Williams, 2000, pp. 132, 142).

In practice the 'image of humanity' conveyed in revelation has to be appropriated by means of the tools of philosophical thought available to a particular culture. Revelation must first be *assimilated* to the corporately held schemata of the society and culture in which it is received. Only then can a process of *accommodation* begin in which revelation begins to shape theology. At this point theology and secular philosophy may start to diverge. This is what took place in the early centuries of Christianity. The culture of Greek philosophy and Roman law did not have the categories to comprehend what had been revealed in Christ about the nature of God. Most of the heresies that arose during the period when the doctrines of the Trinity and the nature of Christ were being hammered out reflect an assimilation of revelation either to the experience of Judaism or the categories of Greek philosophy. The Nicene Creed and Chalcedonian definition rely on definitions of personhood and of God different from anything present in either. However, the content of revelation may not only be distorted by a prevailing culture. It may also influence a culture, as it did western society until the early years of this century. To give just one example, the basic understanding of human life found even in agnostic authors of the nineteenth century such as Eliot and Hardy owes much to the doctrines of Christianity in a way that that found in twentieth-century authors such as Lawrence and Fitzgerald does not.

So far all this is abstract supposition. *If* there is a divine revelation then, recognizing that images of humanity form the foundation of any claims to knowledge, we can expect that revelation to take the form of an interpretation of human life, divinely inspired and therefore authoritative. Nothing in the argument so far establishes whether such a revelation has, in fact, taken place. What we have established, however, is that the unsolved question of anthropology present in every person's pre-conceptual background under-standing of what it is like to be a human being provides the prior possibility or capacity actually to receive revelation. From the theological point of view the content of revelation can be expected to consist of the knowledge of God, impossible to attain without a movement of God himself towards us. Yet this knowledge of God must enter the structure of human knowledge at the point of our conjectures about the nature of humanity.

Thus to understand how revelation might be *received* supplies the key to recognizing the way in which it might be *given*. This conclusion suggests a search for a theological tradition in which the knowledge of God and humanity are given together. This in turn points to two central aspects of Christian theology, the first in the field of anthropology, the doctrine of human nature and being; the second in Christology. First, according to the biblical exposition of creation, human beings, male and female, were made 'in the image of God'. If this is so a true account of humanity will be revelatory of God, since he is the pattern for human life, and moreover the knowledge of God will offer clues to the nature of human beings, made in his image. Second, Christians believe that God has been finally and fully revealed in a human life, that Jesus was both fully human and fully divine at the same time. In his incarnation divinity is revealed cloaked in humanity and the true nature of humanity glimpsed through his divinity. In the following two chapters we will investigate both created human nature and the incarnation of Jesus and find them bound together by the same biblical phrase, 'the image of God'.

Chapter 6

The Image of God

Humanity in God's Image

> When I look at your heavens, the work of your fingers,
>   the moon and stars that you have established;
> what are human beings that you are mindful of them,
>   mortals that you care for them?

In simple but effective poetry Psalm 8 expresses the 'image of humanity' which undergirds the biblical 'story' of God in relation to his creation. The 'story' told by the psalm is that the world is the creation of a sovereign and wise God; human beings, insignificant in themselves, have been granted a special place within creation by God's deliberate decision, a privilege which includes dominion over and responsibility for the animal kingdom.

The Creation Account of Genesis 1

The book of Genesis has two accounts of creation side by side. The first, beginning in chapter 1 with the words, 'In the beginning God created the heavens and the earth', ends in chapter 2 verse 4 with the words, 'These are the generations of the heavens and the earth when they were created.' In form it is highly concentrated hymnic prose. The immediate impression of the narrative is one of structure. The acts of creation are divided into seven days, seven being the number which stands in the Hebrew mind for completion or wholeness. Each day begins with a resolution of God expressed in a command setting creation in motion. Each day ends with the announcement, 'God saw that it was good', and the formula, 'There was evening and there was morning ...'

The structured nature of the prose echoes the emphasis on structure in the content. The creation account is one of dividing, fixing and classifying. In the original formless darkness God brings light into existence, divides it from the darkness and gives both darkness and light a name which establishes its character. Then God divides the waters into two, creating the expanse of the sky between them. On the third day he divides the seas and dry land appears. Then the seas, the sky and the land are filled. The sun, moon and stars, created on the fourth day, separate light from darkness and mark off the seasons, the days and the years. Birds are made for the sky, fish for the sea and animals for the land, classified as domestic animals, wild animals or creeping things, and each are to reproduce 'after their kind'.

The whole account presents the creation by God of an orderly, structured, predictable world out of formless chaos. To these features can be added the goodness of creation, repeatedly affirmed at the end of the account of each day, the equality of men and women and their partnership in the shared task of 'subduing' the earth, and the 'secularization' of creation, the clear implication that what God creates is not in itself God. By means of these features the biblical account of creation provides a distinctive set of 'spectacles' through which to view the world, a 'story' through which to interpret experience.

This story pays particular attention to the place of human beings in the ordered universe. The special status of men and women is signalled in three important ways. First, by the purpose for which they are created, to 'have dominion' and to 'rule' the animal kingdom. While animals, birds and fish each have their own place within the created order, human beings have a freedom within creation to rule it and turn it to their own purposes. The command to have dominion over the earth clearly implies that human beings have a special God-given dignity which sets them apart from the rest of the animal kingdom. The biblical view of the natural world thus contradicts the relatively recent idea that other species have equal rights with human beings.

Secondly, the special place of men and women is indicated by the use of the word *bara* meaning 'to create'. This word is used in Scripture only for what God does (von Rad, 1972, pp. 48–9). While human beings exercise a God-given creativity in 'fashioning', 'forming' or 'making' things just as he does, the word *bara* is used for the creation of the things human beings cannot make. Thus in Isaiah 45:7 the prophet says of God, 'I form light and *create* darkness, I make weal and *create* woe.' It is first used in Genesis 1 of God creating the heavens and the earth. Then it is used of him creating the great sea monsters, thus distancing the biblical creation story from those of other near eastern civilizations, in which Tiamat, the great sea monster, stands for the primordial chaos the gods must overcome before the creation can begin. Finally in Genesis 1:27 the word is used no less than three times at the creation of human beings. While the animals are 'brought forth' by the earth, men and women are 'created' by a special word of God on a par with that which brought the whole universe into being. The children's story which introduces the creation of man and woman with the words, 'Now the earth was ready for people to enjoy,' has the emphasis of the creation account exactly right. Brought on to the stage at the end of the play, the last and therefore most important in a great liturgical procession, the whole account leads up to the formation of creatures of special dignity, so special that the rest of the acts of God in the world centre around them.

Finally the uniqueness of human beings is signalled by the phrase 'the image of God'. This, of the three, comes closest to describing the very nature of humanity. The Hebrew word *selem* meaning 'image' is a concrete word, which can also mean 'statue'. In 1:26 it is qualified by the *demut* or 'likeness' which means 'something like'. Modern commentators take these terms to imply that it is not some particular aspect of humanity, such as reasoning ability, which represents the image of God, but the whole person, including our physical nature. Throughout the Old Testament a person is understood as a psychological–physical unity. Our bodily nature is an important part of our make-up. The term 'image' occurs in two more places in the early chapters of Genesis. In 5:3 Adam passed on the image to his son, implying that all human beings inherit the image from him. In 9:6, speaking to Noah after the Flood, the prohibition against shedding human blood is based on the dignity of the image, in contrast to the animals, which human beings are now allowed to eat for the first time. Thus 'the image of God' expresses the essential nature of humanity and the foundation of that special human dignity but does no more than hint at what this essential nature consists of. It does affirm however that the pattern on which human beings are created is that of God himself. To know of what human nature consists, we need to know more about the God who is its pattern.

The Creation Story of Genesis 2

Genesis 1 is not the only account of creation the Bible gives us. In Genesis 2, or to be more precise from Genesis 2:4b to the end of the chapter, there is another and much older account of creation, which continues in chapter 3 with an account of the disobedience of the first man and woman. In contrast to the structured, liturgical style of chapter 1, in which the orders of creation appear as if in solemn procession, chapter 2 tells a story. Stories work in a variety of complementary ways. They evoke our imagination and draw us in to think and feel along with the characters. Thus when in verse 18 God says, 'It is not good for the man to be alone,' a point of tension is created, a problem is raised which is eventually resolved by the creation of the woman. Like any significant story, this one is full of symbolic features which resonate with experience. The garden, rivers, trees, fruit, precious stones and, in chapter 3, the serpent all evoke a multitude of associations from the accumulated memory of the society in which the story takes shape. Water in the desert is a source of life, so the four rivers flowing from Eden evoke the idea that all life in the world flows from the garden God has made. Finally stories make their point by providing a pattern, a *schema*, as a way of thinking about and interpreting experience. The story in Genesis 2 and 3 invites us to think about human life and our relationship to God in terms of an original state of communion with God in a paradise garden from which men and women are shut out because of their disobedience.

Thus the evocative images and symbolism of the Eden story complement the spare and uncompromising theological directness of Genesis 1. And like Genesis 1, the special place of human beings in creation is signalled in distinctive ways. First, having created a man from the dust of the ground, God 'breathes into his nostrils the breath of life'. The 'breath' of God is the word *ruach* or spirit and the life the man thus receives makes him *nephesh*, a 'living soul'. In contrast the animals, created from the ground in the same way, do not receive the life-giving breath but are brought to the man for him to name them, thus allocating them their nature and place within the creation. The man, though belonging to the natural order by virtue of his creation from the ground, stands over against the rest of creation by virtue of the life-giving breath or spirit of God.

There is another important way in which the two accounts differ. In Genesis 1 God is completely transcendent. He never appears *in* the world but is always completely 'other', creating by sovereign resolution expressed in verbal command. By contrast the story in Genesis 2 and 3 is full of 'anthropomorphisms'. God appears throughout in the guise of a human being. Instead of remaining remote from creation, he gets his hands dirty by making a human being out of clay like a potter. Later he plants a garden, makes animals from earth and leads them to the man, takes a rib out of the man and makes a woman out of it, brings her to him and strolls in the garden in the cool of the day. More significant still, God is perplexed; he notices something wrong in creation and has metaphorically to scratch his head to think of a solution. There is even a first attempt, the creation of the animals, which is not completely successful, before he finally hits on the answer and creates a woman (Gottwald, 1985, pp. 328–9).

The earthy, anthropomorphic presentation of God in Genesis 2 and 3 is not primitive. It is a way of presenting the mystery of God in robust yet human terms which is of a piece with the evocative nature of the stories as a whole. The editor of the book of Genesis has placed the two accounts of creation side by side without suppressing one or the other, allowing them to complement and interpret one another. Like light, which behaves as both waves and particles, God is portrayed both as sovereign and transcendent yet personally involved and responsive to human decision. Moreover the presentation of God in human terms implies an assumption that the fundamental features of human life find their counterpart in the nature of God. Human beings are made 'in his image'.

Human Freedom and Divine Purpose

One of the attributes which the man clearly shares with God in Genesis 2 is freedom of decision. Placed in the garden of Eden to till it and keep it, the implication is that he can make of it what he likes by his skill and effort. The God-given vocation of humankind is to bring the creation to its full potential by work and creativity. God does not supply the animals ready-named but steps back and invites the man to give each their essential nature. Finally and most important, the man and the woman are placed under a command which is first permissive then restrictive. They may eat of the fruit of any tree of the garden except the tree of the knowledge of good and evil. Crucially, they have the freedom to obey or disobey. The world portrayed in both the creation stories is given to mankind to form and to rule for good or evil.

The anthropomorphic presentation of God alongside a man to whom he gives freedom of action is one of several ways in which the Bible treats the relationship between divine sovereignty and providence on the one hand and human freedom on the other. What binds these together is the assumption that God can achieve his purposes in creation through 'double agency'. God is able to work through the free decision and action of human beings without violating human autonomy (Hebblethwaite, 1994, pp. 154–5). 'The human mind plans the way', says Proverbs 16:9, 'but the Lord directs the steps.' And in Proverbs 16:3, 'Commit your work to the Lord and your plans will be established.' One of the most celebrated examples of this viewpoint is the 'Succession Narrative' of 2 Samuel and 1 Kings. This document sets out to explain how Solomon overcame the rival claims of his older brothers to become king in succession to his father, David. At his birth we are told that 'the Lord loved him' (2 Samuel 12:24–5) and at the end of the narrative his older brother Adonijah says, 'You know that the kingdom was mine, and that all Israel expected me to reign; however, the kingdom has turned about and become my brother's, for it was his from the Lord' (1 Kings 2:15). In between is the story of how one brother after another forfeited his claim, in which events move entirely as a result of free human decision. In fact, apart from conventional expressions of piety, the Lord is only mentioned one other time in the course of the story. Hearing that his counsellor, Ahithophel, has joined the rebellion of his son, Absalom, David prays that the Lord would turn his counsel into foolishness. Soon after his prayer David meets his friend Hushai and sends him to Absalom's headquarters to pose as a loyal supporter of Absalom but in fact to oppose Ahithophel. Hushai succeeds and Absalom accepts his inferior advice, as a result of which he loses the ensuing battle and his life, 'For', says the narrative, 'the Lord had ordained to defeat the good counsel of Ahithophel, so that the Lord might bring ruin on Absalom' (2 Samuel 17:14).

The same ability of the Lord to achieve his purpose without affecting human freedom of action is seen in the story of Joseph in Genesis 37–50. Sold as a slave to Egypt as a result of his brothers' jealousy, imprisoned through the lies of his master's wife, released to become Pharaoh's trusted counsellor and agent and able to use his position to save his family from starvation, Joseph later tells his brothers, 'You intended to do me harm, but God intended it for good, in order to preserve a numerous people, as he is doing today' (Genesis 50:20). In the book of Ruth, God saves Ruth and her mother-in-law Naomi from destitution through the good offices of their kinsman, Boaz, into whose field Ruth 'happened' to come (Ruth 2:3). In Isaiah 10 the prophet claims that God is using the armies of the Assyrian empire as the 'rod of his anger' against Jerusalem but that the Assyrians themselves will later be punished for their arrogance (Isaiah 10:5–19). Later in the book the unknown prophet of chapters 40–55 claims that God has raised up the Persian king, Cyrus, to accomplish his purpose even though Cyrus does not know him and has no such intention (Isaiah 45:1–7) (von Rad, 1975, pp. 50–53).

A full biblical view of creation thus requires no less than three 'levels' of explanation for natural and historical events. The first is the laws of cause and effect which are the subject of the natural sciences; the second, 'teleological' explanation, governed by human motivation and purpose. Constrained by the laws of nature, human actions also function as causes in the natural world yet without overriding or suspending its law-governed behaviour. In a similar and perhaps analogous way the third 'level' of explanation, the purpose of God, acts in both the natural and human world without disrupting or invalidating the laws which govern either. The word of God, through which the whole creation was set in motion, achieves its purpose through the agency of human beings and their freely willed decisions and actions. How this is possible remains a mystery wrapped up in the relationship between God and humanity but that it occurs is affirmed throughout the Scriptures.

The freedom of men and women also requires a distinction between two types of relationship between God and humanity. The first is the relation of human beings to God in creation in which God upholds the universe for the benefit of mankind. In this relationship men and women are entirely dependent on the goodness of God for their preservation. But this dependent relationship in which we stand as creatures of the natural world is distinct from that in which we stand as autonomous agents with a God-given freedom. The possibility of knowing God, as well as of sin and redemption, belongs to this second relationship. According to David Kelsey, 'In modern theology, these two kinds of relationships between persons as creatures and God have collapsed into one kind of relationship, consisting in a mode of consciousness or a conscious decision, and admitting of degree' (1982, p. 166). His conclusion is that theologians need both to recover a full-blown doctrine of creation to take the weight of the dependent relationship and make a 'turn' from the person as 'patient' or subject of consciousness to the person as agent. This would allow human freedom its place in the account of sin, salvation and the knowledge of God. It would also allow for the modern consciousness of mankind as autonomous, self-constituting and historically conditioned – the way individuals and societies create the worlds of meaning which they inhabit within the constraints of the inheritance handed down by previous generations.

Human Nature

With the recovery of this distinction, the freedom of humanity not only over against the rest of the created world but also over against God himself can be seen as both an essential feature of creation and the result of God's deliberate purpose. So important is it, in fact, that God will not curtail that freedom even to prevent disobedience and consequent disaster. The autonomy of the agent, inherent in creation, has a high claim to be included in the features of the 'image of God'. The freedom of God, from which the creation itself springs, is mirrored within the creation by the freedom of human beings to shape it to their own purposes. From this freedom flow many of the features of human knowledge. The creation of a psychological world-model through the hermeneutical process of interaction is the work of an active subject shaping the world to his purposes. Even the 'self', the person we understand ourselves to be, is a product of the same process so that in this sense human beings can truly be said to be 'self-constituting'.

Freedom however is not the only inherent quality of humanity; another is the fact of relationships. In Genesis 1:27 the statement, 'God created humankind in his image', is qualified by the further statement, 'male and female he created them'. Karl Barth believed that the second of these statements should be taken as exegesis of the first. His case is strengthened by the observation that the intervening line, 'In the image of God he created them', refers to humanity in God's image as plural. The male–female relationship, Barth believed, was the archetypal encounter and the basis of all the other 'I–Thou' relationships by which human life is constituted (1958, pp. 191–202; 1960, pp. 203–324). The picture of human beings as male-and-female-in-relationship is filled out by those psychoanalytical approaches which recognize *animus*, or masculinity, and *anima*, or femininity, as essential components of all people, male and female alike, so that a sexual element is present in every relationship.

Barth's emphasis on the sexual aspect of the image is in dispute (Gunton, 1997, p. 112). Yet even without the sexual dimension, the creation stories imply that relationships are inherent in human existence. 'It is not good for the man to be alone' (Genesis 2:18). The result is clearly seen in the process of learning, in which all knowing is a 'knowing with'. The schemata by which we come to comprehend the world are formed in relationship with and largely derived from other people, especially significant others such as parents and teachers. The process of psycho-social development, by which identity or self-concept is formed, takes place in relationships. As a person exists in interaction with the natural world so he exists unavoidably in relationship with others. Awareness of 'I' is awareness of being in encounter. Just as God's nature is to exist in relationship, so is it the nature of humanity. To be a 'person' is to exist like God as a 'someone' whose nature, to use the patristic terms, is *hypostatized* by the irreducible 'Who?' or personal subject.

As the essence or fundamental being of God is to exist as three persons in relationship, the nature of that relationship is love. God is not a person who loves, as if love were a detachable quality; God's existence as three mutually constituting persons is the meaning of love. If love is the essence of God, can we say that love is the essence of human personhood also? Not if our experience of the world is anything to go by. Our problem is precisely the lack of enough love to provide everyone with self-esteem and self-worth. The masks we wear, which make up our public *personas*, are attempts to hide from others and even from ourselves the person inside whom we are afraid may be unacceptable. But what the analysis of psycho-social development also implies is that love is precisely what is required for optimum human functioning, including the successful development of identity. The way we develop as people cries out for love, the disinterested nurturing concern first of parents and later of peers. Only by means of love can the potential of our existence in relationships be realized. Existence in relationships is the vestige of a deeper purpose: existence in love. The image of God in human beings consists not simply in the fact that we are constituted by our relationships. It includes the call to love. Love is the completion and fulfilment of the image.

Sin

Leslie Stevenson (1974) shows that every theory of human nature, religious or secular, includes, as well as an assessment of the essential nature of humanity, a diagnosis of the problem of mankind and a prescription for its solution. In Marxism for example the diagnosis of the human predicament is alienation, the separation of a person from the product of his labour. In Christianity the reason for our failure to fulfil the potential to love is called sin. The creation story of Genesis 2 moves straight on to that of 'the fall' in Genesis 3 which, in the same narrative form, explores the origin and effects of human shortcoming. Genesis 3 presents sin as rebellion or disobedience to a command of God and its result as estrangement – the loss of the direct fellowship with him. The story includes an anatomy of temptation, in which by the use of lies and half-truths the serpent induces the woman to abandon her trust in God's goodness and reliability and pursue a good she imagines for herself independent of his provision. It includes an evocative description of the results of the first sinful act, the shame which divides the man and his wife from one another and leads to fear of God. Then there is a brief but expressive summary of the punishment of the act of disobedience. Instead of a life of plenty, the man will have to struggle for his existence and produce food by the sweat of his brow; economics, the science of scarcity, is born. Not only will the woman's experience of childbearing be marred by pain but she will be emotionally dependent on her husband while he will rule over her – power enters the relationship of the sexes and the stage is set for patriarchy and sexism. Finally the couple are banished from the garden and forbidden the tree of life. The direct and satisfying fellowship with God suggested by his walk in the garden in the cool of the evening is lost and human life is henceforth to be lived under the shadow of limitation and death.

Genesis 3 presents sin as a fracturing of the relationship between God and humanity. Because this relationship is broken it is shrouded in mystery. Without the knowledge of God we do not know our own essential nature or value. Nor do we know clearly the essential nature of sin. But as with human nature it is possible to interpret human experience in the light of the biblical account. In human relationships sin can be seen to be a distortion of value, a failure to act from the highest available value or for the highest available good in a given situation, usually because of the competing claims of some end of greater value to oneself. The subjective value or 'salience' of any given object or goal, reflected in the more or less stable attitudes which form predispositions to action, is measured by its contribution to the formation, maintenance and defence of personal identity. To prefer another good, even though it may bring greater well-being to someone else, involves the costly sacrifice of some preferred value to ourselves, though this may be compensated for by the desire to please others or the opportunity to strengthen the image of oneself as a generous or altruistic person. Most fundamental of all, each person is trapped within his own limited world-view or that of his immediate society or reference group.

Confined to our own individual world models, we can never achieve the kind of overview which would enable us to know what is wholly good and pursue it. In the field of economics my surplus may be someone else's scarcity but without knowing how much I need for myself my self-interest encourages me to hold on to what I have. In the world of economic theory the concepts of 'enough' and 'too much' have scarcely any meaning. In the field of relationships the pursuit of my personal goal may be blocked by someone else's pursuit of theirs. The closer the relationship the greater the possibility of one person frustrating the perceived good of another. Thus marriage, the relationship with the greatest potential for love and co-operation, also has the greatest potential for destructive conflict. Parents, on whom children rely for physical and emotional nurture, can also inflict the greatest amount of damage.

The people on whom we depend for the development of our sense of identity are all imperfect. None, even the most loving parents, can supply a perfectly loving upbringing. As a result identity must always be to some degree inauthentic, affected by the scars at least of misunderstanding, possibly of mistreatment. Sooner or later parents fail to understand the needs of the child and she suffers fear or bewilderment. But the child is an autonomous person, capable of her own decisions and judgements. Sooner or later she responds with a judgement on her parents, a perception that her own needs are not always uppermost in their concerns, and perhaps a determination to have her own way. The sin of the human race, which has already affected her from the outside in her less-than-perfect upbringing, takes root in her own psyche. Thus the sinful condition of each generation is passed on to the next, so that Paul could describe the whole human race as being 'in Adam' (1 Corinthians 15:22), tainted with the sin of the man presented in the creation story as its founder and subject to his fate.

At the root of this predicament is the lack of a definitive image of humanity, a clear sense of 'Who I am' or estimate of one's own true nature and value. Estrangement from God, the loss of the relationship based on created human freedom in which knowledge of God is a possibility, means the loss of communication with the one person whose knowledge of us could enable us to develop with a full and correct sense of identity. In the absence of any definite knowledge of the real or underlying self, all value-judgements are based on the need to construct and maintain the social self, the *persona* or *personage*. Sinfulness and the lack of identity turn out to have a common root. In respect of sin, without the knowledge of God, men and women are condemned to choosing on the basis of lesser values. Without the possibility of knowing and choosing God, every act is unavoidably sinful. In respect of identity, 'man' without the knowledge of God becomes a 'problem to himself'.

The implication is that the discovery of our true identity would involve the possibility of freedom from sin. The person whose actions reflect a secure knowledge of their own essential nature and value, though she might not avoid sin automatically, would at least no longer be dominated by the need to maintain an essentially inauthentic identity. In the words of St John, 'Those who have been born of God do not sin, because God's seed abides in them' (1 John 3:9). Knowledge of oneself, which could come about only by revelation, would allow a real possibility of the choice of the highest good. A revelation in which God offered secure and definitive knowledge of ourselves along with knowledge of him would be inextricably tied in with the gracious action by which he moved to deliver us from the effects of sin.

So, having exhaustively laid out the groundwork, let us turn to a joyful celebration of the way that revelation is actually given to us.

The Person of Christ

When the divine Word appears in human flesh the question to be put to him, writes Dietrich Bonhoeffer, is not 'What?' but 'Who are you?' 'The question "Who?" expresses the strangeness and the otherness of the one encountered and at the same time it is shown to be the question concerning the very existence of the questioner ... In theological terms: it is only from God that man knows who he is' (1978, pp. 30–31). Not only is it impossible to express the divine word in the categories of human reason but by his very existence he opens up new categories and poses new questions which expand our understanding of ourselves. The revelation given in Jesus is not of the nature of God conceived in the Greek categories of substance, nor simply the character or personality of God. What is revealed in Jesus is a Person, a 'Who' corresponding to the 'Who?' of the human person beneath the synthetic mask or *persona*.

John's Gospel expresses it in this way: 'The Word became flesh and lived among us, and we have seen his glory, the glory as of a father's only son, full of grace and truth ... No one has ever seen God. It is God the only Son, who is close to the Father's heart, who has made him known' (John 1:14, 18). Influenced by ancient Greek categories of ontology, theologians have taken this passage to affirm that only God can reveal God; the essence of God can only be made known by someone who shares in that essence. But concentration on Greek categories obscures the important point being made here in terms of person-hood. John is saying that by becoming a human being, the person of the Son reveals the person of the Father. The 'glory' which the apostles saw in Jesus refers to a person's 'innermost' being – and the glory of Jesus was at the same time the glory of the Father. As the gospel develops, the theme of glory becomes more and more focused on the cross and resurrection. The leading characteristics of this revelation are 'grace' and 'truth'. In his grace God reaches out to mankind to re-establish the broken relationship and deliver us from sin. In the process the truth is revealed in the person of Jesus who says of himself, 'I am the Truth' (John 14:6) and, 'If you continue in my word ... you will know the truth, and the truth will make you free' (John 8:31–2). The grace embodied in his personal presence among human beings also reveals the truth which liberates. The person of Jesus is the foundation of a certain knowledge which cannot be discovered elsewhere.

Whereas in the Old Testament the phrase 'the image of God' refers to human beings, in the New Testament, except for one passage which uses the Old Testament sense (James 3:9), 'the image of God' always refers to Jesus. In Colossians, Paul writes: 'He is the image of the invisible God, the first born of all creation' (Colossians 1:15) and for the writer to the Hebrews, 'In these last days, [God] has spoken to us by a Son, whom he appointed heir of all things, through whom also he created the worlds. He is the reflection of God's glory and the exact imprint of God's very being, and he sustains all things by his powerful word' (Hebrews 1:2–3). Thus whereas in the Old Testament the image of God is unknown, in the New Testament the image is revealed through the incarnation. As the image of God, Jesus is the representative of the human race. The letter to the Hebrews in particular shows him made 'like his brothers and sisters in every respect' (Hebrews 2:17), 'tested in every respect as we are, yet without sin' (Hebrews 4:15), battling against sin on behalf of men and women and emerging victorious. Moreover whereas mankind has lost the sovereignty over creation which was God's original purpose, Jesus, by his perfect obedience to the Father, has recovered it and now exercises it on behalf of the whole of humanity (Hebrews 2:5–9).

There is a strong tradition, particularly associated with J. B. Lightfoot, in which the title 'image of God' when applied to Christ in texts such as Colossians 1:15 refers to his place in the original creation as the eternal pattern of which mankind is a copy rather than as the pattern of a *new* creation by virtue of his incarnation, death and resurrection (1890, pp. 142ff.). Lightfoot argued that this description, like those in Hebrews 1 and John 1, is an example of 'Wisdom' or 'Logos' Christology, in which Christ is portrayed as the personification of the divine wisdom, through which God made the world. In that case the position of Jesus as image of God would be his *by nature*. G. B. Caird, on the other hand, points out that the New Testament understands Jesus's relationship to mankind as his *by appointment* (1976, pp. 172ff.). In particular, this applies to the title 'first-born,' used in Colossians 1 and derived from Psalm 89:27. In the psalm this is a title bestowed on the king as a result of divine appointment, and this, argues Caird, is its meaning in the New Testament. Christ is 'designated' Son of God by his resurrection (Romans 1:4) and in Colossians 1:18 among other passages he is first-born 'from the dead'. Most important, in Ephesians 1:20–23, which may be taken as a parallel passage, written if not by Paul himself, then by a disciple who was close to him and knew his mind, the cosmic supremacy of Christ is clearly based on his *manhood*. Christ achieves by his earthly life, death and resurrection the sovereignty over the universe for which men and women were created.

At the centre of revelation therefore lies the person of Jesus Christ. God is made known in and identified by the particular human personal identity of Jesus (Bauckham, 1997, p. 174). As the 'image of God' he is the exemplar of true human identity. As such his role precisely meets the requirement that the content of revelation be an 'image of humanity'. Jesus may be described as the 'proper man', 'man as God from the beginning designed man to be' (Caird, 1976, p. 172), a man whose humanity and in particular whose relationship with God serves as a pattern for human self-understanding. Moreover although Jesus had to battle against sin, paying the ultimate cost with his death on the cross, he was not bound by it. For the human race, because of our loss of identity, our knowledge is constructed around and our actions spring from a centre in ourselves. But with his personal centre in the love and the will of God the Father, Jesus broke the confinement brought about by sin. His obedient life, flowing from a full knowledge of and assent to the Father's will, is a vital element in the pattern of humanity of which he is the exemplar. Thus he not only restores the purpose of God for men and women in the old creation, but brings into being a new creation (2 Corinthians 5:14) for those no longer 'in Adam' but, in Paul's terminology, 'in Christ'.

Whereas the primary New Testament meaning of the 'image of God' is Jesus in his incarnation, death and resurrection, secondly and derivatively the image of God is also that into which believers are called by virtue of faith in him. Christians are called to clothe themselves with 'the new self, created according to the likeness of God' (Ephesians 4:24), reminded that they have put on the 'new self, which is being renewed in knowledge according to the image of its Creator' (Colossians 3:10), and told that 'those whom [God] foreknew he also predestined to be conformed to the image of his Son' (Romans 8:29). The destiny of Christian believers is to become like Jesus, to 'put on' his image, 'seeing the glory of the Lord as though reflected in a mirror', to be 'transformed into the same image from one degree of glory to another', something which comes 'from the Lord, who is the Spirit' (2 Corinthians 3:18). As Pinnock writes, 'We are destined to find our true selves in God, in whom we live and move and have our being' (1996, p. 150). Thus while the centre of revelation is the image of God in Jesus Christ, revelation is completed only when Christians receive that image. From the point of view of human experience, therefore, revelation is *the gift of a new identity in the image of Jesus.*

The Spirit of Revelation

The New Testament texts which refer to the gift of a 'new self' or identity modelled on that of Jesus imply that the gift of that identity is the work of the Holy Spirit. The task of the Spirit is to lead his disciples into all truth by revealing Jesus to them (John 16:12–15), to make them aware of their sonship to the Father (Romans 8:15–16; Galatians 4:6). But the work of the Holy Spirit does not bypass human psychology. On the contrary it is in and through the work of the Spirit that divine action and human psychological make-up interact in the process of revelation. This meeting of human and divine throws up a number of questions: what is the psychological process and what changes in our psychological make-up take place as a result of the work of the Spirit? How does a new identity become operational? What changes take place in the self-schema and what changes in self-image, attitude and behaviour can we expect to result? Equally important, how is the essential freedom of humanity in relation to God preserved while the Spirit is at work in the human psyche? And if that freedom is preserved in the area of our knowing, is revelation subject to the activity of assimilation by which all new learning is adapted to the existing pattern of our understanding? What *kind* of knowledge is revelation when we receive it?

Charles Moule describes 'spirit' as a 'bridge word' expressing the human relation with the transcendent (1978, p. 7). In Genesis 2:7 the breath or *ruach* of God is pictured as the source of human vitality. This vitality, Reinhold Niebuhr insists, is not to be confused with the vitality of the non-human creation. The vitality of humanity is a vitality of spirit. It is the spirit which upholds the soul and enlivens the body so that the unity of men and women as soul and body is grounded in spirit (Niebuhr, 1941, pp. 13–15, 27–9, 151–2). 'Spirit' is not to be thought of as a category of substance, as if the spirit were a distinct and separable part of a human being, but a principle of energy (Congar, 1983, p. 3). Biblical psychology pictures the human person as a unity of spirit, soul and body, in which the 'spirit' in human beings is the 'seat of action' or dominant disposition. It is possible to speak of a 'spirit' of intelligence or of wisdom, a spirit of jealousy or of an '"evil" spirit from the Lord'. For this reason also 'spirit' is frequently a parallel with 'heart' where this refers to motive or intention. Our emotional, mental and bodily life all have a 'spiritual' dimension, expressing the same unique relatedness to God the Creator as the phrase 'the image of God' conveys in Genesis 1.

Holy Spirit and Human Spirit

But how exactly are we to understand our relatedness to God in the dimension of the spirit? In the Old Testament *ruach* has three distinct but related meanings. It can refer to natural events like the wind or breathing. Secondly it means the 'spirit' which animates men and women, the principle of life or breath, and derivative of this sense, the dominant disposition or seat of knowledge and feeling. Thirdly the *ruach* is the life of God, the 'spirit of the Lord' by which he acts and causes action. When the second and third of these groups of meaning are confused, the idea of spirit as the principle underlying human life and consciousness comes to be subsumed under that of spirit as the action of God. This happens, for example, in the theology of both Emil Brunner and Karl Barth. 'Man can be person', writes Brunner, 'because and insofar as he has spirit. Personal being is "founded" in the spirit; the spirit is, so to speak, the substratum, the element of personal

being. But what is spirit? ... God *is* spirit, man *has* spirit' (1939, p. 237), and Karl Barth, in his even more radical presentation, declares,

> Man has Spirit. By putting it this way we describe the spirit as something that comes to man, something not essentially his own but to be received and actually received by him, something that totally limits his constitution and thus totally determines it ... Man has Spirit as one who is possessed by it.
>
> (1960, p. 354)

The effect of this position is to perpetuate the confusion to which Kelsey drew attention between the two types of relationship between God and humankind, the relationship of dependence and the relationship of freedom. It makes the very life of a person a divine activity and removes the freedom given to human beings in their created relationship with God. It is true to say that Scripture speaks of the spirit as God's gift and under God's power, its removal resulting in death. But the Holy Spirit, for whose return the author of Psalm 51, for example, prays, is not the principle which upholds the psalmist's very life. Rather he upholds his relationship with God, a relationship characterized by a 'willing spirit' (Psalm 51:10–12). It is not the Holy Spirit who animates a person as creature but the human spirit.

It is the spirit which is the source of human freedom, the foundation of human agency and proper autonomy. 'It is precisely the spirit that furnishes the key to the Biblical understanding of man's self-transcendence; it is spirit that keeps the relation between God and man essentially free and personal' (Hendry, 1957, p. 105). The link between the two senses of *ruach* is that the 'spirit' is the principle which governs *both* the essential vitality of the person as 'ensouled body' *and* the possibility of our relating to God. But the distinction between human dependence on God as creatures and the freedom which applies to the relationship in which we know and respond to God personally must not be ignored. As George Hendry puts it,

> A distinction must be made between man's existential *dependence* on God, which he shares with all living creatures and which applies to him as an 'ensouled body', and man's personal *relation* to God, which can be realised only at the level of spirit ... Man's relation to God, which corresponds to the structure of his being as God's creature, can be realised only by the free act of the human spirit.
>
> (1957, p. 107)

Filled with the Spirit

To begin again with the Old Testament, when God intervenes in human affairs he does so by the infusion of a divine principle of action. In the early stages of Israel's history the Spirit 'comes upon' particular people to enable them to carry out God's will. When the Spirit of the Lord 'takes possession of' Gideon he mounts a successful recruiting campaign and follows it up with victory against the Lord's enemies (Judges 6:33–5; 7:19–22). When the Spirit of the Lord begins to stir in Samson (Judges 13:25) he begins the exploits that dent the power of the Philistines, receiving extra strength when the Spirit of the Lord 'rushes on him' (Judges 14:6, 19; 15:14). Likewise the Spirit of God 'comes in power' upon Saul (1 Samuel 11:6), kindling his anger and moving him to lead Israel into battle. In a rather different way Moses, Joshua, Elijah and Elisha are able to accomplish the tasks they are given because of the spirit that is within them, a spirit which may be transferred to others if God so wills (Numbers 11:16–30; Deuteronomy 34:9; 2 Kings 2:9–15). With the establishment of the kingdom the relationship between the Spirit of the Lord and God's designated servant enters a new phase. At David's anointing, the Spirit of the Lord descends on him *and remains* (1 Samuel 16:13). Meanwhile the prophets grow in visibility and authority, speaking by the Spirit of the Lord (1 Kings 22:24; Micah 3:8). By post-exilic times it had become customary to refer to the Spirit as both the means whereby God had acted and continued to act throughout the whole history of his people in a way consistent with his personality and as the mode of God's presence with his people (Isaiah 63:10–14; Ezekiel 37:14).

As Yves Congar observes, there is a pattern of increasing inwardness in Israel's understanding of her relation with God. When God acts it comes to be understood not simply as directed towards the achievement of a certain political goal, such as military victory, but towards the establishment of a relationship with those of his people who are receptive. Initially the scope of this personal relationship is limited to particular chosen servants, including the prophets. But by post-exilic times it is seen as more widely available, in particular to the 'poor', such as those who speak in such passages as Isaiah 63:7–14. It is the Spirit who supplies the possibility of moral cleansing and of a holy life. In particular, a time begins to be envisaged in which all will share in the personal relationship with God which is the experience of the prophets and in the book of Joel, this hope is extended beyond the boundaries of Israel to embrace 'all flesh' (Joel 2:28–9).

> The 'economy' … to which the Scripture bears witness moves forward in the direction of greater and deeper interiority: 'God all in all'. This progress is clear in the Old Testament. It reaches its conclusion in the New Testament where it is connected with a more perfect revelation and experience of the Spirit.
>
> (Congar, 1983, vol. 1, p. 12)

The New Testament sees the fulfilment of what is foreseen under the Old Covenant. The new age inaugurated with the coming of Jesus is 'the beginning of an eschatological period characterized by the gift of the Spirit to a people of God with a universal vocation' (1983, vol. 1, p. 12). In Galatians 3:14 Paul affirms that it is through the gift of the Spirit that the promise to Abraham is fulfilled. In place of sporadic individual occurrences the Spirit is given permanently and fully in and then through Jesus Christ to lead each of God's people to *teleiosis* – perfection or maturity. Thus in John's Gospel Jesus speaks of the Spirit as a spring of living water welling up in the heart of the believer (John 7:38–9). In Luke and Acts he instructs his disciples to wait until they receive the promise of the Father and are clothed with the power of the Spirit (Luke 24:49; Acts 1:4–5, 8). In Ephesians, Paul or a fellow writer urges all believers to be filled continually with the Holy Spirit (Ephesians 5:18) and in Romans 8:11 he writes that the indwelling Holy Spirit will bring life to their mortal bodies.

As long ago as 1952 Bishop Lesslie Newbigin (1957) pointed out the role of the Pentecostal strand in the theology of the Church. Alongside the 'congregation of the faithful' and the 'Body of Christ', the Church should be understood also as 'the community of the Holy Spirit' and the presence of the Spirit in the Church should be recognized as a fact of present experience. Since then the importance of this strand has increasingly come to be recognized. Its implication is that participation in the Holy Spirit is, along with faith and baptism, an essential mark of every member of Christ's Church. According to James Dunn (1970, pp. 224ff.) baptism in the Spirit is the high point of 'conversion-initiation'. The whole event or process by which a person becomes a Christian involves repentance, faith, forgiveness, baptism, incorporation into Christ and the gift of the Holy Spirit, but it is the gift of the Spirit which both enables and completes Christian conversion and which demonstrates, both to the believer and to others, that a genuine work of God has taken place (Pinnock, 1996, pp. 162–6; Moltmann, 1997, pp. 26–8).

To be filled with the Holy Spirit means not a replacement of substance but the communication of an inner dynamism. The gift of the Holy Spirit introduces a new centre of agency or principle of action into the life of believers yet without in any way constraining or possessing them. This is specifically the point of that passage, beginning in 1 Corinthians 12, in which Paul deals with the gifts of the Spirit in worship. It is, he maintains, the spirits of the 'dumb idols' which his readers previously worshipped which constrain and possess. The Holy Spirit is not to be understood in this way but rather as working according to the character of God, which is love.

In Galatians in particular, Paul maintains that possession of the Spirit brings authentic freedom. It frees us from both the constraints of the Law, which can only condemn, and from the desires of 'the flesh' – the sinful human nature which is hostile to God and leads to 'slavery' to evil desires. The Spirit enables authentic personal choice against a background of sharp dichotomies, light or darkness, faith or works, life or death, and so on. 'We become subjects of a quality of existence and activities which go back to God's sphere of existence and activity' (Congar, 1983, vol. 1, p. 32).

Conformation

The Subjective Aspect of Revelation

This quality of existence has moreover a definite content, which is the person of Christ. In the Old Testament the Spirit was the Spirit of God or of the Lord. Now he is the Spirit of Christ. 'When the Spirit of truth comes,' Jesus declared, 'he will guide you into all the truth ... He will glorify me, for he will take what is mine and declare it to you' (John 16:13–14). As Hendry puts it, 'The Spirit is the subjective counterpart to the objective fact of Christ' (1957, p. 25), and Congar: 'The Spirit makes it possible for us to know and recognise Christ. This is not simply a doctrinal statement. It is an existential reality' (1983, vol. 1, p. 37).

But what kind of knowledge is the knowledge of Christ which is offered to us by the Holy Spirit? What is the process by which it is incorporated into the pattern of schemata which make up our existing knowledge? The clue to the answer comes from the way Paul writes about the work of the Holy Spirit witnessing 'with our spirit' that we are children of God (Romans 8:16). The 'identity' of Jesus, who he 'really' is, is the Son of God. To know him is to know him as God's Son. When we read this in the Bible or hear it in the teaching of the Church it consists of factual information that demands a response. But what the Holy Spirit conveys is not simply that Jesus is God's Son but that we are his children. This knowledge is given to us not as factual, 'explicit' knowledge but as *tacit* knowledge conveyed at the level of *spirit*. The spirit 'witnesses with our spirits'. What we receive is not simply 'saving knowledge', though it is that. We receive a *new identity*, the identity of Jesus himself. He is God's Son, we are 'incorporated' in him as God's children. As Rowan Williams puts it (2000, p. 138), 'to come to be "in Christ" involves a far-reaching reconstruction of one's humanity'. The new dynamic, the new centre of agency, given to us through the Holy Spirit has the 'form' of Jesus himself. It is a gift of Jesus's own identity at a deep level of personality where the Holy Spirit meets, touches or 'impinges' on the human spirit.

This deep level of personality is not the 'me' or known self but the 'I' or knowing subject. Therefore like the knowing subject, the new identity given to us on the pattern of Jesus cannot be known directly. It is given to us as tacit rather than explicit knowledge. It only becomes part of the 'me', the person we know, when we begin to live from it rather than from the old, inauthentic identity. The privilege of becoming children of God is 'more than we can tell'. But tacit knowledge is actively organized. It consists of a readiness to respond to situations. The tacit knowledge that I am a child of God forms a readiness to respond to familiar situations in new ways and, having done so, to see myself, others and the world in a new light.

The gift of new identity with Jesus as its exemplar begins a process Paul calls the 'renewal of the mind' through which God the Holy Spirit gradually changes our whole mental and emotional make-up. The identity schema provides continuity between the way we remember the past and the way we envisage the future, and controls the way the schemata of our memory relate to one another. To draw on an example I quoted earlier, a person who changed his mind about fox-hunting would need to 're-relate' his fox-hunting schema from the complex to do with healthy outdoor country sports to the complex associated with unjustified cruelty or vice versa. In the same way, a change in the way we see ourselves has the power to produce a whole series of readjustments in our world-model, our emotions and our actions. 'You'd never have caught me with this bunch of people a few months ago', comments one recent convert. Another discovers a new love for the Bible as it feeds his new sense of identity. A third, richer than most, begins to give away large quantities of money to those she now recognizes for the first time to be in need. A fourth discovers a new vocation to serve young people and changes his job to become a teacher.

Changed into His Likeness

In Protestant theology, 'salvation', which can also be understood as 'healing' or 'making whole', traditionally involves two aspects, 'justification' and 'sanctification'. 'Justification' may be seen as 'objective', involving the restoration of a relationship between God and mankind and conferring upon the believer a new status before God. 'Sanctification' is 'subjective', involving an actual change in the life of the believer. Without sanctification, justification is incomplete and inauthentic. A merely forensic theory of the atonement fails to relate either the need for or the means of amendment to the action of God in Christ. On the other hand, without justification sanctification is impossible. The problem is to relate the two so as to show that they imply one another as parts of the one process of salvation or making whole. Here we see that justification consists of the gracious gift of a new identity, that of Jesus himself. At a stroke we are changed from God's enemies into his beloved children, sinners clothed in the 'righteousness of Christ'. But this new identity is more than a theoretical change in the way God sees us. In the power of the Holy Spirit it is a capacity for change. Justification is only the first step on the journey of sanctification (Pinnock, 1996, pp. 156–7).

The 'subjective' dimension of revelation, involving the gradual conformation of the believer to the image of Christ, is an aspect of sanctification (Abraham, 1997, pp. 211–13). The non-believer is trapped within an inauthentic self-understanding. Our identity is formed by interaction with the imperfect world. Broken and damaged, we cannot escape a partial and distorted world-view. Sinful thoughts, sinful choices and sinful actions are unavoidable. But with the gift of the Holy Spirit a new and liberating self-understanding becomes available. This new identity, based on that of Jesus himself, offers the possibility of genuine freedom from sin. However, it must be progressively worked out in the life of the believer, making possible a gradual change in both inward self-image and outward behaviour in the direction of the character of Christ himself. The pattern of such change is that we become what we already are. What we are before God by virtue of incorporation into Christ and the gift of his identity we gradually become before men and women by means of inner transformation. The public self is to reflect increasingly the nature of the new life which springs up from the hidden depths of the personality, the inner person where the Holy Spirit dwells.

The dynamic of this process of transformation may be illustrated by the experience of penitence. Repentance constitutes the gateway to the Kingdom of God. It was repentance which lay at the heart of the preaching of John the Baptist, of Christ himself and of the apostles. But genuine penitence for sin is difficult to attain. Indeed, without the incarnation and its extension in the work of the Spirit it is impossible. Christ however shoulders the burden of a life of perfect penitence. Then this attitude of penitence before God is made available to humanity by means of the gift of the Spirit. Penitence is the attitude towards God which places a person in right relationship towards him. It is not simply one attitude among others but a vital aspect of our self-understanding in relationship to God.

The experience of penitence suggests a dual role for the Holy Spirit in the process of conformation. First the Spirit enlightens. Charles Colson recalls the moment when he first saw his whole life in an entirely different perspective:

> During the throes of Watergate, I went to talk with my friend, Tom Phillips. I was curious, maybe even a little envious, about the changes in his life. His explanation – that he had 'accepted Jesus Christ' – baffled me. I was tired, empty inside, sick of scandal and accusations, but not once did I see myself as having really sinned. Politics was a dirty business, and I was good at it. And what I had done, I rationalised, was no different from the usual political manoeuvring. What's more, right and wrong were relative, and my motives were for the good of the country – or so I believed.
>
> But that night when I left Tom's home and sat alone at my car, my own sin – not just dirty politics, but the hatred and pride and evil so deep within me – was thrust before my eyes, forcefully and painfully. For the first time in my life, I felt unclean, and worst of all, I could not escape. In those moments of clarity, I found myself driven irresistibly into the arms of the living God.
>
> (1985, p. 138)

The Greek word *metanoia*, usually translated 'repentance', literally means 'a change of mind'. Here is an example of the Holy Spirit bringing about a new view of the self in relation to God. He thus provides the change of mind essential for a reorientation of a person's world-model in which his attitudes and values come increasingly to reflect those of Jesus Christ.

Secondly the Holy Spirit enables. The Spirit makes available to the individual a divine centre of agency or principle of action by means of which he is enabled to do things he would otherwise find impossible. Having been led by the Spirit to a change of *mind* about our actions or motives, the underlying change in *attitude* which will make the difference to our behaviour is usually beyond our power to accomplish. Attitudes lie too deep in the psyche for voluntary control. *Metanoia* must lead to the prayer that God, by his Spirit, would accomplish the necessary change of 'heart'. When we pray in this way, we acknowledge the lordship or authority of Christ over the particular area of life in which the Spirit has revealed a sinful attitude or action, resolving to take Jesus as our model.

Made Whole in His Image

What the Holy Spirit does not do is take away human freedom. The divine principle of action which he makes available never becomes a compulsion. The preservation of human freedom over against the Spirit allows the possibility of misunderstanding and rejection, of differences of interpretation and degrees of obedience. The enlightening work of the Spirit may enable us to see with a clarity otherwise impossible the need for change. But it is up to us at each juncture to choose whether to follow the demands of Christian character or our own natural inclination. In the terminology of Romans 8, this means living 'according to the Spirit' rather than 'according to the flesh'. For example, faced with the need to forgive someone who has hurt us, we have a choice. We can live from the new life of Christ within and extend the forgiveness we ourselves have received to others. Or we can continue to respond in a pre-Christian way, hold on to what we imagine to be our rights and refuse forgiveness. In times of material need, the Spirit's assurance that we are children of a generous heavenly Father allows the possibility of living without anxiety and giving generously to others. The alternative is to hold on to what we have in fear of not having enough for ourselves.

There may be considerable barriers to personal change in the direction of conformation to Christ. Lack of experience of a stable family during childhood often prevents people as adults from relating satisfactorily to God as a heavenly Father. Between intellectual comprehension of the biblical assurances of God's paternal (and maternal) love and the testimony of the Holy Spirit at the deepest levels of personality may lie a lifetime's accumulation of attitudes to oneself and others which flatly contradict this revelation. The work of psychotherapy is to enable people to bring to consciousness these destructive attitudes and by reflecting on them change them. The ministry of inner healing accomplishes a similar change. It is a way of bringing the Holy Spirit into painful memories, depriving them of their power to shape our image of ourselves. In the words of one woman who had been the victim of rape, 'I can still remember everything that happened, but it is as if it happened to someone else.' The guilt and sense of uncleanness associated with the memory had been removed.

Thus while Christian conversion and nurture is comparable in many respects to secondary socialization, in others it is more comparable to resocialization. Some aspects of Christian growth involve the relatively painless process of the addition of further skills and insights, a process of gradual internalization of Christian norms. At other times a complete reworking of previous areas of personality and understanding is required. Like any process of resocialization, this kind of painful transformation requires a degree of affectivity and corporate support. As the family is the matrix of primary socialization, resocialization, involving change in deeply held beliefs and attitudes, requires the support of a family-like community for its success. A ministry of healing to broken and damaged people can only be effective in churches where strong, loving and non-judgemental support structures exist.

This process of 'conformation' is not the same as mere imitation of Christ. Simply to read about the example of Jesus in the gospels and to attempt to follow it as the rest of the New Testament urges us to do can be done in the power and energy of the old self. In this case, outward success may easily lead to self-righteousness and condemnation of others. Only when the process is undertaken under the lordship of Christ and by the prompting by his Spirit within does it lead to true holiness, a partaking of the nature of Christ himself. For Clark Pinnock, 'It is not so much a matter of an imitation of Christ as our being the locale for the realization and radiation of his love through the Spirit' (1996, p. 177), and Dietrich Bonhoeffer warns,

> Formation comes only by being drawn into the form of Jesus Christ. It comes only as formation in his likeness, as *conformation* with the unique form of him who was made man, was crucified and rose again.
>
> This is not achieved by dint of efforts to 'become like Jesus', which is the way in which we usually interpret it. It is achieved only when the form of Jesus Christ itself works upon us in such a manner that it moulds our form in its own likeness (Galatians 4:19). Christ remains the only giver of forms. It is not Christian men who shape the world with their ideas, but it is Christ who shapes men in conformity with Himself. But just as we misunderstand the form of Christ if we take him to be essentially the teacher of a pious and good life, so, too, we should misunderstand the formation of man if we were to regard it as instruction in the way in which a pious and good life is to be attained. Christ is the Incarnate, Crucified and Risen One whom the Christian faith confesses. To be transformed in His image (2 Corinthians 3:18, Philippians 3:10, Romans 8:29 and 12:2) – this is what is meant by the formation of which the Bible speaks.
>
> (1965, pp. 80–81)

The form of Jesus, conveyed by the Holy Spirit, lies at the heart of revelation. Here we find the centre and the key to the kind of knowledge that revelation is.

Our main conclusion is now established. Revelation is the transforming gift of a new identity on the pattern of Jesus himself accomplished by the indwelling Holy Spirit. Several questions, however, remain to be answered and in the next chapter I will examine some of these in the light of the understanding of revelation proposed here. First, what are we to make of the claims for revelation in the non-Christian religions? Are these to be taken with equal seriousness? Do they even invalidate the claim of Christianity to a unique and authoritative revelation? Or is there some generally available knowledge of God outside of Christian revelation, of which the non-Christian claims to revelation are special instances? Secondly, the claim that Jesus in his incarnation is the primary locus of revelation implies that history is capable of supplying truths of decisive importance. This is something which for the past two hundred years has been taken by many theologians as axiomatically false. What are we to say about the role of history in revelation? Finally, although the Bible has been extensively quoted, virtually no mention has been made of its status in regard to revelation. What are we to make of the Bible? Is it revelation in itself, as many Christians believe? If not, what role does it play in revelation? Can the claim of inspiration be upheld and in what sense? To these questions we now turn.

Chapter 7

The Jesus of Faith and History

A Universal Knowledge of God?

One of the biggest hurdles for the idea of definitive revelation in Jesus Christ to negotiate is the presence of other world religions all claiming a revelation of their own. In the modern world it is widely assumed that every claim to revelation must be treated on a par with all the others. A final and definitive truth relevant to every man and woman on earth is held to be unattainable. All the proponents of a given 'revelation' can hope to do is to commend their own tradition as a point of view from which to make sense of human experience and as a pattern for living. So powerful and widespread is this assumption that even some Christian theologians find it necessary to accept it without serious question (Ward, 1994).

In contrast to what could be seen as capitulation to the spirit of the age, the idea that the content of Christian revelation is a definitive 'image of humanity' capable of answering the deepest questions of human identity is consistent with the traditional Christian claim that in Jesus Christ, God has acted in a unique and decisive way for the salvation of the whole of humanity. The argument does not entail the claim that Christians have sole rights to the revelation given in Jesus nor that Christianity as taught by any of its representatives is infallible. On the contrary, I have argued that there is plenty of scope for error in the way Christians have understood the revelation given in Christ. Revelation can only be received and appropriated in the context of the culture of a particular time and place and the twin processes of assimilation and accommodation operate in the reception of revelation just as they do in all learning (Williams, 2000, p. 132).

Nevertheless the implication of the argument is that other claims to revelation, such as those which undergird Islam or Buddhism, are not on a par with that available in Jesus Christ. Before the claim to a unique authoritative revelation can be accepted it is necessary *to provide an explanation for these alternative claims*. The purpose of this section is to examine the idea of a knowledge of God universally available and what kind of knowledge this could be, thereby to illuminate the claims to revelation of other religions.

Natural Theology or General Revelation?

In classical Christian thought a distinction was maintained between natural
and revealed theology. This distinction was given its most authoritative
expression by Thomas Aquinas. Thomas assumed that revelation consisted
of a body of truths about God and the world made available to us in verbal
form through the Scriptures and the doctrinal pronouncements of the
Church, in particular in the creeds. Most of these propositions can only be
known by revelation but some, such as the existence of God and his
providential care of the world, are also available to unaided human reason.
Natural theology is the activity of clarifying and demonstrating those parts
of the divine revelation that can be grasped by human reason.

The idea of natural theology as preliminary and preparatory to revelation
is still an important element in Roman Catholic theology. For many,
especially Protestant, theologians, however, the earlier distinction between
natural and revealed theology has been abandoned in favour of one between
general and *special* revelation. General revelation refers to a knowledge of
God shared by all as part of the conditions of creation whereas special
revelation is given as a result of God's saving activity. Upholders of both
natural theology and general revelation subscribe to the idea of a universal
knowledge of God. The difference lies in the fact that 'natural theology' is
taken to be reliable as far as it goes whereas the knowledge given by
'general revelation' is usually taken to be distorted because of human
sinfulness. Whereas revealed theology is taken to supplement and complete
natural theology, special revelation *corrects* those ideas of God which arise
from general revelation. In both cases, however, the act of God in revelation
or special revelation is a means of grace, an integral part of the offer of
salvation, which cannot be achieved by either natural theology or general
revelation (d'Costa, 1997, pp. 118–19).

What Kind of Knowledge?

The foundations for a belief in a universally available knowledge of God are
threefold. First, there are arguments from experience. For example, it is
possible to point to the universal experience of moral constraint and the
virtually universal phenomenon of religious belief. Secondly, there are
arguments from Scripture. Certain passages imply that God makes himself
known to all people, especially through the works of creation and the
experience of moral demand. In Psalms 8 and 19 the heavens proclaim the
handiwork of God. In Malachi 1:11 the prophet implies that God is known

and worshipped throughout the world. Preaching to the crowd in Lystra, Paul declares that God has left a witness to himself in creation and general providence and in Athens that the urge to worship is planted in people by God himself (Acts 14:15–17; 17:22–9). In the epistle to the Romans he argues that the eternal power and deity of God are plain to all from his works in creation but that people suppress this knowledge because of wickedness (Romans 1:18–20) and in a later passage implies that the conscience is a witness to the requirements of God's law (Romans 2:12–15). Finally there is an argument from the concept of revelation itself. Without a generally held concept of God prior to revelation, it is argued, revelation itself would be unintelligible. Before the more particular ideas to be conveyed in revelation, such as God acting in various ways for particular purposes, could be understood, there must exist a generally held concept of 'God' to which such ideas could be referred, and this concept could only arise as the result of a prior revelation available to all (Temple, 1937, pp. 96–7).

Despite these arguments, including the support given from Scripture, great difficulties arise when it comes to specifying what this universal knowledge of God actually consists of. Again there are three possible ways of understanding the concept of general revelation (Helm, 1982, pp. 2–6). First there is the idea of a revelation of God in nature along the lines of that hinted at by the Psalms and by Paul. The problem here lies in specifying what mankind is supposed to understand from nature and how. In the eighteenth century David Hume produced the classic refutation of the claim that we can argue from the existence of creation to that of a Creator. In fact, he claimed, it is as easy to ascribe the creation of the world we experience to a committee of bunglers as to a single omnipotent God (Hume, 1748, p. 39). Without some divine illumination on the subjective side telling us what we are supposed to conclude from the created world, any revelation conveyed in creation remains vague and ambiguous.

The second possible understanding of general revelation – a series of propositional truths available to everyone – fares little better. Aquinas thought that the existence and goodness of God and his general providence were to be included as propositions available to natural theology. But in the modern world the sheer diversity of belief displayed by the world's religions makes the task of uncovering a common core of propositional truths formidable.

This leaves the third suggestion: a universal knowledge of God as a feature of human psychological make-up. John Baillie was among those who argued for a kind of innate knowledge of God or 'mediated immediacy' (Baillie, 1939, pp. 178–218). According to Baillie, the knowledge of God is analogous to our knowledge of other selves. The existence of another rational person is incapable of proof; some portion at least of our belief in the existence of others with minds like ourselves rests on intuitions which we cannot support logically. In the knowledge of God there is, he believed, both an intuitive and a logical element. God is known 'in, with and under' other objects of experience. There is an immediate, intuitive knowledge of God corresponding to the intuition which tells us of the presence of another person but that knowledge becomes effective only as it is mediated by our knowing of the world. In every act of knowing, he believed, four subjects of knowledge are present together: the self, others, the world and God. Thus consciousness of God arises *through* experience.

General Revelation as Tacit Knowledge

The difficulties with all three of these attempts to give content to general revelation arise from the fact that they depend on an ideal of *explicit* knowledge. However, Baillie's analysis of the way we know other people moves in the direction of the concept of a different type of knowledge. It becomes entirely intelligible if this knowledge of God 'in, with and under' the knowledge of ordinary things is seen as an element of *tacit* rather than explicit knowledge. This would mean that general revelation is something rooted in the necessities of the human cognitive make-up. Our awareness of God is not derived simply or directly from experience but from the need to set experience within a comprehensible frame of reference.

    One of the roles of the schema in the process of learning is the provision of a range of expectations. The schema represents 'set' or orientation; it provides an 'outline' of the situation, a readiness to respond to information or experience of a particular type. Included in that outline are what Stuart Hampshire calls 'necessities of discourse' (Hampshire, 1959, pp. 13–14). These arise from the fact that people are agents with purposes. Their necessity is a logical outcome of the decision to treat people as acting subjects.[1] The existence of an external physical world is incapable of logical proof; we know that it exists simply because our mode of existence is to be acting on it. The existence of other people with minds like our own is

---

[1] Immanuel Kant included in the *Critique of Pure Reason* a complex and authoritative argument for the position that the existence of God has to be understood as a 'regulative principle of reason' (1787, pp. 500–507). The foundation of Kant's argument is the same as Hampshire's. The individual must be understood as a knowing subject who contributes certain elements to their own knowledge. The concept of God is part of that contribution.

similarly incapable of logical proof; we know it because we experience language as a means of communication. Finally the existence of ourselves is something we take for granted. Even the radical sceptic Descartes was forced to concede the existence of the thinking self. Yet of what that self consists remains a mystery. Every schema thus includes the readiness to encounter the self, others and the world and rarely, if ever, are these expectations overthrown. To the three 'necessities of discourse' proposed by Hampshire, Baillie adds a fourth: an expectation of the existence of a supreme Being, the origin and perhaps the source of purpose in the universe. In its strongest form this expectation may generate a readiness to encounter 'God'.

Psychologist of religion James Fowler refers to a person's total psychological world within which all his individual schemata operate as the 'ultimate environment'. Fowler uses a dramatic metaphor to describe this 'ultimate environment'. It is, he says,

> The largest theatre of action in which we act out our lives. Our images of the ultimate environment determine the way we arrange the scenery and grasp the plot in our life's plays. Furthermore, our images of the ultimate environment change as we move through life. They expand and grow, and the plots get blown open or have to be linked in with other plots.
>
> (1981, p. 29)

To the individual's ultimate environment there corresponds, for the culture or perhaps for particular communities within a given culture, the 'symbolic universe' (Berger and Luckmann, 1966, pp. 110–46). Symbolic universes are shared schemata expressing the perspective of a given reference group, a shared 'ultimate environment'.

'Ultimate environments' and 'symbolic universes' provide a perspective on the unknown transcendent. They are the schemata in which the great questions of human existence are asked and the answers to these questions related to one another. In the quest for self-understanding, concludes Stephen Toulmin, the philosopher may have to become a myth-maker since it is in the form of myths that insights beyond the range of theorizing have generally been preserved (1976, pp. 308–10). Such 'myths' are the means by which men and women attempt to cope with the unanswered questions of human existence such as the problem of evil and apparently purposeless suffering and the questions of human significance and destiny. Fowler describes the forms such constructions take in a variety of ways. He draws attention to 'centres of value', 'images of power' and, in particular, 'master stories'. He describes a conversation in a taxi with a man who told him,

> The way I see it, if we have any purpose on this earth, it is just to keep things going. We can stir the pot while we are here and try to keep things interesting. Beyond that, everything runs down: your marriage runs down, your body runs down, your faith runs down. We can only try to make it interesting.
>
>   (Fowler and Keen, 1978, p. 36; Fowler, 1981, p. 30)

Fowler suggests that this man's 'master story' could be summed up in the word 'entropy'. Such fundamental beliefs form the backdrop against which the significance of life and the various commitments it entails are measured. They may be tacit and unexamined or explicit in story, symbol, myth, ritual, philosophical theory or full-blown religious commitment.

One of the most important features of master stories is that they are self-involving. The need for overarching explanation is more than simply cognitive but also emotional and spiritual. They are the means by which people attempt to cope with the unanswered questions of human existence. 'Ultimate environments' or 'symbolic universes' express a particular set of beliefs about the place of the individual or humanity as a whole in the scheme of things. They represent an orientation to the world along the lines of Erikson's 'basic trust'. Since they are self-involving, master stories form an element of the identity schema. The way individual people and whole societies picture the transcendent is an element of corporate or individual identity.

It follows that every individual and society can be said to have a schema for God, not in the explicit sense of articulated religious belief but as a feature of tacit knowledge. The schema need not include a fully-worked-out idea of the transcendent. It may or may not include the idea of a personal God. Neither the idea of the 'man upstairs' looking down on us nor the 'God' of the ontological or cosmological arguments for his existence measure up to the full content of the God revealed in Jesus Christ. The schema consists simply of a readiness to respond to questions about the origin, significance and destiny of the world, a background of expectations against which talk of God makes sense.

Consequences of Accepting General Revelation

The model given here helps to ground various theological assertions relating to general revelation by requiring their translation into the terms of a theoretical framework for human cognition. We can affirm with Jean Calvin that 'a sense of deity is indelibly engraved on the human heart' (1536, I.iii.3) but only in the sense that a readiness to respond to the divine is part of human make-up. Against this background of tacit knowledge, we may affirm the physical and human creation as a *witness* to God's existence, while conceding, with Hume, that such evidence does nothing to *compel* belief in a personal divine Creator. For the same reason we can affirm that all experience is potentially revelatory. An awareness of the transcendent and the problems and questions associated with it lies at the heart of our awareness of the world and forms the ultimate context of all our experience.

Another corollary is the distortion of the universal sense of deity as a result of human sinfulness. There is no support in this position for the idea of a 'natural theology' consisting of the inference of reliable propositions about God from the evidence available in creation. The effect of sin is to confine each individual and society within a relative point of view, so that final and definitive knowledge is impossible. It could be achieved only as the result of the realization by an individual or group of their true identity, bringing the quest for meaning in the universe to a definitive end. Finally, this understanding of general revelation also affirms what Emil Brunner called human 'responsibility' before God (Brunner, 1939, pp. 53, 60–63, 70–74; 1947, pp. 50–57). Every person may be said to exist *before God* in the sense that their life is governed by a search for identity which is, at one and the same time, a search for God. Men and women are thus conditioned by their relationship to God even though the terms of this relationship consist, on the human side, of ignorance.

Because the awareness of deity contained in a general revelation is a feature of tacit rather than explicit knowledge, the argument offers no support for the idea of universal belief in God, as proposed by Paul Tillich among others. In his declaration that 'Man is immediately aware of something unconditional which is the *prius* of the separation and interaction of subject and object' (1959, p. 22) Tillich appears to recognize Calvin's 'universal sense of deity' and interprets this awareness as a universal belief in God rather than openness to questions of the transcendent. 'God', he declared, 'is the presupposition of the question of God' (1959, pp. 12–13). Truth, wrote Tillich, is the presupposition of philosophy and God is truth, while for Charles Hartshorne, 'God is the name for the uniquely good, admirable, great, worship-eliciting being' (1953, p. 7). The idea that the awareness of God is an element of tacit knowledge does not imply however that human ideas of truth, beauty and so on serve as incognitos for the divine. Rather, they arise in the course of a quest for the meaning of life prompted by the tacit awareness of mystery and the need for a secure sense of identity. They serve as preparations for revelation, not substitutes for it.

General revelation is to be understood as an outcome of human creation in the image of God. Because we are created in God's image, human beings have a spiritual dimension, which comes to expression in the awareness of an underlying 'I' or 'true self'. The spiritual dimension of human life also generates an awareness of the transcendent, a 'sense of deity'. This awareness of a transcendent dimension in human existence and of the need for an explanation for that dimension is a feature of *tacit* rather than *explicit* knowledge. In cognitive terms it consists of a 'set' or 'expectation' for a certain aspect of identity, one which places the person or society in an overarching scheme of things and which accounts for personal and corporate origin and destiny. Human explanations of all kinds, including the philosophical systems with which the early Christian apologists were faced, and the great world religions which form an increasingly important element in the experience of modern western men and women, may contain a significant amount of truth arising out of profound insight into the human condition. But such truth does not, in itself, constitute revelation. Such truth as exists in the world's great religious and philosophical systems could be recognized as truth only when seen to be grounded in the definite truth of revelation itself. This definitive truth, though active in the renewal of individuals and communities, could only be arrived at conceptually by a process of interpretation. The awareness of a question of God or, in Calvin's terms, that sense of deity engraved on the human heart constitutes an expectation of further revelation to come and a possibility of receiving such a revelation. But it does not of itself constitute such a revelation. Nothing in this state of things *requires* a revelation in the sense of compelling God to act. But 'general revelation', in whose interpretation all men and women err, requires a 'special' or definitive revelation for its completion.

The Historical Christ

The claim that the incarnate Jesus Christ is the content of divine revelation and the exemplar for the formation of Christian identity involves a claim about the role of history both in revelation and in human and particularly Christian formation. The propriety of basing religious faith wholly or in part on historical knowledge is hotly contested (Evans, 1993, p. 134). The problem is not a new one however. Throughout the New Testament the assumption is to be found that Jesus, who even for the first Gentile converts was already an historical figure from a semi-alien culture, was nevertheless available as a focus of faith. Can this claim be substantiated at a distance of nearly two thousand years?

Philosophy of History

Of all the sciences dealing with human life, history deals with men and women at their most concrete. The subject of its enquiry is the whole person rather than an abstracted aspect of personal life. The material of history consists of a web of causal connections of a particular kind. They are not the connections of natural causation familiar to the natural scientist but consist of a complex interplay of psychological motivation, a 'constant interaction of conscious efforts' (Troeltsch, 1913, p. 719). The web of historical causality is thus the outcome of that elusive quality of human life, the power of agency. One of the most powerful justifications of the historical enterprise is its contribution to the study of human identity, through the infinite variety of motivation and outcome which forms its subject matter. History is the hermeneutical science *par excellence*. Its goal is the discovery, by means of the structure of cause and effect in human affairs, of the key to the nature of human action and human being. If the definitive nature of human being is to be revealed, not only is history the appropriate medium for its revelation but the methods of the historian best suited to its reception. As Bauckham puts it, 'Since it is as personal agent and personal presence in the world that God becomes identifiable within the world, God's identity can only be adequately conveyed by narration of God's agency and presence with God's people' (1997, p. 190).[2]

---

[2] Denials of the appropriateness of history as a vehicle for the knowledge of God are usually based on inadequate theories of knowledge. One of the most important examples is Gotthold Lessing (1956), who claimed that an 'ugly ditch' lay between contingent historical fact and the 'necessary' truths of reason, in which he believed Christianity consists. Lessing's 'ugly ditch' has recently been examined in detail by Gordon E. Michalson Jr (1985, esp. pp. 23–47), who shows that Lessing identifies but confuses three separate types of 'ditches': first, the temporal ditch between the events of the past and the standpoint of the present; second, the disjunction between types of truths, the contingent or 'accidental' truths of historical reporting and the 'necessary' truths of reason; and third, the disjunction between the type of truth conveyed in Christological statements and the events which are supposed to prove or add weight to such statements. The first two types of ditch, argues Michalson, are mutually exclusive in terms of their significance. The first is based on a strict empiricist view of the possibilities of historical testimony, the second on a strict rationalist interpretation of truth. The raising of problems of the second kind makes problems of the first kind irrelevant.

The third type of ditch has perhaps the greatest significance for modern approaches to historical revelation. This is the supposed disjunction between 'events' and 'truth' which appears to sever the connection between the 'Jesus of history' and the 'Christ of faith'. It is this idea that, in the words of Michalson's summary, ' "Events" simply do not produce "truths"', which emerges from Lessing's inadequate theory of knowledge. Events are always grasped by means of a framework of expectations. Their significance and interpretation is a

Philosophy of history takes the form of comparison and criticism of historical method. For this reason its study is closely bound up with both the writing of history itself and the examination of the work of particular historians. Two distinct orientations are to be discerned, which form the subject respectively of *substantive* and *analytical* philosophy of history (Atkinson, 1978, pp. 4–13). In the substantive philosophy of history the 'meaning' of the historical process is sought for in an overall interpretation of historical movement on a broad scale. Some writers, such as Arnold Toynbee, have attempted to show a cyclical pattern in history. Others prefer a linear pattern, as represented by various versions of the theory of historical progress. Still others however deny any pattern to history, finding in the course of events, as H. A. L. Fisher memorably put it, only 'one damn thing after another'. Theirs is an analytical philosophy, which finds the meaning of history in the pattern of internal connections and the light thrown by such connections on human character and motivation. The difference between the two approaches is a question of balance or emphasis. Neither orientation can escape the dialectical relation between evidence and presupposition. While he brings to his task a particular world-view, the historian must be prepared for that world-view to be corrected and refined in the course of engagement with the evidence itself. A substantive philosophy of history represents a relative confidence on the part of the historian in his particular view of human nature and destiny; the analytic a confidence in the ability of the study of historical events to mould and correct that world-view.

The Bible Writers as Historians

In terms of these two types of history writing, the biblical writers belong to the first. Theirs is a substantive rather than analytical philosophy of history, demonstrating a confidence in a particular tradition of interpretation. The main characteristic of this tradition, or set of traditions, as they developed within the history of Israel and were taken over by the Christian Church, is

---

function of the schema brought to their comprehension. Thus, events *always* produce truths of some kind; no event involving human beings has ever gone uninterpreted. In this context the importance of Jesus's claim to fulfil the Scripture can readily be appreciated. The gospels are full of evidence of precisely this type of question asked about him by contemporaries. 'Are you he who is to come or should we look for another?', a question Jesus answered with a reference to the Old Testament Scripture. Jesus's life and claims throw a new light on the Scripture, in which light his teaching and actions stand out as of immense significance. It is precisely the fulfilment of Scripture in this unexpected way which is the principal theme of the Gospel accounts.

the claim to interpret history from the point of view of the purposes of God. The concern of the biblical writers was not to allow the past to 'speak for itself' as an analytic historian might. Their purpose was to use an account of historical events as a means to express the nature and purposes of God.

At the same time they believed that certain events, in particular the deliverance of the Israelites from Egypt and later the Babylonian exile, were themselves the means by which God's character was revealed. The knowledge of God becomes available in history as the outcome of a process of both event and interpretation or, as William Temple put it, 'The essential condition of effectual revelation is the coincidence of divinely controlled event and minds divinely illumined to read it aright' (Temple, 1937, p. 107). In the Bible, God becomes involved in events through the intervention of a divine principle of action in the cycle of human purpose and outcome. But revelation is incomplete without a similar divine involvement on the side of interpretation. Thus biblical history is 'prophecy'. It requires the interpretation of past and present events by men (and possibly women) who claimed, like Jeremiah, to have 'stood in the council of God' (Jeremiah 23:18, 22). The work of these men and women was further refined and developed within the several traditions to which they gave rise. Within these traditions the prophetic books were both edited and supplemented and historical books such as the great cycle from Joshua to 2 Kings, compiled before and during the Babylonian exile, came into being.

While biblical history is comparable to history as it is understood in the modern age in that it consists of a pattern of event, interpretation and reinterpretation, there is also a decisive difference. The modern historian deals with his material with the aim of discovering and/or commending a particular understanding of the human condition. The biblical writers present theirs in the confidence that the events with which they deal and the interpretation they offer spring from and are themselves a part of the revelation of the nature and purpose of God and his relation to humanity. In relation to the modern historian, the Bible claims to offer a definitive perspective on human nature. From the perspective of revelation, biblical history may be said to be the centre of world history in that it furnishes the key to the understanding of all other history (Cullmann, 1951, pp. 19–23, 177–214).

Jesus in Faith and History

Although the New Testament was written from the standpoint of the Easter faith, this does not make it unhistorical. Like any other history, it is written from a particular point of view, offering an interpretation of past events. Its special character as history lies in the claim that the events around which it centres – the life, death and resurrection of Jesus – constitute God's decisive intervention in human affairs. For the New Testament writers, the experience of the resurrection and the outpouring of the Holy Spirit provided a framework for the interpretation of the life of Jesus not available at the time the events of his life actually took place. But this does not make that framework inauthentic. It is, in fact, a continuation of the prophetic framework within which biblical history is written. The work of the Holy Spirit in the Christian believer enables him to interpret Jesus as 'the Messiah, the Son of God' and fulfilment of the Old Testament Scriptures. The incarnation, death and resurrection of Christ are the events in and by which all previous revelatory events are fulfilled. But the interpretation of this event is not now available only to a select group of inspired individuals but to all who, as a result of their response to Christ, receive the indwelling Holy Spirit.

The incarnate Christ who is the content of revelation is thus to be understood as a figure in history. Access to him is by means of history. It comes through the written record of his life, his words and his impact on those around him. Moreover a process of historical interpretation is required in order to understand him better. His actions and teaching can only be correctly understood in the context of his own culture. And in fact the process of historical study continues to yield valuable insights. It shows us more clearly Jesus the Jew in the culture of his time. It enables us to ask questions about Jesus in relation to special concerns, highlighting his care for the poor and his respect for women. But no amount of confidence in the significance of Jesus's life can render the judgements on which that significance depends invulnerable to the possibility of reinterpretation in the light of further evidence.

At the same time Jesus is a super-historical figure. His life is the culmination of a process of divine revelation, in the light of which the meaning of history is disclosed. This means that any interpretation of Jesus is potentially self-involving. The gospel narratives have what Edward Farley calls 'intrinsic facticity': they present facts which involve the reader personally and require a decision (Farley, 1965, p. 433). 'These things are written', concludes the fourth evangelist, 'that you might believe . . .' Mark's gospel, it has been remarked, revolves around the question 'Who do you say that I am?' The question concerns not simply the identity of Jesus but of oneself as well. The answer the reader gives will express not a disinterested evaluation of Jesus but willingness or otherwise to become a follower, to re-evaluate one's own life in the light of Jesus's claims (Stroup, 1984, pp. 14ff.). For the reader who is personally involved, the question 'What is man?' which lies at the heart of historical interpretation has become 'Who am I?' The history is no longer impersonal and disinterested. It is, in Richard Niebuhr's phrase, 'internal history' (Niebuhr, 1960, p. 59). The definitive self-understanding offered by Christian revelation forms the framework within which all history, including the history of Christ, is interpreted. Within this framework, the particular historical facts of Christ are capable of revealing, to the person whose own identity is in the course of formation by means of them, a set of truths of decisive personal significance.

Turning back to the pages of the New Testament, we find this understanding of history implicit there also, especially in the fourth gospel. For most of the gospel John is content to play fast and loose with the facts of history. The cleansing of the Temple is moved from the end of Jesus's ministry to its beginning, the call of Peter from the beginning to the end. Important events like Jesus's baptism and transfiguration and the agony in Gethsemane are hardly touched on except in the form of meditative comments on their significance. Instead the gospel highlights the drama of confrontation between Jesus and his followers, the crowds and his enemies. In fact, the Jesus of John's gospel is not so much the historical Jesus but the risen, reigning Lord who confronts people in the present through the Holy Spirit and the testimony of his followers.

At the cross and resurrection, however, the evangelist becomes very particular about the truth of his testimony, insisting on the evidence of the eye-witness, the beloved disciple. This is because the actuality of these events is of central importance. The fact that the Word became flesh and dwelt among us, that Jesus was crucified and rose again, is at the heart of the gospel. The dual importance of historical fact and personal response emerges most clearly in the resurrection accounts of chapter 20. The first story is the account of Peter's run to the tomb with the beloved disciple. John describes in detail the position of the grave-clothes in the empty tomb and rounds off his account with the reaction of the beloved disciple who 'saw and believed'. The message is clear: the tomb was really empty, Jesus's body really raised and the historicity of this event is crucial for Christian faith. In contrast, John's second story is about personal encounter. Mary Magdalene stands weeping outside the tomb. Seeing Jesus, she is slow to recognize him until he calls her by name. Her response is to acknowledge him as teacher and Lord and to worship him. In the juxtaposition of these two stories the evangelist suggests that the historical evidence of the empty tomb is not sufficient on its own to make a disciple. It requires also the personal encounter in which Jesus, the Good Shepherd, calls his sheep by name and they follow him.

The last story in the chapter illustrates the same point. After Jesus's first appearance to his disciples Thomas refuses to believe in his resurrection until he has seen him face to face. A week later Jesus appears to him bearing the marks of his crucifixion and invites him to handle them to be sure of their reality, whereupon Thomas worships him and makes the Christian profession, 'My Lord and my God.' Thomas stands for all who are asked to believe in Jesus on the basis of the testimony of others. The story shows him convinced by the evidence of his senses but offers a blessing to those who believe without such evidence. While Christian faith rests on the historical reality of Jesus's life, death and resurrection, his truth can only be discovered in personal encounter.

Revelation and the Bible

Is the Bible Revelation?

In her autobiography, *Child of the Covenant*, Michele Guinness recounts the story of how she first read the Bible. As the child of an orthodox Jewish family, it was a book she was forbidden to read. To find out about Jesus she had to take her old school Bible to bed and read by torchlight.

> I began to read, slowly at first, struggling with the quaint, archaic language, then faster as the story began to unfold, until, almost despite myself, I was so enthralled that I could not stop but read on and on into the night ... That night, as I read about him for the first time, Jesus Christ lived for me. This was no remote, historical character of two thousand years ago, but someone who was vibrantly alive now, in the present. He became as real to me as the people I sat next to on the bus every day, with the difference that none of them was like this man. He was utterly unique, totally compelling. Every gesture, every word mattered, not just because they made sense of the mess our world seemed to be, but because they spoke directly to me.
>
> (Guinness, 1985, pp. 74–6)

Stories like this, of which there are many, bearing witness to the power of the Bible to change lives and put people directly in touch with God, not only suggest that the Bible is a locus of revelation but support the claim that the Bible itself *is* revelation.

Revelation is something which breaks into the hermeneutical circle of human self-interpretation and offers a definitive foundation for understanding both ourselves and the world, a truth which serves as the basis for the interpretation of all experience. This is precisely what is claimed, in the Calvinist tradition, for the Bible. In Calvin's view, although the knowledge of God is available to all in creation, that knowledge is suppressed because of human sinfulness. The external witness to God's power and love is insufficient. Before men and women can truly know God they must be 'enlightened through faith by an *internal* revelation from God'. It is the Bible which provides that necessary internal revelation. Scripture is God's providential remedy for the lack of true knowledge of him within human experience. The Bible acts as a 'pair of spectacles' through which we are enabled to interpret aright the signs of God in creation as well as the history of God in redemption (Calvin, 1536, I.i.6).

In the 1970s Michael Green served as editor of the *I Believe* series of basic introductions to areas of Christian doctrine from an evangelical standpoint. Chatting about the series at a meeting of the Church of England Doctrine Commission, he was challenged by Professor Geoffrey Lampe, who remarked, 'I hope you are including one on "I Believe in Revelation".' 'I am not sure that we were at that stage,' writes Green, 'but thereafter it seemed inevitable' (Morris, 1976, p. 7). In the resulting book Professor Leon Morris sets out the classic conservative position. 'Revelation' is to be understood as the process which led to the composition of the Old and New Testaments and ceased with the formation of the closed canon (1976, pp. 42–4). It is doubtful if this is what Professor Lampe had in mind. The problem with the position articulated by Calvin, Morris and many others is that it fails to take account of the task of biblical interpretation. It requires the truth of Scripture itself to be, in Calvin's words, 'as obvious as black and white' (1536, I.i.6–7). Calvin thus allows the Bible to interpret the world for us but does not allow a place for our interpretation of the Bible. Yet the scope for divergent and downright mischievous misinterpretation in a book like the Bible is enormous. From earliest times heretics of all colours have taken their stand on passages from the Bible, only to be accused of misinterpretation by the representatives of orthodoxy. Perhaps as a direct result of its approach to Scripture, the conservative tradition has fragmented into a multiplicity of sects each claiming absolute authority for its own style or principles of biblical interpretation.

The conservative position is buttressed by an appeal to the 'inward testimony of the Holy Spirit'. However, there are broadly two alternative ways in which this doctrine may be understood and the difference between them is crucial. For Calvin, the testimony of the Holy Spirit takes the form of an internal witness to the *authority* of Scripture. Conviction of the truth of

Scripture, he believes, rests not on human testimony, especially not on that of the Catholic Church, but on that of God himself. While unaided human reason may provide *evidences* of divine authorship, 'the certainty which faith requires' comes only from the Spirit (I.i.7). The logic of this position is that Christians must *first* accept the authority of the Bible on the basis of the Spirit's inward testimony and *then*, on the basis of the Bible's testimony, believe the claims of Jesus. Not only does this place the authority of the Bible above that of Jesus, but it leads to an anxious defence of the accuracy of Scripture in its smallest details. The fear is that if the Bible can be shown to be wrong in points of detail we are on a slippery slope which will lead to the undermining of its witness to the vital truths of salvation.

The alternative is to allow the Holy Spirit a role in the *interpretation* of Scripture. In this understanding the Holy Spirit supplies the 'inward revelation' necessary not only for true self-knowledge and the knowledge of God but for the interpretation of Scripture itself. The testimony of the Spirit is not to the authority of Scripture directly but to Christ. Acceptance of the authority of Scripture is an indirect result of the recognition in the pages of the Bible of the same Christ to whom the Spirit bears witness as the source of the believer's new identity and relationship with God. As Emil Brunner maintains, it is by a single act of revelation that there is created in the believer both faith in Christ and confidence in Scripture (1947, pp. 164–76). The principle of interpretation needed for the correct understanding of the Bible is the incarnate Jesus Christ; it is to Christ that the Spirit bears witness. Rather than believing in Christ on the authority of the Bible, we believe in the Bible on the authority of Christ.

Bible and Church

This means that we need to understand the Bible not on its own as the single authoritative and indeed miraculous witness to the truth but in the context of a broader work of God in revelation. We have already looked at the formation of the Old Testament, the incarnation of Jesus, outpouring of the Holy Spirit and the apostles' witness. It remains to look at the Bible in relation to the formation of the Church and the preservation and handing on of Christian tradition. Protestants in general have been uncomfortable with the observation that the Bible is the 'Church's book'. Yet it is undeniable that it was the Church that fixed the limits of the canon, recognizing in certain books an authority which it denied to others; undeniable also that certain books such as James and Revelation, like Esther in the Old Testament, hovered on the edge of canonical recognition for some time before finally being accepted.

Is the Church, in accepting the canonicity of a certain set of books and rejecting others, simply *conferring* authority on those particular books or is it *recognizing* in them an inherent authority which they possess by virtue of a certain relationship to Christ? This question was raised in its sharpest form by David Kelsey (1975, pp. 89–119). The idea of 'Christian Scripture', he claimed, is logically related to the idea of 'Christian Church'. A book like the Bible is only 'Scripture' because the Church has decided to accept its authority. Conversely, part of what it means to belong to the Church is to accept the authority of the Bible. Thus the authority of Scripture is not something inherently present in the books themselves. It is something conferred upon it by the Church as an outcome of the role of these particular books in its formation.

The strengths and weaknesses of Kelsey's analysis are those of the philosophy of Wittgenstein on which it is based. Wittgenstein believed that there was no way of establishing the relationship between words and any reality which underlies them. The 'meaning' of a word is the way it is used in language. Thus, for Wittgenstein, the real meaning of the word 'God' is not the person religious people suppose to exist. Its meaning is whatever is distinctive about religious language. The question of whether God exists or not in the conventional sense cannot be settled. Wittgenstein might have said it is not really important. God 'exists' because the word 'God' has a meaning for the people who use it. In its own terms then, Kelsey's analysis is accurate. 'Christian Church' and 'Christian Scripture' *do* imply one another. The Bible is the Scripture because that is the way the Church uses it and the Church is that group of people who accept the authority of the Bible. But this does not rule out the possibility that what the Church believes about the Bible may be true (in the sense we ordinarily understand 'truth'): that it may indeed possess some inherent authority as a result of divine revelation.

Inspiration

The idea that the Bible possesses an authority inherent in itself rather than simply conferred by the Christian community rests on a theory of inspiration explaining how Israel's tradition and later that of the early Church came to be formed in the correct direction in line with the truth about God. For the conservative evangelical, the idea of divine inspiration is taken to mean that the Bible was 'written' by God. What the Bible says, God says. In support of this, conservatives can point to the fact that Paul writes of the Scriptures as 'God-breathed' (2 Timothy 3:16), and that Jesus calls God the author of the early chapters of Genesis (Matthew 19:4–5). On the other hand what are we to make of the frequent mistakes and apparent contradictions in the biblical text and how are we to come to terms with the rather unsavoury portrayals of God in some places?

To answer these questions it is necessary to give careful attention to the meaning of the word 'inspiration'. William Abraham (1981, esp. pp. 58–69) points out that 'inspiration' has an ordinary, everyday use which does *not* mean the same as 'written'. The example he uses is the inspiration of a student by a particularly influential teacher. To say that a piece of the student's work was 'inspired' by that teacher does not mean that it was written by the teacher but that it was in some way a response by the student to that teacher. 'Inspiration' is not an action in itself; it is the effect of other actions, such as explaining or demonstrating. It may not even be deliberate on the part of the teacher. Moreover the fact of inspiration by no means rules out the possibility of error. The influence of the teacher will be limited by the capacity of the student both to understand what the teacher intended to convey and to respond to it. The student's work will reflect his own particular style of thought and expression, his cultural background and the limits of his understanding. In fact, there may well be a considerable degree of divergence between the work of different students, who may be more or less inspired and who may comprehend the teacher to a greater or lesser degree. But despite these differences we could expect a degree of unity between the students, reflecting the intention of the teacher.

When we apply a term like 'inspiration' to God we do so by analogy, making such changes as the nature and character of God require. But it is possible to see straight away that there are a number of close parallels between 'inspiration' understood in this way and the role envisaged for the Holy Spirit in the formation of Scripture. None of the biblical writers sets out to explain how they were inspired, though some describe dreams and waking visions. None of the prophets tell us what the experience of 'hearing' the 'word of the Lord' was. They and the later editors of their books were far more interested in the content than the experience. But from what we can glean, the idea of inspiration in and through actions like explaining and showing seems more likely than that of dictation to a passive recipient.

This model of inspiration moreover preserves a vital element in the Spirit's operation – freedom of response. The differences in style and emphasis between biblical writers can be understood as the result of the latitude allowed to human autonomy in their response to the experience of inspiration. It also allows for the progressive formation of a tradition based on successive experiences of revelation. As the written record of that developing tradition, the Bible preserves descriptions of events taken to be the result of divine intervention; of primary religious experience, such as that of the prophets; as well as successive layers of interpretation within the community. It is the record of a process of formation by means of successive experiences of revelation and subsequent interpretation and reinterpretation so that the tradition is progressively moulded, deepened and enriched in the resources it contains for understanding the nature of God and his relationship to mankind (Brown, 1994, pp. 123–30).

Bible and Tradition

The Bible itself contains tradition. The Old Testament records progressive stages in the development of several traditions, such as those of the prophets, the wisdom teachers and in the formation of the ritual and ethical laws. In the New Testament Paul draws attention to traditions he passed on both *from* Jesus himself and *about* him (1 Corinthians 11:2, 25; 15:3). Elsewhere in his letters he includes without acknowledgement passages which there is good reason to believe were based on traditional formulations (Romans 1:2–4; Philippians 2:6–11). For the gospels, the achievement of the form critics was to show how each is made up of skilfully edited units of tradition. Tradition is, at its heart, a relationship between giver and receiver, often between one generation and the next, a relationship in which each successive generation is formed by the inheritance of the past. In the words of Colin Gunton, it is 'a process of giving and receiving in which the very shape of our being is at stake' (1995, p. 89).

Moreover, as in science, knowledge progresses when the tradition is thoroughly digested and becomes the foundation for further progress. As Gunton again remarks, 'Most secure and rational forms of progress and innovation are to be found where there is fundamental trust in the tradition' (1995, p. 90). In the case of Christian tradition there is at its heart a record of certain unrepeatable events, the life, death and resurrection of Jesus. These can only be fully understood when read against the background of the Old Testament, which is preparatory for the revelation of God in Christ. Yet the Old Testament can itself only be fully understood when read in the light of what is revealed in Jesus. The illumination of this particular hermeneutical circle is just one part of ongoing Christian tradition. In the generation following the resurrection the apostles gave their testimony to Jesus and the traditions of the earliest Church came into being. The early Church had before it the example of the Jews, who, in fixing the canon of the Hebrew Bible, had attempted to distinguish between traditions which genuinely reflected the acts and the mind of God and those with a large admixture of human, in particular Greek, philosophy. It is apparent from works such as the apocryphal gospels as well as the disputes of Paul with his opponents that the formation of the canon of the New Testament was a sifting process by which genuine apostolic traditions were distinguished from an accumulation of fantasy, myth and error. Thus the New Testament came to be acknowledged as the centre of Christian tradition and the touchstone by which the authenticity of later developments was to be judged.

Just as the Bible arose from the milieu of a developing tradition, so that tradition, now centred on the Bible, continues to develop. As David Brown insists, a sharp contrast between tradition and revelation is unsustainable. 'Scripture', he maintains, 'has only ever had authority in the church as a moving stream, not as a changeless deposit' (1999, p. 127). The Holy Spirit continues to guide the developing tradition, although, since a characteristic of his involvement with mankind is the preservation of human freedom, his role is not a guarantee against error. Brown sees God 'interacting' with the recipients of his revelation so that the way people read the Bible 'is a function not just of the divine will or of historical circumstances but of what God can get the individual to see on the basis of his reflection both upon the context and upon the biblical text' (1994, p. 140). Ideally Christians need to know how to avoid error in the interpretation of the Bible and use it for its correct purpose, which is the formation of the 'new self' based on the image of Christ (Colossians 3:10, 16; 2 Timothy 3:16–17). Thus at the heart of tradition lies the author of Scripture, namely the Holy Spirit. His task is to witness to Jesus (John 14:26; 16:14). His is the 'internal witness' enabling Jesus's disciples to understand the Scripture. And just as the Spirit enables us to understand the Bible, the Spirit enables the Church to discern in developing tradition what is compatible with biblical revelation and what is contrary to it. The Spirit points not *to* Scripture but *through* it to Jesus.

Conclusion

Divine Communication

The term 'revelation' may be used to describe an action of God as communicator, an experience of human beings as the receivers of communication and an authoritative content as the information communicated. One of the problems of theology is its variety of models of communicator, receiver and content. A coherent account of revelation as divine communication requires a harmonious account of all three terms. On the side of divine action, revelation does not consist of just one thing; God accomplishes revelation through many acts including creation, the incarnation, death and resurrection of Jesus and the work of the Holy Spirit and promises a final revelation still to come at the parousia (Abraham, 1997, p. 206). On the side of the receiver, too, revelation is more than one thing; learning includes a wide variety of psychological and social elements and both learning and revelation spring out of and express the mystery of personhood. 'The Christian claim about revelation in Christ has to be understood, then, as part of a comprehensive vision of ourselves and our predicament which shapes the very form and character of that revelation' (Abraham, 1997, pp. 212–13).

The method I have adopted has been to begin with an examination of the capacity of human beings as the potential receivers of revelation. The resulting model of human beings as learners forms the background against which I have drawn on the resources of theology to suggest an account of God as communicator and the content of his communication, which answers to both human need and constitution. My conclusion is that the content of revelation is to be understood as a definitive 'image of humanity'. A tacit 'image of humanity' is expressed in every particular culture or set of social institutions, provides the explicit or unexpressed foundation of every significant paradigm in the natural or human sciences and lies behind the hermeneutical principles of historical or literary interpretation. Behind the great questions of science, literature, history or philosophy lies a pre-reflective understanding of the nature of mankind irreducible to explicit formulation. The most sophisticated philosophical system fails to give adequate expression to the elusive quality 'humanity'. Instead the philosopher is obliged to create 'myths' in order to express the deepest levels of meaning in human life. The content of revelation may be understood precisely as the information required to set human speculation in a single unified framework.

The anthropological question at the heart of culture is paralleled by the role of the elusive personal subject as the source of cognitive and affective coherence. The attempt to elucidate the pre-reflective image of humanity which lies behind a given culture or society is paralleled by the quest for secure personal identity. It is at this level, the deepest level of human personality, that revelation is appropriated. In theological terms this is the level of spirit, that element of human being which governs both the essential vitality of the person and the possibility of our relating to God. Revelation consists of the gift of personal identity, but since it is given at the level of the personal subject, revelation is given not as explicit but as tacit knowledge. The content of revelation, the Christian believer's new identity with Jesus Christ as its exemplar, is not known directly but must be gradually appropriated in the course of subsequent learning until it becomes the core of a person's self-image.

Before the content of revelation can be grasped explicitly in such a way as to inform theology, a process of interpretation is required in which previously incomplete or erroneous images of humanity, those of contemporary philosophy and culture, provide the only categories initially available for its comprehension. The appropriation of revelation thus involves the twin processes characteristic of learning, assimilation and accommodation. The witness of Scripture to the works of God, especially in Jesus, and the experience of rebirth in the Holy Spirit may at first be only partially or even incorrectly understood, depending as this process does on the previous experience of the individual believer or the cultural inheritance of the theologian. But the assimilation of God's self-communication in revelation to the categories of philosophy and culture may lead to the complementary process of accommodation by which those categories are themselves transformed by the implications of revelation. The appropriation of revelation is thus a progressive process, not immune from the possibility of error, through which the individual, the community of faith and, conceivably, the culture is gradually formed in its image of humanity and understanding of God.

As in the normal processes of learning, the learning characteristic of revelation expresses the autonomy proper to human beings in their relationship with God. Human autonomy is not abolished or eclipsed in the reception of revelation, but upheld and established. The power of agency characteristic of human beings is expressed by the possession of spirit. Since the Lord breathed into the first man the 'breath of life', spirit sums up the essence of humanity both in its distinction from nature and in the unique relationship of human beings with their Creator. The spirit is the centre of both agency and self-knowledge, the locus of that elusive 'I' which is the seat of true identity. The spirit is also that element of human personality uniquely open to the influence of God by the Holy Spirit. It is through the agency of the Holy Spirit that revelation is made available at that deep level of personality where the Spirit meets, touches or 'impinges' on the human spirit.

The gift of the Holy Spirit is an integral part of the action of God for the salvation of the world. The resulting gift of revelation must be seen as an element of salvation and inseparable from it. Revelation is to lead to discipleship and discipleship to sanctification, the realization of revelation in concrete form in the life of the individual believer and the Church as a whole.

To sum up, the actions of God in revelation are many and various and include the incarnation, death and resurrection of Jesus Christ, the activity of inspiration which brought the Scriptures into being and set in motion a tradition of interpretation and the gift of the Holy Spirit to Christian believers. The content of revelation is the person of Jesus Christ, witnessed to in the Bible and given as new identity through the indwelling Spirit. The experience of revelation is the receiving of the Holy Spirit, both initially and continually, and the way in which the new identity he gives is worked out in all the ways by which Christian formation takes place.

Above or Within?

Within practical theology the study of discipleship is the sphere of Christian education. The model of revelation I have presented here is intended to address one of the key questions for Christian education, the involvement of God himself in the Christian learning process (Astley, Francis and Crowder, 1996, pp. xiv–xv; Astley, 2000, pp. 15–16). Are we justified in seeing Christian education as a proper sphere of divine intervention; and if so, what is the nature of God's intervention? Does the Holy Spirit undermine or bypass the natural processes of human learning, leaving the outcome of human effort dependent on 'a personal decision that rests in the mystery of God' (Miller, 1980, p. 162)? Or does the Spirit respect and work with the natural processes of learning, so that 'religion is learned according to the way the learner learns' (Lee, 1973, p. 58)?

The answer I have consistently aimed at throughout the course of the argument is that the natural processes of human learning are precisely those through which revelation is received. The subjective experience of revelation is learning about and being formed by our knowledge of God, just as we learn about and are formed by our knowledge of other people and the world in general. It is a learning that takes place at every level of personality, open to the work of the Holy Spirit but using at every point our natural learning capacities. The autonomy through which individual men and women shape and form their world is preserved and upheld by the action of the Spirit. The motivating and forming effect of the search for secure identity remains a vital factor in stimulating and directing learning. The influence of the community from which schemata of understanding are taken over and in which attitudes are formed is just as great in the sphere of revelation as in other learning. The schemata of the understanding – cognitive and affective, knowledge of facts, opinions, values and attitudes – are precisely those which are formed by revelation in the power of the Spirit. Revelation is a learning process, which uses all the natural processes of human learning, but in which the subject is God himself through Jesus Christ and in which the dynamism of the Holy Spirit is added to the natural agency of the human individual.

A second and related concern is whether the supposed supernatural action of God by means of the Holy Spirit, arresting and redirecting the learning process, constitutes an alien intervention in the course of human life for which no theological basis of understanding exists. Here it is important to remember the doctrine of creation through which men and women are constituted in two types of relationship with God. There is a relationship of dependence on God as the Creator, through whom all things exist and in whom 'we live and move and have our being' (Acts 17:28). There is also a relationship of independence expressed in human autonomy through which we obey the command to shape and subdue the world. As a result of these two relationships all human beings exist in a relatedness to God characterized not simply by dependence but by free personal response, even where that response takes the form of hostility or estrangement. It is within the parameters of this relatedness that the work of the Holy Spirit takes place.

The relationship between the Holy Spirit and human spirit which makes revelation possible is the key to the link between nature and grace, the natural and the supernatural. There is an enormous difference between a view of the universe as contingent and dependent for its operation on the continual upholding of a divine Creator and one in which nature is governed only by its own inherent lawfulness. From the perspective of the latter view the actions of God in redemption and revelation are alien intrusions redirecting the course of a self-sufficient system. From the point of view of a doctrine of creation, however, not only does the universe exist for a particular purpose but its natural lawfulness is both a reflection of and a means to the achievement of that purpose. The plausibility of divine 'intervention' can be maintained if the intervention in question can be shown to uphold that lawfulness and achieve that purpose. The whole aim of this book has been to show that the mode of divine revelation is one that maintains the lawfulness of the created universe, rightly interpreted to include a doctrine of human nature in which men and women are constituted by God as agents in relationship. Further, the purpose of God in revelation to re-establish the sovereignty of human beings over the created world and the possibility of a free and loving relationship with himself and one another is precisely the purpose of God for the whole creation. The sonship which belongs to Jesus by right is now available to all by adoption. Revelation is an integral part of the whole movement of God to the world in the incarnation of Jesus Christ and the gift of the Holy Spirit. Through it he calls out a people for his own to enjoy his love and to be formed into the image of his Son (Abraham, 1997, pp. 205–7).

Theology or Social Science?

The need to relate disciplines to one another has been a major feature of my argument. What I have sought to demonstrate is that every field of study is conceptually linked to every other. The point at which social science meets theology is anthropology, the study of humanity. The fundamental models of the social sciences consist of certain 'images of humanity'. Theology criticizes these images and brings its own into the conversation, contending that these images offer potentially greater explanatory power over a wider range of issues than do those of social science. But theology does not deny the applicability of the images of social science, nor should theologians resist the demand that their own images be tested by empirical observation. Thus the decision to view human beings as agents with purposes best understood by means of teleological explanation has both an empirical and a theoretical foundation. I have argued that it makes more sense of the role of schemata in memory, recognition and perception as well as the phenomenon of selective attention. I have argued, with philosophers like Hubert Dreyfus (1992) and John Searle (1980), that there is more in what it means to be human than can be reduced to computation. Finally, I have tried to show

how the autonomy of humanity coheres with a theological understanding of human beings as creatures 'in the image of God'. In the task of applying theological statements about humankind to experience, of selecting and appraising the evidence by which such statements are to be validated, theology and social science must go hand in hand.

If theology and social science meet in dialogue over their respective images of human life, it is with respect to the image of the learner that the theological and social science approaches on Christian education come together. While Miller, for example, sees the learner from the theological point of view as a 'person-in-relation-to-God', Lee sees the learner as learner as the relevant anthropology. Lee's position requires more than empirical justification if it is to become operative in Christian education. It requires a theological justification for the use of the best techniques of teaching and learning. This, in fact, is what Lee implicitly provides. His justification for it rests not merely on empirical verification of the most effective approach to teaching and learning, but on a certain theological understanding of the teaching–learning situation. The statement that religion is learned naturally, the way the learner learns, is dependent on the belief that natural ways of learning are not supernaturally overridden. The 'social science approach' requires for its justification a theology of immanence.

In this respect it is clearly a more adequate theological statement than much of what lies behind the theological approach. It includes a well-developed conception of God's work in and through the conditions of creation. There is a close relation between the social science criticism of the appeal to the Holy Spirit as 'primary proximate cause' in the process of Christian learning and the protest of one of the father-figures of Christian education in the United States, Horace Bushnell, against the supernaturalism of nineteenth-century revivalism which 'allowed no place for the organic powers God has consituted as vehicles of grace' (Bushnell, 1861, p. 187). A theology that ignores creation and *begins* with an image of people as sinners in need of grace rather than as created human beings sharing a common human nature is clearly inadequate not simply for Christian education but as theology.

Once it is realized that social science is in dialogue with theology, the way is open for a genuine practical theology, incorporating the methods of social science into an overall practical perspective. The images of human life thrown up by theology become the starting point for empirical research and enter dialogue with the interpretations of secular social scientists. In this book I hope I have succeeded to some extent in showing the potential of that conversation. The nature of human self-understanding is such that there can be no fixed point of certainty from which theorizing can begin. Sara Little anticipates the move towards the 'practical theology' of today when she writes that the relationship between theology and education 'is possible only when theology and education are both viewed as dynamic, not static, processes' (1976, p. 38). Similarly although Wyckhoff writes from within the theological approach when he sees Christian education as 'an enquiry into teaching and learning as modes and means of response to revelation' (1967, p. 173), he does not thereby dismiss the various contributory disciplines in the field of education as irrelevant. He recognizes the interdisciplinary nature not only of education but Christian education also. 'Religious education', he writes, 'belongs in the context of a total education' (1967, p. 177). Moreover his proposal for a discipline of Christian education involves the practitioner becoming conversant with a number of fields each with its own sphere of relevance to the overall task. Within a fully interdisciplinary practical theology, Christian education needs a thorough understanding of the relationship between the two disciplines in order to draw on the insights of both.

Good Theory and Good Teaching

Traditional transmissive strategies in Christian education tend to draw their rationale from a view of revelation as an authoritative deposit of truth, usually in propositional form. The Protestant evangelical version of this approach identifies Scripture, if not as revelation *per se*, at least as the primary repository of the saving truth to be handed on to each succeeding generation. The Roman Catholic version of the same model gives correspondingly more weight to tradition and the Church's teaching authority. This view of revelation is appealed to explicitly or implicitly to justify the emphasis on preaching and traditional content-based teaching methods.

Theological liberals are more likely to be found espousing an alternative approach using methods centred on the learner's experience. From the point of view of this approach, the Christian story is much less likely to be seen as a 'metanarrative' capable of providing a total world outlook. The aim of Christian education within this tradition is more likely to be to provide the 'paintbox' rather than the full picture, the resources needed to recreate a coherent Christian faith for the current situation rather than the fully digested wisdom of previous generations (Astley, 1992, p. 42).

Which approach to Christian education receives the greatest justification from the theory of revelation and learning I have presented here? The answer is paradoxically 'both' and 'neither'. In some respects my theory of revelation is an apologetic for a traditional Christianity. I have tried to show that the 'image of humanity' required by the human learning process is supplied by the traditional understanding of Jesus Christ in his relationship both to God and humankind. Christianity may properly be understood as a total and unifying perspective capable of making sense of the world. The revelation we have in the incarnation, death and resurrection of Jesus supplies a truth capable of anchoring human speculation and supplying definitive human identity. Moreover the Bible as interpreted by the indwelling Holy Spirit provides the means by which we receive that perspective.

However, I have also tried to show that revelation is appropriated through the natural processes of human learning. In very few circumstances is straightforward authoritative transmission an effective strategy for teaching and learning. As Leon McKenzie observes, 'In too many places, teaching is apprised as authoritative telling; learning is equated as listening and accepting. The faith-process becomes the receiving of a cultural hand-me-down and not the wrestling with Jacob's angel that leads to authentic commitment' (1982, p. 11). Effective learning requires every stage of the learning cycle: experience, reflection, conceptualization and action. However authoritative the teacher may perceive the content of the faith to be, religious learners need to be encouraged to take part in the 'wrestling' McKenzie speaks of and provided with the tools for it to take place. Moreover the natural order of learning is not that of the textbook; it is dictated by 'the way the learner learns', which in turn is influenced by the learner's prior experience and their motivations for learning.

'Both' the liberal and the traditional approaches to Christian education are correct then to an extent; and yet 'neither' is correct, because neither has the essential key which has been central to my theory of learning and revelation. This is that revelation is given as *tacit* rather than explicit knowledge; it must therefore be *taught* as tacit knowledge. The central truth, which most Christians spend the whole of their Christian lives learning and relearning, consists of our identity in Jesus Christ. This is given to us deep down at the level of 'spirit', the elusive 'I' of personal identity. Christian learning takes place when this identity is applied in experience. The Bible, the key authoritative source of explicit knowledge of Jesus and this new identity, is not structured for us as a textbook but as a resource. It is arguable that what the new convert requires is a basic introduction to the essential truths of Christian faith authoritatively passed on and equally arguable that the gospels – at least the Synoptic Gospels – are intended precisely as teaching manuals for the instruction of new disciples. Yet even the essential truths of Christian faith must be individually grasped or 'passionately embraced' if they are to become operative in the way a person actually lives his life and relates to the world of experience (Astley, 2002, pp. 25–34).

As Bonhoeffer writes (1965, pp. 80–88), Christian life consists not so much in the 'imitation' of Christ but in 'conformation' to the form of Jesus Christ, a being drawn into his image. Such conformation takes place as the identity of Christ given to us through the Spirit and the cognitive and attitudinal perspectives based on that identity become increasingly operative in our lives. 'Whatever is the given with which theology works, it must be "grist to the mill" of our lives. We discover what theology is as it thus emerges in the midst of our experience' (Orr, 2000, p. 78). A man or woman may become extremely knowledgeable in the facts and values of Christian faith but fail to live them out. He may even be a pillar of the church on Sundays or in mid-week activities but fail to make any impact on his family or working environment or may even bring the name of Christ into disrepute by his failure to live out the truths he proclaims. Christian growth does not consist of learning to look *at* the truths of Christian faith so as to reproduce them in sermons, Bible study groups and conversations with Christian friends but in learning to look at the world *through the perspective* of those truths so that they become a part of the way we think about the world and respond to it. Christian faith thus becomes a *habitus* or wisdom for living (Farley, 1983, pp. 35–7) consisting of tacit rather than explicit knowledge.

The task of Christian education is thus to teach Christian faith, or rather to enable people to learn Christian faith, *as tacit rather than explicit knowledge*. When Thomas Kühn wanted to know what enabled his students to learn most effectively, he discovered that it was the ability to see the new information they were learning as *like* an already familiar, previously understood situation. Their *effective* as opposed to their *theoretical* knowledge grew not explicitly but tacitly through the acquisition of new exemplars. In the words of Michael Polanyi, 'While tacit knowledge can be possessed by itself, explicit knowledge must rely on being tacitly understood or applied' (1966b, p. 7). Tacit knowledge includes the skill of being able to apply existing knowledge to interpret new situations, the capacity of 'judgement' which Immanuel Kant remarked was the key to applying knowledge of universals to the concrete instance (1787, p. 178). The aim of Christian education must be to enable Christian disciples to apply their theology – their experience and understanding of God – to their everyday lives, to allow theology to become 'grist to the mill' of their lives. Their new Christian identity given by the Holy Spirit must provide the spectacles through which they habitually interpret the world.

Michael Williams, who spent over ten years as Director of the Manchester-based Northern Ordination Course, once observed,

> One of the most frustrating things in ordination training is seeing people pass through a two or three year programme of studies where they enjoy the debate, relish new ideas, learn new skills, but after six months into ordained ministry they revert to the same set of beliefs and ministerial practices that they had on day one of the course.
>
> (1996, p. 22)

This experience is not uncommon and its principal cause is the lack of effective teaching and learning in theological training. As a former teacher, training at theological college for the Anglican ministry and seeking to raise the profile of Christian education as a resource for both staff and students, my impression was that the principal obstacle to progress was simply incomprehension. Like most people without educational training, the staff taught as they themselves had been taught – by the transmission of information. Straightforward telling however lacks the power to enable students to learn their faith as tacit knowledge. In ministerial training, as in every context of Christian education, what is required is the skill to enable Christian disciples to interpret their lives and experiences through the spectacles of their faith; in other words, the skills of good teaching (Heywood, 1997, p. 50; Orr, 2000, p. 87).

An approach to Christian education based on *teaching skill* is both more effective educationally and better theologically than either the traditional transmissive or liberal experiential approach. A Christian education method based on authoritative telling is clearly deficient but so too is an approach that acknowledges neither the unique authority of Christian revelation nor the supernatural source of the power of Christian transformation. A well-informed confidence in the content and power of Christian revelation; a well-developed Christian *habitus*; a commitment to conformation and a life in the process of transformation – these are some of the essential requirements for those who would seek to teach others. But in addition, teaching skill is based on a thorough appreciation of 'how the learner learns', a feel for the teaching–learning situation that goes beyond the learning of the textbook. It involves imaginative ways of applying the learning cycle to a given subject or situation. It involves an eye for the learner's preferred *styles* of learning and skill in adapting the learning *cycle* to make use of these. It includes a receptivity to the world of the learners; a mind and heart tuned to the possibility of drawing parable and example from experience. The good teacher knows how to work *towards* a systematic understanding rather than from it. She designs the curriculum to lead gradually from easier concepts to more difficult ones. She understands the learning that can take place through the hidden values of the curriculum and pays attention to these. She stays in touch with and relates all new learning to the learners' existing experience and sets tasks which require the learners to apply what they are learning to familiar situations. Teaching skill is what enables the learner not only to appropriate the content of a given lesson or to reflect on a given experience but to respond in such a way as to make these effective in her life. It is an informed 'walking alongside' the learner in the Christian way. My passionate hope is that as the Church faces the challenge of a new century, teaching skill will be given the recognition it deserves as an essential resource in equipping Christian people for the discipleship to which Jesus calls them.

Discipleship

What then will be the characteristics of a Christian education based on the model of revelation and learning I have described. A full answer to this question requires a book in itself. All that can be given here is the briefest possible account of its characteristics, each of which requires extensive exploration and qualification.

It will first of all be *Trinitarian*. It will recognize the Spirit as the dynamic of the new life, the One through whom God's gift of new identity is given. It is the Spirit who supplies the power to renew the 'new self ... in knowledge according to the image of its creator' (Colossians 3:10). The transformation brought about by the 'renewal of the mind' (Romans 12:2) can be accomplished only in his power not by human effort.

The gift of the Spirit makes real in human experience our adoption as God's children (Galatians 4:5–6) and enables every Christian to acknowledge God as Father (Romans 8:15–16). At the heart of Jesus's own basic teaching for disciples, given in the Sermon on the Mount, is the Fatherhood of God. His exhortations to trust God for food and clothing and the fundamentals of life point to the possibility of a trust in God capable of bringing healing and restoration in the area of 'basic trust'. Where the degree of basic trust established in the first stage of psycho-social development is imperfect or even lacking altogether, the Spirit supplies a new security and possibility of self-esteem.

Finally Jesus himself is the exemplar of the new Christian identity. He is the 'proper man', 'man as God from the beginning designed man to be' (Caird, 1976, p. 172). To the disciple he is 'Rabboni', teacher and lord, the title given him by Bartimaeus, the blind man who became his follower on the road leading to the cross (Mark 10:51–2), and Mary Magdalene, the first witness to his resurrection (John 20:16). The goal of discipleship is to become like Jesus in his outlook, values and attitudes, to 'know him' in 'the power of his resurrection' and the 'fellowship of his sufferings' (Philippians 3:10), to 'take up the cross' and 'follow him' (Mark 8:34). Jesus is the 'pioneer and perfecter' (Hebrews 12:2) of the life of discipleship.

The life of discipleship will secondarily be *informed by the Bible* as witness to Jesus and the character of God. For Christian teachers throughout the centuries the Bible has been so integral to Christian learning and lifestyle that it has been seen as the agent of change in itself. For St John Chrysostom, for example, Scripture frees from vainglory, cures and consoles (Congar, 1966, p. 380). To the present day, readers of the Bible testify to the same effects:

> The Bible is ... no ordinary book. It reaches out and grabs me by the scruff of the neck. Through it, God loves me, tells me off and trips me up. The Bible promises me things, opens my eyes to the suffering of the world and kicks me into action. It makes me a better person, a better husband, a better father. It rummages through my pockets, tells me to 'phone my Mum, and calls me to work for justice.
>
> (Mayfield, 1990, p. 50)

The Bible has these effects because through it the Spirit is showing us our God-given identity, whose exemplar is Jesus. Through the Bible this identity, which is an item of tacit knowledge, becomes clear as the Spirit, the inspirer and interpreter of Scripture, enables us to understand what we read. Without the Bible to give it shape, the experience of the Spirit might easily end up in unguided or misguided enthusiasm.

Discipleship takes place in *community*. The 'story' of the Bible is the story of a community, chosen by God, taught, blessed, protected and disciplined by him, recipients of numerous promises finally fulfilled in the coming of Jesus. As the earliest Church was heir to the Old Testament community, so the present-day community of faith is to be formed by the biblical 'story' in its understanding of and response to God. The Church is a reference group, to which people are attracted (or repelled) both by the people who belong and the perspective they share in common. An important element of Christian learning is socialization into the ways of thinking and acting reflected in the life of the local church.

John H. Westerhoff III is a proponent of the 'faith community' approach to Christian education, in which the principal dynamic of Christian formation is the life of the community. The learner is perceived as 'a communal being, whose identity and growth can only be understood in terms of life in a community that shares a common memory, vision, authority, rituals and family-like life together' (Westerhoff, 1983, p. 50). Christianity is 'caught' rather than 'taught'. The 'hidden curriculum' of church life, made up of shared attitudes and ways of behaving, is likely to be more powerful than what is explicitly taught from the pulpit or in other formal contexts of Christian learning. The beliefs of the community about such things as worship, mission, the place of children and what it means to be a Christian disciple will be reflected in the patterns of interaction that make up the Church's life. The task of the educator is to ensure that the Church remains faithful to the norms and inheritance of Christian faith (Heywood, 1988).

As well as socialization, another dimension of Christian learning is resocialization. Alongside the learning of new attitudes, values and ways is an element of unlearning. The Christian disciple brings to the life of faith a certain amount of 'baggage' – attitudes formed through experiences which contradict the truths of faith and create sometimes formidable barriers to their acceptance. It is not easy to trust in the love of God as Father if one's own father was absent, neglectful, demanding, cruel or otherwise a poor model of what fatherhood ought to be. It is not easy to accept the love of fellow Christians if one's capacity for relationships has been damaged by past experience or to believe oneself loved unconditionally if one has grown up with low self-esteem. The learning characteristic of discipleship includes an element of *healing*, especially of the hurts of past memories, for which the concrete love and acceptance of the community of faith is a pre-requisite.

Another element is the discovery of *vocation*. God's gift of new identity is not an 'identikit'. Although based on the exemplar of Jesus, every believer is created with their own unique personality and receives from God through the Spirit their own particular calling, gifts and passions. An important aspect of the journey of discipleship is the discovery of God-given vocation (see O'Connor, 1968; Dewar, 1988). Finally the field in which the life of discipleship is lived is not confined to the community of faith. Discipleship is lived out *in the world*. For most Christians their God-given vocation will be to some task in the everyday world: teacher, shopkeeper, homemaker. Christian education needs to be directed towards helping every disciple to be effective and fulfilled as they live the Christ-like life in the times and places in which they find themselves. The most effective agent of revelation to the wider community is the person whose own life is in the process of being formed by it, being transformed into the image of the Lord 'from one degree of glory to another' (2 Corinthians 3:18).

Bibliography

Abelson, R. P. (1981), 'The psychological status of the script concept', *American Psychologist*, **36**, 715–29.

Abraham, W. J. (1981), *The Divine Inspiration of Holy Scripture*, London: Oxford University Press.

Abraham, W. J. (1982), *Divine Revelation*, London: Oxford University Press.

Abraham, W. J. (1997), 'Revelation reaffirmed', in Avis, Paul (ed.), *Divine Revelation*, London: Darton, Longman & Todd, pp. 201–15.

Allport, G. (1935), 'Attitudes', in Murchison, C. (ed.), *Handbook of Social Psychology,* Worcester, Mass: Clark University Press, pp. 798–844.

Anderson, J. R. (1995), *Cognitive Psychology and its Implications*, 4th edn, New York: W. H. Freeman & Co.

Aronson, E. (1999), 'Dissonance, hypocrisy and the self-concept', in Harmon-Jones, E. and Mills, J. (eds), *Cognitive Dissonance: Progress on a Pivotal Theory in Social Psychology*, Washington, DC: American Psychological Association, pp. 103–26.

Aronson, J., Cohen, G. and Nail, P. R. (1999), 'Self-affirmation theory: an update and appraisal', in Harmon-Jones, E. and Mills, J. (eds), *Cognitive Dissonance: Progress on a Pivotal Theory in Social Psychology*, Washington, DC: American Psychological Association, pp. 127–47.

Astley, J. (1980), 'Revelation revisited', *Theology*, **83** (695), 339–46.

Astley, J. (1987), 'On learning religion: some theological issues in Christian education', *Modern Churchman*, **29** (2), 26–34.

Astley, J. (1992), 'Tradition and experience: Conservative and Liberal models for Christian education', in Astley, J. and Day, D. (eds), *The Contours of Christian Education*, Great Wakering, Essex: MacCrimmons, pp. 41–53.

Astley, J. (1994), *The Philosophy of Christian Religious Education*, Birmingham, Ala: Religious Education Press.

Astley, J. (2000), 'Aims and approaches in Christian education', in Astley (ed.), *Learning in the Way: Research and Reflection on Adult Christian Education*, Leominster: Gracewing, pp. 1–32.

Astley, J. (2002), *Ordinary Theology*, Aldershot: Ashgate.

Astley, J., Francis, L. J. and Crowder, C. (eds) (1996), *Theological Perspectives on Christian Formation*, Leominster: Gracewing.

Atkinson, R. F. (1978), *Knowledge and Explanation in History*, Ithaca, NY: Cornell University Press.

Austin, J. L. (1946), 'Other minds', *Proceedings of the Aristotelian Society Supplement XX, 1946,* 148–87.

Austin, J. L. (1962), *Sense and Sensibilia*, London: Oxford University Press.

Ayer, A. J. (1940), *The Foundations of Empirical Knowledge*, London: Macmillan.

Ayer, A. J. (1956), *The Problem of Knowledge*, Harmondsworth: Penguin.

Ayer, A. J. (1963), *The Concept of a Person and Other Essays*, London: Macmillan.

Baddeley, A. D. (1999), *Essentials of Human Memory*, Hove: Psychology Press.

Baillie, J. and Martin, H. (eds) (1937), *Revelation,* London: Faber & Faber.

Baillie, J. (1939), *Our Knowledge of God*, London: Oxford University Press.

Baillie, J. (1956), *The Idea of Revelation in Recent Thought*, New York: Columbia University Press.

Ballard, P. and Pritchard, J. (1996), *Practical Theology in Action: Christian Thinking in the Service of the Church and Society*, London: SPCK.

Bandura, A. (1974), 'Behaviour theory and the models of man', *American Psychologist*, **29**, 859–69.

Bannister, D. (1966), 'Psychology as an exercise in paradox', *Bulletin of the British Psychological Society*, **19**, 21–6.

Barber P. J. and Legge, D. (1976), *Perception and Information*, London: Methuen.

Barbour, I. (1966), *Issues in Science and Religion*, London: SCM Press.

Barbour, I. (1974), *Myths, Models and Paradigms*, London: SCM Press.

Barth, K. (1958), *Church Dogmatics III/1,* Edinburgh: T. and T. Clark.

Barth, K. (1960), *Church Dogmatics III/2*, Edinburgh: T. and T. Clark.

Bartlett, F. C. (1932), *Remembering*, Cambridge: Cambridge University Press.

Bauckham, R. (1997), 'Jesus the revelation of God', in Avis, P. (ed.), *Divine Revelation*, London: Darton, Longman & Todd, pp. 174–200.

Baumohl, A. (1984), *Making Adult Disciples*, London: Scripture Union.

Benjafield, J. G. (1997), *Cognition*, 2nd edn, Upper Saddle River, N.J: Prentice-Hall.

Berger, P. and Luckmann, T. (1966), *The Social Construction of Reality*, Harmondsworth: Penguin.

Bly, B. M. and Rumelhart, D. E. (eds) (1999), *Cognitive Science*, New York: Academic Press.

Boden, M. A. (1970), 'Intentionality and physical systems', *Philosophy of Science*, **37**, 200–213.

Boden, M. A. (1979), 'The computational metaphor in psychology', in Bolton, N. (ed.), *Philosophical Problems in Psychology*, London: Methuen.

Bonhoeffer, D. (1965), *Ethics*, trans. N. H. Smith, New York: Macmillan.

Bonhoeffer, D. (1978), *Christology*, trans. E. Robertson, Glasgow: Fontana.

Braine, M. D. S. (1978), 'On the relation between the natural logic of reasoning and standard logic', *Psychological Review*, **85**, 1–21.

Braithwaite, R. B. (1971), 'An empiricist's view of the nature of religious belief', in Mitchell, B. (ed.), *The Philosophy of Religion*, London: Oxford University Press, pp. 72–91.

Brim, O. G. Jr and Wheeler, S. (1966), *Socialisation after Childhood*, New York: John Wiley & Sons.

Brim, O. G. Jr (1968), 'Socialisation through the life cycle', in Gordon, C. and Gergen, K. J. (eds), *The Self in Social Interaction,* New York: John Wiley & Sons, pp. 227–40.

British Council of Churches (1976), *The Child in the Church*, London: BCC.

Brown, D, (1985), *The Divine Trinity*, London: Duckworth.

Brown, D. (1994), 'Did revelation cease?', in Padgett, A. G. (ed.), *Reason and Religion: Essays in Honour of Richard Swinburne*, Oxford: Clarendon Press, pp. 121–41.

Brown, D. (1999), *Tradition and Imagination*, London: Oxford University Press.

Brown, D. (2000), *Discipleship and Imagination*, London: Oxford University Press.

Brown, S. (ed.) (1974), *Philosophy of Psychology*, London: Macmillan.

Browning, D. S. (1991), *A Fundamental Practical Theology*, Minneapolis: Fortress Press.

Bruner, J. S. and Postman, L. (1949), 'On the perception of incongruity: a paradigm', *Journal of Personality*, **18**, 206–23; also in Anglin, J. M. (ed.), *Beyond the Information Given,* London: George Allen & Unwin, 1974, pp. 68–83.

Bruner, J. S. (1951), 'Personality dynamics and the process of perceiving', in Blake, R. R. and Ramsey, G. V. (eds), *Perception: An Approach to Personality,* New York: Ronald Press Co., pp. 121–47; also in Anglin, J. M. (ed.), *Beyond the Information Given,* London: George Allen & Unwin, 1974, pp. 89–113.

Bruner, J. S. (1962), *On Knowing: Essays for the Left Hand*, Cambridge, Mass: Harvard University Press.

Bruner, J. S. (1974), *Beyond the Information Given*, ed. J. M. Anglin, London: George Allen & Unwin.

Bruner, J. S. (1975), 'The ontogenesis of speech acts', *Journal of Child Language*, **2**, 1–19.

Bruner, J. S. (1983), *In Search of Mind: Essays in Autobiography*, New York: Harper & Row.

Bruning, R. H., Shraw, G. J. and Ronning, R. R. (1995), *Cognitive Psychology and Instruction*, Englewood Cliffs, NJ: Prentice-Hall.

Brunner, E. (1939), *Man in Revolt: A Christian Anthropology*, trans. O. Wyon, London: Lutterworth Press.

Brunner, E. (1947), *Revelation and Reason*, trans. O. Wyon, London: Lutterworth Press.

Bushnell, H. (1861), *Christian Nurture*, Grand Rapids, Mich: Baker Book House, 1979.

Caird, G. B. (1976), *Paul's Letters from Prison*, London: Oxford University Press.

Cairns, D. S. (1953), *The Image of God in Man*, London: SCM Press.

Calvin, J. (1536), *Institutes of the Christian Religion*, Philadelphia: Westminster Press, 1960.

Cavell, S. (1984), *Themes Out of School: Effects and Causes*, San Francisco: North Point Press.

Chase, W. G. and Simon, H. A. (1973), 'The mind's eye in chess', in Chase (ed.), *Visual Information Processing*, New York: Academic Press, pp. 215–81.

Clark, L. F. and Woll, S. B. (1981), 'Stereotype biases', *Journal of Personal and Social Psychology*, **41**, 1064–72.

Coare, P. and Thomson, A. (eds) (1996), *Through the Joy of Learning: The Diary of 1,000 Adult Learners*, Leicester: NIACE.

Coleridge, S. T. (1975) *Bibliographia Literaria*, ed. G. Watson, London: J. M. Dent & Son.

Colson, C. (1985), *Who Speaks for God?*, London: Hodder & Stoughton.

Congar, Y. M-J. (1966), *Tradition and Traditions*, London: Burns & Oates.

Congar, Y. M-J. (1983), *I Believe in the Holy Spirit*, 3 vols, London: Geoffrey Chapman.

d'Costa, G. (1997), 'Revelation and world religions', in Avis, P. (ed.), *Divine Revelation*, London: Darton, Longman & Todd, pp. 112–39.

Cullmann, O. (1951), *Christ and Time*, London: SCM Press.

Dewar, F. (1988), *Live for a Change*, London: Darton, Longman & Todd.

Donaldson, M. (1978), *Children's Minds*, Glasgow: Fontana.

Downing, F. G. (1964), *Has Christianity a Revelation?*, London: SCM Press.

Dreyfus, H. L. (1992), *What Computers (Still) Can't Do: A Critique of Artificial Intelligence*, Cambridge, Mass: MIT Press.

Dunn, J. D. G. (1970), *Baptism in the Holy Spirit*, London: SCM Press.

Eagly, A. H. and Chaiken, S. (1998), 'Attitude structure and function', in Gilbert, D. T., Fiske, S. T. and Lindzey, G. (eds), *The Handbook of Social Psychology*, vol. 4, New York: McGraw-Hill, pp. 269–322.

Erikson, E. H. (1959), *Identity and the Life Cycle: Psychological Issues No.1*, New York: International Universities Press, pp. 197–207.

Erikson, E. H. (1963), *Childhood and Society*, Harmondsworth: Penguin.

Erikson, E. H. (1964), *Insight and Responsibility*, New York: W. W. Norton & Co.

Erikson, E. H. (1968), 'Identity and identity diffusion', in Gordon, C. and Gergen, K. J. (eds), *The Self in Social Interaction*, New York: John Wiley & Sons, pp. 197–204.

Evans, C. S. (1979), *Preserving the Person*, Leicester: Inter-Varsity Press.

Evans, C. S. (1993), 'Empiricism, rationalism and the possibility of historical religious knowledge', in Evans, C. S. and Westphal, M. (eds), *Christian Perspectives on Religious Knowledge*, Grand Rapids, Mich: Wm. B. Eerdmans, pp. 134–60.

Evans, D. D. (1968), 'Differences between scientific and religious assertions', in Barbour, I. G. (ed.), *Science and Religion: New Perspectives on the Dialogue*, London: SCM Press, pp. 101–33.

Farley, E. (1965), 'The work of the Holy Spirit in Christian education', *Religious Education*, **60**, 427–36, 479.

Farley, E. (1983), Theologia: *The Fragmentation and Unity of Theological Education, Philadelphia: Fortress Press.*

Farley, E. (1985), 'Can church education be theological education?', *Theology Today*, **42**, 158–71; also in Astley, J., Francis, L. J. and Crowder, C. (eds), *Theological Perspectives on Christian Formation*, Leominster: Gracewing, 1996, pp. 31–44.

Fazio, R. H., Zanna, M. P. and Cooper, J. (1977), 'Dissonance and self-perception: an integrative view of each theory's proper domain of application', *Journal of Experimental Social Psychology*, **13**, 464–79.

Festinger, L. (1957), *A Theory of Cognitive Dissonance*, Palo Alto, California: Stanford University Press.

Fishbein, M. and Ajzen, I. (1975), *Belief, Attitude, Intention and Behaviour*, New York: Addison-Wesley.

Fowler, J. W. and Keen, S. (1978), *Life Maps: Conversations on the Journey of Faith*, Waco, Texas: Word Books.

Fowler, J. W. (1981), *Stages of Faith*, San Francisco: Harper & Row.

Gill, J. H. (1969), 'The tacit structure of religious knowing', *International Philosophical Quarterly*, **9**, 533–59.

Gillespie, V. B. (1979), *Religious Conversion and Personal Identity*, London: Routledge & Kegan Paul.

Goffman, E. (1974), *Frame Analysis*, Harmondsworth: Penguin.

Gottwald, N. K. (1985), *The Hebrew Bible: A Socio-Literary Introduction*, Philadelphia: Fortress Press.

Greenwald, A. G. and Ronis, D. L. (1978), 'Cognitive dissonance: a case study of the evolution of a theory', *Psychological Review*, **85**, 53–7.

Guinness, M. (1985), *Child of the Covenant*, London: Hodder & Stoughton.

Gunton, C. (1995), *A Brief Theology of Revelation*, Edinburgh: T. & T. Clark.

Gunton, C. (1997), *The Promise of Narrative Theology*, 2nd edn, Edinburgh: T. & T. Clark.

Hacking, I. (1981), *Scientific Revolutions*, London: Oxford University Press.

Hamlyn, D. W. (1967), 'The logical and psychological aspects of learning', in Peters, R. S. (ed.), *The Concept of Education*, London: Routledge & Kegan Paul, pp. 24–43, reprinted in Hamlyn (ed.), *Perception, Learning and the Self: Essays in the Philosophy of Psychology*, London: Routledge & Kegan Paul, 1983, pp. 71–90.

Hamlyn, D. W. (1971), 'Epistemology and conceptual development', in Mischel, T. (ed.), *Cognitive Development and Epistemology*, New York: Academic Press, pp. 3–24; reprinted in Hamlyn (ed.), *Perception, Learning and the Self: Essays in the Philosophy of Psychology*, London: Routledge & Kegan Paul, 1983, pp. 107–31.

Hamlyn, D. W. (1974), 'Human learning', in Brown, S. C. (ed.), *The Philosophy of Psychology*, London: Macmillan, pp. 139–57; reprinted in Hamlyn (ed.), *Perception, Learning and the Self: Essays in the Philosophy of Psychology*, London: Routledge & Kegan Paul, 1983, pp. 132–48.

Hampshire, S. (1959), *Thought and Action*, London: Chatto & Windus.

Hanson, N. R. (1958), *Patterns of Discovery*, Cambridge: Cambridge University Press.

Hanson, N. R. (1961), 'Is there a logic of scientific discovery?', in Feigl, H. and Maxwell, G. (eds), *Current Issues in the Philosophy of Science*, New York: Holt, Rinehart & Winston, pp. 20–42.

Hanson, N. R. (1969), *Perception and Discovery*, San Francisco: W. H. Freeman & Co.

Hardy, D. D. (1980), 'Christian affirmation and the structure of personal life', in Torrance, T. F. (ed.), *Belief in Science and the Christian Life: The Relevance of Michael Polanyi's Thought for Christian Faith and Life*, Edinburgh: Handsel Press, pp. 71–90.

Hardy, D. W. (1985), 'Religious education – truth claims or meaning given?', in Felderhof, M. C. (ed.), *Religious Education in a Pluralistic Society,* London: Hodder & Stoughton, pp. 101–20.

Harmon-Jones, E. and Mills, J. (1999), 'An introduction to cognitive dissonance theory and an overview of current perspectives on the theory', in Harmon-Jones and Mills (eds), *Cognitive Dissonance: Progress on a Pivotal Theory in Social Psychology,* Washington, DC: American Psychological Association, pp. 3–21.

Hartshorne, C. and Reese, W. L. (eds) (1953) *Philosophers Speak of God,* Chicago: University of Chicago Press.

Harvey, D. (1990), *The Condition of Postmodernity,* Oxford: Basil Blackwell.

Hebblethwaite, B. (1994), 'The communication of divine revelation', in Padgett, A. G. (ed.), *Reason and Religion: Essays in Honour of Richard Swinburne,* Oxford: Clarendon Press, pp. 143–59.

Helm, P. (1982), *The Divine Revelation,* London: Marshall, Morgan & Scott.

Hendry, G. S. (1957), *The Holy Spirit in Christian Theology,* London: SCM Press.

Henle, M. (1962), 'The relationship between logic and thinking', *Psychological Review,* **69**, 366–78.

Heron, A. (1983), *The Holy Spirit,* London: Marshall, Morgan & Scott.

Heywood, D. S. (1988), 'Christian education as enculturation: the life of the community and its place in Christian education in the work of John H. Westerhoff III', *British Journal of Religious Education,* **10** (2), 65–71.

Heywood, D. S. (1992), 'Theology or social science? The theoretical basis for Christian education', in Astley, J. and Day, D. (eds), *The Contours of Christian Education,* Great Wakering, Essex: MacCrimmons, pp. 99–116.

Heywood, D. S. (1997), 'Ministerial education and teaching skill', *British Journal of Theological Education,* **9** (1), 44–51.

Hirst, P. H. (1965), 'Liberal education and the nature of knowledge', in Archambault, R. D. (ed.), *Philosophical Analysis and Education,* London: Routledge & Kegan Paul, pp. 113–38.

Hirst, P. H and Peters, R. S. (eds) (1970), *The Logic of Education,* London: Routledge & Kegan Paul.

Hirst, P. H. (1972), 'Christian education: a contradiction in terms', *Learning for Living,* **11**, 6–11.

Hirst, R. J. (ed.) (1959), *The Problems of Perception,* London: George Allen & Unwin.

Hobbes, T. (1651), *Leviathan,* ed. J. Plamenatz, London: Collins, 1962.

Hull, J. M. (1985), *What Prevents Christian Adults from Learning?,* London: SCM Press.

Hume, D. (1739), *A Treatise of Human Nature*, ed. L. A. Selby-Bigge, Oxford: Clarendon Press, p. 1888.

Hume, D. (1748), *An Enquiry Concerning the Human Understanding*, Oxford: Clarendon Press, p. 1962.

Kant, I. (1787), *Critique of Pure Reason*, trans. N. Kemp Smith, London: Macmillan, p. 1929.

Kant, I. (1974), *Anthropology from a Practical Point of View*, The Hague: Martinus Nijhoff.

Kelsey, D. (1975), *The Uses of Scripture in Recent Theology*, London: SCM Press.

Kelsey, D. (1982), 'Human being', in Hodgson, P. and King, R. (eds), *Christian Theology*, London: SPCK, pp. 141–67.

Kerr, F. (1986), *Theology after Wittgenstein*, Oxford: Basil Blackwell.

Kolata, G. (1982), 'How can computers get common sense?: two of the founders of the field of artificial intelligence disagree on how to make a thinking machine', *Science*, **217**, 1237–8.

Kolnai, A. (1968), 'Agency and freedom', *Royal Institute of Philosophy Lectures, vol. 1: the Human Agent*, London: Macmillan, pp. 20–37.

Knox, I. P. (1976), *Above or Within? The Supernatural in Religious Education*, Mishawa, Indiana: Religious Education Press.

Körner, S. (1955), *Kant*, Harmondsworth: Penguin.

Kühn, T. S. (1969), *The Structure of Scientific Revolutions*, 2nd edn, Chicago: University of Chicago Press.

Kühn, T. S. (1970), 'Logic of discovery or psychology of research?', in Lakatos, I. and Musgrave, A. (eds), *Criticism and the Growth of Knowledge*, Cambridge: Cambridge University Press, pp. 1–22; also in Schlipp, P. A. (ed.), *The Philosophy of Karl Popper*, La Salle, Illinois: Open House Publishing Company, 1974, pp. 789–819; also in Kühn, *The Essential Tension*, Chicago: University of Chicago Press, 1977, pp. 266–92.

Kühn, T. S. (1974), 'Second thoughts on paradigms', in Suppé, F. (ed.), *The Structure of Scientific Theories*, Urbana: University of Illinois Press, pp. 459–82; also in Kühn, *The Essential Tension: Selected Studies in Scientific Tradition and Change*, Chicago: University of Chicago Press, 1977, pp. 293–319.

Lakatos, I. (1970), 'Falsification and the methodology of scientific research programmes', in Lakatos, I. and Musgrave, A. (eds), *Criticism and the Growth of Knowledge*, Cambridge: Cambridge University Press, pp. 95–190.

Lee, J. M. (1971), *The Shape of Religious Education*, Birmingham, Ala: Religious Education Press.

Lee, J. M. (1973), *The Flow of Religious Education*, Birmingham, Ala: Religious Education Press.

Lee, J. M. (1986), *The Content of Religious Education*, Birmingham, Ala: Religious Education Press.

Lessing, G. (1956), 'On the proof of the spirit and of power', in Chadwick, H. (ed. and trans.), *Lessing's Theological Writings*, London: A. & C. Black, pp. 51–6.

Lewin, K. (1935), *A Dynamic Theory of Personality*, New York: McGraw-Hill.

Lewis, H. D. (1969), *The Elusive Mind*, London: George Allen & Unwin.

Lightfoot, J. B. (1890), *St Paul's Epistles to the Colossians and to Philemon*, London: Macmillan.

Lindbeck, G. A. (1984), *The Nature of Doctrine: Religion and Theology in a Post-Liberal Age*, London: SPCK.

Lippitt, R. (1968), 'Improving the socialisation process', in Clausen, J. E. (ed.), *Socialisation and Society,* Boston: Little, Brown & Co., pp. 345–8.

Little, S. (1976), 'Theology and religious education', in Taylor, M. J. (ed.), *Foundations for Christian Education in an Era of Change*, Nashville: Abingdon.

Locke, J. (1690), *An Essay Concerning Human Understanding*, Oxford: Clarendon, 1975.

Loder, J. E. (1981), *The Transforming Moment: Understanding Convictional Experiences,* San Francisco: Harper & Row.

Lossky, V. (1974), *In the Image and Likeness of God*, New York: St Vladimir's Seminary Press.

Lowe, G. (1972), *The Growth of Personality*, Harmonsworth: Penguin.

Lyotard, J.-F. (1984), *The Postmodern Condition*, Manchester: Manchester University Press.

McDonagh, E. M. (1976), 'Attitude change and paradigm shifts', *Social Studies of Science*, **6**, 51–76.

McFadyen, A. I. (1990), *The Call to Personhood: A Christian Theory of the Individual in Social Relationships*, Cambridge: Cambridge University Press.

McIntyre, J. (1957), *The Christian Doctrine of History*, Edinburgh: Oliver & Boyd.

McKenzie, L. (1982), *The Religious Education of Adults*, Birmingham, Ala: Religious Education Press.

Macnamara, J. (1972), 'The cognitive basis of language and learning in infants', *Psychological Review*, **79**, 1–13.

Macnamara, J. (1982), *Names for Things: A Study of Human Learning*, Cambridge, Mass: MIT Press.

Markus, H. (1977), 'Self-schemata and processing information about the self', *Journal of Personality and Social Psychology*, **35,** 63–78.

Marshall, I. H. (1977), *I Believe in the Historical Jesus*, London: Hodder & Stoughton.

Martin, D. A. (1971), 'The status of the human person in the behavioural sciences', in Preston, R. H. (ed.), *Technology and Social Justice*, London: SCM Press, pp. 237–65.

Marwick, A. (1970), *The Nature of History*, London: Macmillan.

Mayfield, T. (1990), *Thank God for That*, London: Bible Reading Fellowship.

Mead, G. H. (1934), *Mind, Self and Society from the Standpoint of a Social Behaviourist*, Chicago: University of Chicago Press.

Mey, M. de (1982), *The Cognitive Paradigm*, London: Reidel.

Michalson, G. E. Jr (1985), *Lessing's 'Ugly Ditch': A Study of Theology and History*, University Park, Pa: Pennsylvania State Press.

Miller, G. A. (1956), 'The magical number seven, plus or minus two: some limits on our capacity for processing information', *Psychological Review*, **63,** 81–96.

Miller, R. C. (1950), *The Clue to Christian Education*, New York: Charles Scribner & Sons.

Miller, R. C. (1953), 'Christian education as a theological discipline and method', *Religious Education*, **45,** 409–14; reprinted in Westerhoff, J. H. III (ed.), *Who are We? The Quest for a Religious Education*, Birmingham, Ala: Religious Education Press, 1978, pp. 110–22.

Miller, R. C. (1980), *The Theory of Christian Education Practice,* Birmingham, Ala: Religious Education Press.

Minsky, M. (1967), *Computation: Finite and Infinite Machines*, New York: Prentice-Hall.

Minsky, M. (1975), 'A framework for representing knowledge', in Winston, P. H. (ed.), *The Psychology of Computer Vision*, New York: McGraw-Hill, pp. 211–77.

Mischel, W. (1973), 'Toward a cognitive social learning re-conceptualisation of personality', *Psychological Review*, **80,** 252–83.

Mitchell, B. and Wiles, M. (1980), 'Does Christianity need a revelation?', *Theology*, **83,** 103–14.

Moberly, R. C. (1901), *Atonement and Personality*, London: John Murray.

Moltmann, J. (1997), *The Source of Life: The Holy Spirit and the Theology of Life*, London: SCM Press.

Moray, N. and Fitter, M. (1973), 'A theory and the measurement of attention', in Kornblum, S. (ed.), *Attention and Performance IV,* New York: Academic Press.

Morris, L. (1976), *I Believe in Revelation*, London: Hodder & Stoughton.

Moule, C. D. F. (1978), *The Holy Spirit*, Oxford: Mowbrays.

Neisser, U. (1976), *Cognition and Reality*, San Francisco: W. H. Freeman & Co.

Neisser, U. (1988), 'What is ordinary memory the memory of?', in Neisser, U. and Winograd, E. (eds), *Remembering Reconsidered: Ecological and Traditional Approaches to the Study of Memory*, Cambridge: Cambridge University Press, pp. 356–73.

Neisser, U. (1997), 'The future of cognitive science: an ecological analysis', in Johnson, D. M. and Erneling, C. E. (eds), *The Future of the Cognitive Revolution*, London: Oxford University Press, pp. 247–60.

Newbigin, L. (1957), *The Household of God*, London: SCM Press.

Niebuhr, H. R. (1960), *The Meaning of Revelation*, London: Macmillan.

Niebuhr, R. (1941), *The Nature and Destiny of Man*, New York: Charles Scribner's Sons.

Norman, D. A. (1968), 'Toward a theory of memory and attention', *Psychological Review*, **75**, 522–36.

Norman, D. A., Gentner, D. R. and Stevens, A. L. (1976), 'Comments on learning schemata and memory', in Klahr, D. (ed.), *Cognition and Instruction*, Hillsdale, NJ: Laurence Erlbaum, pp. 177–96.

O'Connor, E. (1968), *Journey Inward, Journey Outward*, New York: Harper & Row.

Odom, R. D. and Guzman, R. D. (1970), 'Problem solving and the perceptual salience of variability and constancy: a developmental study', *Journal of Experimental Child Psychology*, **9**, 156–65.

Odom, R. D. and Corbin, D. W. (1973), 'Perceptual salience and children's multi-dimensional problem solving', *Child Development*, **44**, 425–32.

Odom, R. D., Astor, E. C. and Cunningham, J. G. (1975), 'Effects of perceptual salience on the matrix task performance of four- and six-year-old children', *Child Development*, **46**, 758–62.

Odom, R. D., Cunningham, J. G. and Astor, E. C. (1975), 'Adults thinking the way we think children think, but children don't always think that way: a study of perceptual salience and problem solving', *Bulletin of the Psychonomic Society*, **6**, 545–8.

Oldham, J. H. (1952), 'Approach to adult Christian education', *Adult Education (London)*, **25**, 38–46.

Orr, M. (2000), 'The role of the teacher in the theological education of the laity', in Astley, J. (ed.), *Learning in the Way: Research and Reflection on Adult Christian Education*, Leominster: Gracewing, pp. 72–89.

Pannenberg, W. (1970), *What is Man?*, Philadelphia: Fortress Press.

Pannenberg, W. (1976), *Theology and the Philosophy of Science*, London: Darton, Longman & Todd.

Pannenberg, W. (1985), *Anthropology in Theological Perspective*, Edinburgh: T. & T. Clark.

Parkes, C. M. (1986), *Bereavement*, 2nd edn, Harmondsworth: Penguin.

Peacocke, A. (1993), *Theology for a Scientific Age*, 2nd edn, Oxford: Blackwell.

Peck, D. and Whitlow, D. (1975), *Approaches to Personality Theory*, London: Methuen.

Peck, J. R. and Strohmer, C. R. (2001), *Uncommon Sense: God's Wisdom for our Changing and Complex World*, London: SPCK.

Penrose, R. (1989), *The Emperor's New Mind: Concerning Computers, Minds and the Laws of Physics*, London: Oxford University Press.

Peters, R. S. (ed.) (1967), *The Concept of Education*, London: Routledge & Kegan Paul.

Peters, R. S. (ed.) (1973), *The Philosophy of Education*, London: Oxford University Press.

Petty, R. E. and Wegener, D. T. (1998), 'Attitude change: multiple roles for persuasion variables', in Gilbert, D. T., Fiske, S. T. and Lindzey, G. (eds), *The Handbook of Social Psychology*, vol. 4, New York: McGraw-Hill, pp. 323–90.

Pinnock, C. (1996), *Flame of Love: A Theology of the Holy Spirit*, Downer's Grove, Illinois: InterVarsity Press.

Polanyi, M. (1958), *Personal Knowledge: Toward a Post-Critical Philosophy*, London: Routledge & Kegan Paul.

Polanyi, M. (1959), *The Study of Man*, London: Routledge & Kegan Paul.

Polanyi, M. (1961a), 'Faith and reason', *Journal of Religion*, **41**, 237–47.

Polanyi, M. (1961b), 'Knowing and being', *Mind*, **70**, 458–70; also in Grene, M. (ed.), *Knowing and Being*, London: Routledge & Kegan Paul, 1969, pp. 123–37.

Polanyi, M. (1962), 'The unaccountable element in science', *Philosophy*, **37**, 1–14; also in Grene, M. (ed.), *Knowing and Being*, London: Routledge & Kegan Paul, 1969, pp. 105–20.

Polanyi, M. (1965), 'The structure of consciousness', *Brain*, **88**, 799–810; also in Grene, M. (ed.), *Knowing and Being*, London: Routledge & Kegan Paul, 1969, pp. 211–24.

Polanyi, M. (1966a), 'The creative imagination', *Chemical and Engineering News*, **44**, 85–93.

Polanyi, M. (1966b), 'The logic of tacit inference', *Philosophy*, **41**, 1–18; also in Grene, M. (ed.), *Knowing and Being*, London: Routledge & Kegan Paul, 1969, pp. 138–58.

Polanyi, M. (1967), *The Tacit Dimension*, London: Routledge & Kegan Paul.

Polkinghorne, J. (1994), *Science and Christian Belief: Theological Reflections of a Bottom-Up Thinker*, London: SPCK.

Polkinghorne, J. (1998), *Science and Theology: An Introduction*, London: SPCK.

Popper, K. (1959), *The Logic of Scientific Discovery*, London: Hutchinson.

Pylyshyn, Z. W. (1980), 'Computation and cognition: issues in the foundation of cognitive science', *Behavioural and Brain Sciences*, **3**, 111–69.

Quine, W. V. O. (1961), *From a Logical Point of View*, 2nd edn, New York: Harper & Row.

Rad, G. von (1972), *Genesis*, trans. J. H. Marks, revised J. Bowden, 2nd English edn, London: SCM Press.

Rad, G. von (1975), *Old Testament Theology Volume One*, trans. D. M. G. Stalker, 2nd English edn, London: SCM Press.

Ramsey, I. T. (1955), 'The systematic elusiveness of "I"', *Philosophical Quarterly*, **5**, 193–204.

Ratzsch, D. (2001), *Science and Its Limits: The Natural Sciences in Christian Perspective*, Downer's Grove, Illinois: InterVarsity Press.

Richard of St Victor (1959), *De Trinitate, Sources Chrétiennes 63*, Paris: Editions du Cerf.

Rosch, E. (1975), 'Cognitive reference points', *Cognitive Psychology*, **7**, 532–47.

Rosch, E. and Mervis, C. B. (1975), 'Family resemblances: studies in the internal structure of categories', *Cognitive Psychology*, **7**, 573–605.

Rose, A. (1962), 'A systematic summary of symbolic interaction theory', in Rose (ed.), *Human Behaviour and Social Processes: An Interactionist Approach*, London: Routledge & Kegan Paul, pp. 3–13.

Rubin, D. C. (1988), 'Go for the skill', in Neisser, U. and Winograd, E. (eds), *Remembering Reconsidered: Ecological and Traditional Approaches to the Study of Memory*, Cambridge: Cambridge University Press, pp. 374–82.

Rumelhart, D. E. and Ortony, A. (1977), 'The representation of knowledge in memory', in Anderson, R. C., Spiro, R. J., and Montague, W. E. (eds), *Schooling and the Acquisition of Knowledge*, Hillsdale, NJ: Laurence Erlbaum, pp. 99–129.

Rumelhart, D. E. and Norman, D. A. (1978), 'Accretion, tuning and restructuring: three modes of learning', in Cotton, W. J. and Klatsky, R. L. (eds), *Semantic Factors in Cognition*, Hillsdale, NJ: Laurence Erlbaum, pp. 37–56.

Ryle, G. (1963), *The Concept of Mind*, Harmondsworth: Penguin.

Sampson, E. E. (1981), 'Cognitive psychology as ideology', *American Psychologist*, **36**, 730–43.

Schank, R. C. (1972), 'Conceptual dependency: a theory of natural language understanding', *Cognitive Psychology*, **3**, 552–631.

Schank, R. C and Abelson, R. P. (1977), *Scripts, Plans, Goals and Understanding: An Enquiry into Human Knowledge*, Hillsdale, NJ: Laurence Erlbaum.

Schank, R. C. (1981), 'Language and memory', in Norman, D. A. (ed.), *Perspectives on Cognitive Science,* Norwood, NJ: Ablex, pp. 105–46.

Schleiermacher, F. D. E. (1799), *On Religion: Speeches to its Cultured Despisers*, New York: Harper and Row, 1958.

Schleiermacher, F. D. E. (1811), *Brief Outline of the Study of Theology*, Atlanta: John Knox Press, 1966.

Schleiermacher, F. D. E. (1821), *The Christian Faith*, Edinburgh: T. & T. Clark, 1928.

Schleiermacher, F. D. E. (1829), *On the* Glaubenslehre*: Two Letters to Dr Lucke, Chico*, California: Scholars Press, 1981.

Schlenker, B. R. (1980), *Impression Management: The Self-Concept, Social Identity and Interpersonal Relations*, Monterrey, California: Brooks/Cole.

Schutz, A. (1970a), 'Concept and theory formation in the social sciences', in McIntyre, A. and Emmet, D. (eds), *Sociological Theory and Philosophical Analysis*, London: Macmillan, pp. 1–19.

Schutz, A. (1970b), 'The problem of rationality in the social world', in McIntyre, A. and Emmet, D. (eds), *Sociological Theory and Philosophical Analysis*, London: Macmillan, pp. 89–114.

Searle, J. R. (1980), 'Minds, brains and programmes', *Behavioural and Brain Sciences*, **3**, 417–57.

Seymour, J. L. and Miller, D. E. (eds) (1982), *Contemporary Approaches to Christian Education*, Nashville: Abingdon.

Shibutani, T. (1962), 'Reference groups and social control', in Rose, A. (ed.), *Human Behaviour and Social Processes: An Interactionist Approach*, London: Routledge & Kegan Paul, pp. 128–47.

Shotter, J. (1975), *Images of Man in Psychological Research*, London: Methuen.

Siegel, L. S. and Brainerd, C. J. (1978), *Alternatives to Piaget: Critical Essays on the Theory*, New York: Academic Press.

Smith, E. R. (1998), 'Mental representation and memory', in Gilbert, D. T., Fiske, S. T. and Lindzey, G. (eds), *The Handbook of Social Psychology*, vol. 4, New York: McGraw-Hill, pp. 391–445.

Smith, F. (1982), *Understanding Reading*, 3rd edn, New York: Holt, Rinehart & Winston.

Sponheim, P. (1984), 'The knowledge of God', in Braaten, C. E. and Jenson, R. W. (eds), *Christian Dogmatics*, Philadelphia: Fortress Press, pp. 197–264.

Stevenson, J. (ed.) (1966), *Creeds, Councils and Controversies*, London: SPCK.

Stevenson, L. (1974), *Seven Theories of Human Nature*, London: Oxford University Press.

Strawson, P. F. (1966), *The Bounds of Sense: An Essay on Kant's* Critique of Pure Reason, London: Methuen.

Stroup, G. (1982), 'Revelation', in Hodgson, P. and King, R. (eds), *Christian Theology*, London: SPCK, pp. 88–114.

Stroup, G. W. (1984), *The Promise of Narrative Theology*, London: SCM Press.

Swinburne, R. (1992), *Revelation: From Metaphor to Analogy*, Oxford: Clarendon Press.

Taylor, C. (1964), *The Explanation of Behaviour*, London: Routledge & Kegan Paul.

Taylor, C. (1971), 'Interpretation and the sciences of man', *Review of Metaphysics*, **25**, 3–51; also in Beehler, R. and Drengson, A. R. (eds), *Philosophy of Society*, London: Methuen, 1978, pp. 159–98.

Taylor, C. (1980), 'Understanding in human science', *Review of Metaphysics*, **34**, 25–38.

Tedeschi, J. T., Schlenker, B. R. and Bonoma, T. V. (1971), 'Cognitive dissonance: private ratiocination or public spectacle?', *American Scientist*, **26**, 685–95.

Temple, W. (1937), 'Revelation', in Baillie, J. and Martin, H. (eds), *Revelation*, London: Faber & Faber, pp. 86–121.

Tillich, P. (1958), *Dynamics of Faith*, New York: Harper & Row.

Tillich, P. (1959), 'The two types of philosophy of religion', in Kimball, R. C. (ed.), *Theology of Culture*, New York: Oxford University Press, pp. 10–29.

Tomasello, M. and Farrar, M. J. (1986), 'Join attention and early language', *Child Development*, **57**, 1454–63.

Torrance, A. J. (1996), *Persons in Communion: Trinitarian Description and Human Participation*, Edinburgh: T. & T. Clark.

Torrance, T. F. (1969), *Theological Science*, London: Oxford University Press.

Toulmin, S. (1970), 'Does the distinction between normal and revolutionary science hold water?', in Lakatos, I. and Musgrave, A. (eds), *Criticism and the Growth of Knowledge*, Cambridge: Cambridge University Press, pp. 39–47.

Toulmin, S. (1971), 'The concept of "stages" in psychological develop-ment', in Mischel, T. (ed.), *Cognitive Development and Epistemology*, New York: Academic Press, pp. 25–60.

Toulmin, S. (1976), *Knowing and Acting: An Invitation to Philosophy*, London: Macmillan.

Tournier, P. (1973), *The Meaning of Persons*, New York: Harper & Row.

Troeltsch, E. (1913), 'Historiography', in Hastings, J. (ed.), *Encyclopedia of Religion and Ethics*, vol. 6, Edinburgh: T. & T. Clark, pp. 716–23.

Turner, R. H. (1962), 'Role-taking: process v. conformity', in Rose, A. (ed.), *Human Behaviour and Social Processes: An Interactionist Approach*, London: Routledge & Kegan Paul, pp. 20–40.

Vygotsky, L. S. (1962), *Thought and Language*, Cambridge, Mass: MIT Press.

Vygotsky, L. S. (1978), *Mind in Society: The Development of Higher Psychological Processes*, Cambridge, Mass: Harvard University Press.

Walker, A. (1991), 'The concept of the person in social science: possibilities for a theological anthropology', in Heron, A. (ed.), *The Forgotten Trinity: A Selection of Papers Presented to the BCC Commission on Trinitarian Doctrine Today*, London: British Council of Churches, pp. 137–57.

Wallace, W. T. and Rubin, D. C. (1988), 'The Wreck of the Old "97": A real event remembered in song', in Neisser, U. and Winograd, E. (eds), *Remembering Reconsidered: Ecological and Traditional Approaches to the Study of Memory*, Cambridge: Cambridge University Press, pp. 283–310.

Ward, K. (1994), *Religion and Revelation: A Theology of Revelation in the World's Religions*, Oxford: Clarendon Press.

Weber, M. (1970), *The Interpretation of Social Reality*, London: Michael Joseph.

Weldon, D. E. and Malpass, R. S. (1981), 'Effects of attitudinal, cognitive and situational variables on recall of biased communications', *Journal of Personality and Social Psychology*, **40**, 29–42.

Wertsch, J. V. (1979), 'From social interaction to higher psychological processes: a clarification and application of Vygotsky's theory', *Human Development*, **22**, 1–22.

West, L. (1996), *Beyond Fragments*, London: Taylor & Francis.

Westerhoff, J. H. III (1976), *Will Our Children Have Faith?*, New York: Seabury.

Westerhoff, J. H. III (1978a), 'Christian education as a theological discipline', *St Luke's Journal of Theology*, **21** (4), 280–288.

Westerhoff, J. H. III (1978b), *Who Are We? The Quest for a Religious Education*, Birmingham, Ala: Religious Education Press.

Westerhoff, J. H. III (1983), *Building God's People in a Materialistic Society*, New York: Seabury.

White, V. (1996), *Paying Attention to People*, London: SPCK.

Williams, M. (1996), 'Theological education and ordination training', *British Journal of Theological Education*, **8** (1), 22–6.

Williams, R. (2000), *On Christian Theology*, Oxford: Blackwell.

Winch, P. (1958), *The Idea of a Social Science and Its Relation to Philosophy*, London: Routledge & Kegan Paul.

Wisdom, J. (1953), *Philosophy and Psychoanalysis*, Oxford: Basil Blackwell.

Wisdom, J. (1965), *Paradox and Discovery*, Oxford: Basil Blackwell.

Wittgenstein, L. (1921), *Tractatus Logico-Philosophicus*, London: Routledge & Kegan Paul, 1974.

Wittgenstein, L. (1929), 'A note on logical form', *Proceedings of the Aristotelian Society Supplement*, **9**, 162–71.

Wittgenstein, L. (1958), *Philosophical Investigations*, 2nd edn, Oxford: Basil Blackwell.

Wood, C. M. (1993), *The Formation of Christian Understanding*, Valley Forge, Penn: Trinity Press International.

Woolley, B. (1992), *Virtual Worlds*, Oxford: Basil Blackwell.

Wyckhoff, D. C. (1967), 'Religious education as a discipline', *Religious Education*, **62**, 387–94. Reprinted in Westerhoff, J. H. III (1982), *Who Are We? The Quest for a Religious Education*, Birmingham, Alabama: Religious Education Press.

Zajonc, R. B. (1980), 'Feeling and thinking', *American Psychologist*, **35**, 151–75.

Zizioulas, J. D. (1985), *Being as Communion*, London: Darton, Longman & Todd.

Zizioulas, J. (1991), 'The doctrine of God today: suggestions for an ecumenical study', in Heron, A. (ed.), *The Forgotten Trinity: A Selection of Papers Presented to the BCC Commission on Trinitarian Doctrine Today*, London: British Council of Churches, pp. 19–32.

Name index

Subject index